HARRY A. BULLIS,
Champion American

Other Books in the "Men of Achievement" Series:

J. Edgar Hoover, Modern Knight Errant

John Foster Dulles, Peacemaker

Bob Mathias, Champion of Champions

Charles F. Kettering, Inventor and Idealist

Herbert Hoover, Humanitarian

Carl Sandburg, Poet and Patriot

William L. McKnight, Industrialist

Conrad Hilton, Hotelier

Lowell Thomas, Adventurer

J. C. Penney, Merchant Prince

Dr. Albert Schweitzer, Medical Missionary

Ernest Hemingway, Man of Courage

Dr. Frank H. Krusen, Pioneer in Physical Medicine

Nathaniel Leverone, Pioneer in
Automatic Merchandising

Dr. Norman Vincent Peale, Minister

Men of Achievement Series

HARRY A. BULLIS,
Champion American

A Biography of a Business Leader Who
Was a Champion of Human Rights

by
GLADYS ZEHNPFENNIG
With an Introduction by Paul G. Hoffman

* * *

Publishers
T. S. DENISON & COMPANY, INC.
Minneapolis

First Printing, September 1964
Second Printing, March 1965
Third Printing, February 1966
Fourth Printing, March 1967

Printed in the U.S.A.
By The Brings Press

1 6

Library of Congress Catalog Card Number: 63-21944

INTRODUCTION

Harry A. Bullis, Champion American, is fascinating reading. It is a "Rags to Riches" story with Horatio Alger overtones, but Harry Bullis did not marry the boss' daughter. Instead, he built a philosophy that enriched his life and the lives of all who were privileged to know him. It also contributed to his noteworthy success in business, national and international affairs.

Harry Bullis' philosophy shines forth in this biography not only in words, but in deeds. Any attempt to put it into capsule form inevitably would result in the loss of much of its salty flavor. It can be fully appreciated only by noting the impact it had day by day in his family life, in his relationships with his associates and with all people, high and low, whose paths crossed his.

The underlying motivation for Harry Bullis' actions seem to have been a passion for people and a passion for facts. The brotherhood of man was not a sterile phrase, but a goal to be striven for eagerly. As for facts —they were elusive—but if you didn't get them, they would get you.

Never was there a more determined seeker for facts than Harry Bullis. Prior to making any decision, he took time, all the time needed, to get all the facts. Then he would, to quote his watchwords, "Drive Straight Ahead with a Positive Mental Attitude." He was never arrogant or intolerant of the views of others, but once he made up his mind, it wasn't easily changed. For fourteen years he was a director of the National Association of Manufacturers, a very conservative organization, but he retained a liberal outlook. On the other hand, he spent much time in academic circles where business was not held in high repute, but his conviction that private enterprise had a vital part to play in the making of a good society never waivered, and he never hesitated to give voice to this conviction.

From a personal standpoint, the quality of Harry Bullis that most endeared him to me was his courage. For a just cause he would not only take a stand, but he would fight for it, no matter how unpopular it might be. He foresaw the coming of World War II and urged early United States participation at a time when many of his friends were "America-firsters." He didn't like McCarthyism and didn't hesitate to say so. He believed that only through freer trade could we have a stronger free world and was willing at a drop of the hat to battle this issue with the most ardent protectionists.

He also was ready to do battle any time for the United Nations. He recognized that the spectacular advances in communication and transportation were rapidly making the world one neighborhood and he knew that we had to be good neighbors.

Anyone who knew Harry Bullis was a better man for having known him, and the world is a better place in which to live because of his manifold activities.

—Paul G. Hoffman

CONTENTS

ACKNOWLEDGMENTS

It would be impossible to list all of the gracious people who have contributed to the preparation of this biography. Foremost among them is Mrs. Harry Bullis whose kindness and understanding are typical of this great lady. I am grateful to all of Mr. Bullis' secretaries who helped to compile his scrapbooks over the years, and especially to Miss Gladys Leight who recently assembled and transferred much vitally necessary material to me.

In addition to satisfying my curiosity, Mr. A. Louis Champlin, Jr., of the General Mills Public Relations Department, provided me with enlightening literature. Both Harry Bullis and I appreciated being conducted on a grand tour of the General Mills Home Service Department by Mrs. Mildred Kranz.

My special thanks go to all of Mr. Bullis' correspondents whose letters have given me a well-proportioned picture of a tall, enthusiastic man with a host of friends in every area of endeavor.

I am grateful to the Handley Library at Winchester, Virginia, for allowing the copy of William C. Edgar's **The Story of a Grain of Wheat** to repose high in the stacks for almost a half-century—until I needed it.

Two important reference sources were **Manifesto for Americans**, by Harry A. Bullis (McGraw-Hill), and **Business Without Boundary**, by James Gray (University of Minnesota Press). Also consulted were **Encyclopedia Britannica** and Funk and Wagnall's **Universal Standard Encyclopedia.**

Quoted with due credit are excerpts from reviews and features in **The Northwestern Miller, Time, The Saturday Review, Banco Yearly Times, Fortune, The Modern Millwheel, Commercial West, General Mills Horizons, The Minneapolis Star-Tribune**, and various other newspapers, magazines and milling periodicals.

Chapter One

An All-American Boy

If you looked for Harry Bullis in a crowded room, your intuition would have told you that he was the very tall, erect man whose face was lively with anticipation of each moment's fresh developments. Unaware that he dominated the room with his hale and hearty presence, he would have been honestly surprised at the miracle of your instant recognition. A random recollection stirred in your mind, and you thought to yourself: "Jack Armstrong has grown up, and here he is!"

Delightfully fabulous was Harry Bullis' reputation as a Jack Armstrong type of enthusiast, counselor and abettor of "Betty Crocker," and a zestful advocate of the good life for the human family.

What gave this admirable fellow such a healthy portion of Jack Armstrong alertness and so much "Breakfast of Champions" spirit? Why is it natural to think of this dynamic Midwesterner in terms of a cheerful little ditty that goes rollicking down the years, still tantalizing the ears of little boys who have grown to manhood since Jack Armstrong, the All-American Boy, was saluted coast-to-coast on the radio by the famous Wheaties Quartet:

"Have you tried Wheaties—
They're whole wheat with all of the bran.
Won't you try Wheaties—
For wheat is the best food of man.
They're crispy and crunchy, the whole year through—
The kiddies never tire of them and neither will you.
So just buy Wheaties, try Wheaties—
The best breakfast food in the land!"

Most of all, what was there about Harry Bullis that made him an easy man to meet? From the first handshake, he ceased to be a stranger to be contemplated with awe. Distinguished citizens of the world called him by his first name, and he had dined and danced under the glittering chandeliers of the White House. Still, he was a man who could stride comfortably along the glory road—"nor lose the common touch" of which Kipling spoke.

Whether you think of him in terms of "The Breakfast of Champions," as a champion American businessman in the Horatio Alger tradition, as an international champion of human rights and dignity, or as a buoyant champion of the optimistic viewpoint, Harry Bullis exerted his energy and talents to "drive straight ahead with a positive mental attitude" toward the winner's circle where the laurel wreaths of achievement are bestowed on the industrious and the wise.

Even though his name has become so synonymous with General Mills that a stranger once tried to call him "General Bullis," the future President and Chairman of the Board of that mighty corporation was not born with a silver spoon in his mouth. The rugged road was not made smooth with wealth or family privilege; hard work, determination and self-discipline were the forces that took Harry Bullis over the ruts and boulders on his hazardous ascent to the magnificent heights of achievement.

For many years Harry Bullis' watchwords were "Drive Straight Ahead with a Positive Mental Attitude." With so vigorous a slogan, he was equipped to tackle a multitude of challenges with stout-hearted faith in his God, his nation, and his own destiny.

Harry Amos Bullis' Canadian-born father was a reliable, honorable man, with an eighth grade education. The elder Bullis earned a humble, subsistence living, first as a house painter and later as a sewing machine salesman. His mother, of English, Scotch and Irish ancestry, was an extraordinarily resourceful, highly intelligent, and devotedly religious lady. Seventy-one years later, Harry dedicated a book to her with these words: "To my wonderful Mother who radiated the spirit of the America I love, and the world I want to live in."

George Amos Bullis and Ella Gould were married in Council Bluffs, Iowa, in 1888. Miss Gould had been a bookkeeper in the Singer Sewing Machine Company office there, and George Bullis was a salesman operating out of the Council Bluffs office.

Photographs from that picturesque era show Ella Gould Bullis as a fine-featured young woman with a becoming cluster of curls crowning her forehead.

"Dad" was a poised-looking young man with a well-tended mustache, dressed in his black Sunday suit and high stiff collar.

Two enchantingly handsome little boys, their curly heads close together, are featured on one of the "Instantaneous Portraits of Children" that reveal the photographer's art of the 1890's. Roe McClude Bullis, who was born in York, Nebraska, in 1889, was three years old when the picture was taken. The "portrait" shows Harry Amos Bullis as a wide-eyed two-year-old. He was born in Hastings, Nebraska, on October 7, 1890.

As the Bullises moved from one town to another in Nebraska, George Bullis continued to sell sewing machines. Several years after Harry was born, the family moved back to Council Bluffs, where George had courted and married Ella. In the thriving little Iowa city, seat of Pottawattamie County, the Bullis brothers spent most of their boyhood years.

Before Harry Bullis arrived there, Council Bluffs was already famous for several very remarkable developments in the history of the nation. Indians had held their council meetings, for many centuries, on those bluffs above the Missouri. There the Indians smoked the peace pipe with Lewis and Clark in 1804. Lusty, eager Forty-Niners had used Council Bluffs as a departure base, during the California Gold Rush. Directly across the Missouri, Iowa's natural boundary on the west, was the great sister-city of Omaha, Nebraska. In the civic-minded enthusiasm of their youth, Roe and Harry Bullis delighted in dubbing Council Bluffs "the capital of the world."

Shortly after he started trying to talk, little Harry Bullis ran into his first frustration. The words wouldn't come out right. When he followed Roe into the public school in Council Bluffs, the teachers discovered that Harry was a very bright boy, but he was handicapped by a tendency to stammer. Neighbors would assure his parents that he was exceptional in his spirit and serious beyond his age, but the handicap and impediment made him miserable.

Between Harry and his mother there was a sensitive communion of minds. Ella Bullis took an attentive interest in encouraging his efforts to speak properly. "She seemed to be the only one who had any faith in me," he recalled.

In almost every difficulty or illness, a mother can somehow alleviate a portion of the discomfort. In the case of a stammering child, she must press her own lips tightly together, aching with silent helplessness at her inability to relieve the long-drawn moments of poor articulation. This is a battle a child must fight for himself, even though he may be too young to fight battles. Young Harry would see the constant concern in his mother's eyes, and she would not allow him to forget that he was a healthy, intelligent, quick youngster. Perhaps it was his quickness, his breathless eagerness to speak the many exciting thoughts crowding his mind, that caused the difficulty.

His mother's encouragement helped Harry to realize early in life that he must develop himself and that he could not lean upon others. He must practice discipline. Possessed by an overwhelming desire to speak correctly, his life during this period was not child's play. It was a man's game directed to the attainment of good speaking and good reading. Seeking the aid of the most Infinite Power, he knew he needed God, and he often prayed.

The youngster did not take time to brood about his difficulties. At the turn of the twentieth century, "The Council Bluffs Nonpareil" was not yet printing any feature stories about Harry A. Bullis, but he had already made close contact with that local newspaper. When he was eleven, he shouldered the heavy paper bag that separates the young fellows who are in business from the ones who are still in bed on icy mornings. Both Harry and Roe got up at four o'clock and set out delivering papers before school.

Part of his mind kept concentrating on his speech difficulties. It was an impediment that made him a miserable boy and would continue to make him an uncomfortable teen-ager. He acknowledged that God had cast him in the role he was to play, but he would not accept himself with the stammering weakness. In his determination to cure his speaking deficiency, his overpowering goal became "To speak and read perfectly and easily and well." The attainment of this goal was the master passion of his existence for the first twenty-five years of his life, until he finally felt that he had dominated the stubborn handicap. As he disciplined himself so rigorously, always straining for perfection, he was unconsciously strengthening his character and preparing himself for a future in which people would marvel at his stamina and perseverance.

Like other normal brothers, Roe and Harry had their share of fist fights. Roe won all of them until, at the age of eleven, there came a day when Harry knocked his older brother out. After that, there were no more fights.

Roe and Harry were "getting along in years"—Harry would be twelve in October—when their parents presented them with a baby sister on June 11, 1902. On her "growing-up pictures," Jennie Gould Bullis was a pretty little girl, with a puckish smile and long, lustrous curls on her shoulders.

For several years Harry had been shooting up out of his clothes. As though his speech difficulty were not enough cause for mortification, he felt like a Gulliver in a world of Lilliputians by the time he was twelve years old and almost six-feet-two. He recalled himself as "a skinny kid, built like a beanpole, and as round-shouldered as a fishhook.'" Terribly self-conscious, and always awkwardly aware that he was taking up more vertical space than his peers, he kept trying to hunch himself down, to cramp himself into the physical dimensions of his young classmates. Over a period of months, he grew more and more stoop-shouldered.

One day, at the request of his understanding mother, he took his dog up to a wooded hilltop and prayed to God for guidance. Harry had studied his Bible, and he listened now for the voice of God with the unequivocal faith of a Noah or an Abraham of the Old Testament, expecting the Lord to speak to him in words best suited to his understanding. As he waited on that hill in the clear blue of an Iowa day, the message seemed to come back, "Harry, straighten up your shoulders. Instead of looking for nickels on the ground, look straight ahead and you will find much better returns." Just as the Lord had given Noah the proper specifications for building a reliable ark, he was giving Harry the proper specifications for building a reliable young man.

Returning home, the boy started a series of vigorous setting-up exercises designed to straighten his shoulders. It was a long-drawnout, painful procedure. Finally Harry Bullis achieved the erect posture that marked him with that "champion look" in a crowded room.

The effervescent spirit of young Harry Bullis is preserved in some faded ledger pages, dated August 1903. He had jotted down some brief notes about a secret society called "The Jolly Skeletons." Since it was a secret society, it probably was considered discreet not to put much of anything in writing.

On the first page of the old notebook, a twelve-year-old boy proclaims to the world:

"Harry Bullis is my name,
America is my nation.
Council Bluffs is my dwelling place,
And Christ is my salvation.
When I am dead and all my bones are rotten,
It's you that will remember me
Or else I'll be forgotten."

There are some paper route collection entries—standing like minor monuments to customers who have lived their honest lives and gone to their rewards long years ago. Harry was buying his own clothes, and the future "man of figures" kept careful track of his "charge account" credits and debits.

Young Bullis finished the elementary grades and then took a semester at the Council Bluffs High School. In the meantime, he had been out of school for a year, working on a farm that was the property of a German-born, dawn-to-dark, Iowa farmer. Even though he was not in the classroom during that period, his mind was occupied with self-education and Bullis-improvement.

Hours at a stretch, as he guided a horse-drawn cultivator between interminable rows of corn, the boy would speak memorized lines to correct his speech impediment. Alone in the barn, when he was milking cows, Harry would recite Biblical and other stories, without that distressing halt and embarrassing stammer. Worthy of repetition was the sublime assurance that "There is nothing but God and His Manifestation," which he repeated over and over again. It was more than a lip-challenging sentence to be articulated glibly after long periods of practice. Constant declaration of this faith—that he was a part of the nature of God—would remain with him through all of his years. From the heart-warming conviction that he, stammering Harry Bullis, was part of the dynamism of the whole wide world, derived his spiritual strength to be able to do all things necessary for growth and advancement.

Even as he was throwing back his shoulders to stand at his full height, as straight as the tall cornstalks in the fields of his home state, he was elevating his mind upward and away from petty irritations and distractions. He might even have said, "Lord, I thank you for giving me so many big problems—I'd hate to waste all this excess energy on a batch of small ones!"

In 1906, George Bullis became seriously ill for a whole year, and it was necessary for his young sons to find full-time work. Harry learned that the Citizens Gas and Electric Company wanted an office boy and he took the opening.

From office boy, he climbed to storekeeper, handling the inventory of appliances and services. Then he progressed to bookkeeper, in charge of posting the four-foot open ledgers. Here he was casting a shadow of the future Bullis, in a niche that suited his natural inclinations. As a bookkeeper, he wore the green eyeshade which was the symbol of his profession, and he sat on a high stool to record the utility company's business in pen and ink on those enormous pages.

After he discovered in his work at the Gas and Electric Company that he had a flair for figures, Bullis was eager to continue his interrupted education. The local high school principal, a Mr. Thomas who taught mathematics, was a great friend of Harry's mother. The ambitious young bookkeeper told Mr. Thomas that he would like to obtain his high school credits in mathematics by studying the problems alone at home at night. He asked Mr. Thomas to give him the book of answers to the problems and arranged to take the required high school examinations at Mr. Thomas' home at night.

Much to Mr. Thomas' surprise, Harry figured out the mathematical progressions necessary to bridge the gap between the problems and the answers, and he passed the examinations with a scholarly flourish.

Harry worked at the Gas and Electric Company

from eight to five o'clock, six days a week. With pages of mathematics problems waiting for him at home, he was in no mood to work overtime as several of the other clerks did. Jealously protective of those minutes after five o'clock, he devised new methods of handling his work with competent dispatch. His boss took note and increased his work load—but Harry turned that out with efficiency too.

After he left his bookkeeper's stool for the day, Bullis took a walk of several miles and then went home to dinner. After dinner he studied every night until midnight. Then he went out in his back yard and practiced setting-up exercises for a half hour. This boy really was whipping himself into shape for any challenges the future might hold!

During that five-year period, he was utilizing every possible method to cure his stammering. He took Yogi breathing exercises. He remembered devising a breath control machine, by fitting one large container into another container filled with water. "When you blew into the first container," he explained, "it arose from the water and registered the number of pounds of breath." Years later, as a freshman at the University of Wisconsin, when Harry Bullis took the required physical examination, he astounded the doctors by the high record he reached when he blew into their breath-control machine!

Under the circumstances, Harry Bullis might have been expected to side-step anything faintly resembling public speaking. Looking ahead in the story of his life, it is obvious that Bullis was inclined to make the unexpected choices, to defy the inevitable. He would "beard the lion in his den" instead of beating a fast retreat. Aware of his stammering handicap, how much courage it must have taken to join the Lowell Literary Society at Simpson College Academy and become involved in speaking and debating programs! He had time for only one outside activity, and he chose the most difficult and emotionally demanding one. In fact, he practiced speaking on the Lowell programs as often as possible.

Two years later, when he became a member of the freshman class at the University of Wisconsin, he deliberately joined the Philomathean Literary Society to continue practicing public speaking, and he participated in numerous debates.

Subsequent developments in the career of the remarkable Mr. Bullis will show that a semi-articulate lad behind the plow might some day stand before the most distinguished of audiences and deliver messages of great impact "perfectly and easily and well."

When Bullis set out to cure his stammering handicap, he was also strengthening his spirit and building up his self-confidence. The disciplines and the constant striving for success developed attitudes and characteristics which undoubtedly enabled him to climb up the "Mountain of Achievement" to the very summit, instead of remaining on one of the lower levels.

Young people who are afflicted with a handicap should not despair but should strive to overcome it, or at least become adjusted to it. The measure of victory they achieve will expand their personalities and develop increased powers for them. Harry Bullis became a man with a delightfully expanded personality, liberally endowed with talents and powers that have become almost legendary. But, early in 1911, he was still busy marking figures in that huge ledger and studying mathematics at night. Only in his imagination could he see a high school diploma with the name "Harry Amos Bullis" on it.

Chapter Two

Why Stay in the Lowlands?

At the age of twenty, Harry Bullis did not have his high school diploma, but he had already conceived the idealistic notion that "the good future of this country and the world lies with the highly educated man" —an extremely far-fetched theory for a former ninth grader who should have been proud of his safe, dependable bookkeeper's job in Council Bluffs.

Seventy-five dollars a month was a whopping good salary in 1911, but the "education bug" kept buzzing around Harry Bullis' ears as he bent his head over an enormous ledger at the Citizens Gas and Electric Company. In addition to proficiency with figures, he had an imagination that kept shooting questions at him. If, as, and when he might be able to go to a University, what course would he take? Because he was associated with engineers, he at first considered becoming an engineer. When he learned that Mr. A. L. English, manager of the Gas and Electric Light Company, was employing graduates of the Massachusetts Institute of Technology for sixty dollars a month, while his own salary was seventy-five dollars a month, the idea of becoming a straight engineer did not appear so attractive.

Bullis became his own "guidance counselor." He began to concoct a revolutionary course of study for himself, based on a solid combination of engineering, economics and business subjects. What if no one had ever heard of such a concoction before? It would best suit his interests and aptitudes. There was nothing foggy about Harry Bullis' reasoning. In the process of learning self-discipline, he had trained himself to think about his future while he was doing a highly efficient job of handling his everyday duties. These were no idle daydreams; his aspirations were as clear and intelligible to him as the figures he kept entering in the ledger before him.

One of the dominant characteristics of Harry Bullis, by his own admission, has always been his bull-dogged tenacity. At eighteen, he set his goal toward becoming a new kind of scientific engineer in economics and business. He was telling himself in no uncertain terms: "Define your purpose. Then drive straight ahead with a positive mental attitude." This was the earliest philosophy of operation that Bullis adopted, and it is highly significant. It was the slogan with which he everlastingly coupled scientific research and a high level of human understanding—of others, as well as himself.

When Bullis named his destination and steered straight toward his objective—to become an engineer in industrial management—nothing could stop him. It would not be a happy-go-lucky adventure; it would be in the same category with his valiant struggles to control his stammering and to achieve good posture.

Bullis had perceived, long before many of his peers, that while experience was invaluable, the key for getting ahead—the best vertical motion technique—was education. This was the indispensable equipment that a man must carry in his tool kit when he sets out to tackle the wide variety of problems presented by the growing complexities of American society and industrial development.

It was characteristic of Harry Bullis to take a careful survey of the road ahead. He has always been a great man for measuring "the lay of the land" with an analytical eye. His mind had already jumped beyond the first hurdle, high school. Perched on his bookkeeper's stool in the Gas and Electric Company, he was asking himself which college might offer him the prime combination of courses in engineering, economics and business operation. M.I.T., Harvard, Wisconsin, and a number of other colleges attracted him.

Harry's "mental slide rule" indicated that the University of Wisconsin would be a wise choice. In economics, Professor Richard Ely was nationally recognized; John R. Commons was famous as a progressive labor specialist; Edwin A. Ross was tops in sociology, a science then emerging from philosophy, psychology and economics; and William Scott, with Professor Stephen Gilman, headed the excellent University of Wisconsin School of Business.

With his eyes firmly "On Wisconsin," there was that little matter of finishing his high school or preparatory work. Since the Bullises were Methodists,

Harry knew all about Simpson College and Simpson College Academy at Indianola, Iowa, about one hundred and twenty miles east of Council Bluffs. The Academy, which had been in operation before Simpson College was founded, provided a convenient institution for older farm boys and girls who had been out of school for awhile. It would suit Harry's purposes to perfection.

Harry's chief wasn't a mind reader, so he hadn't guessed what was going on in the brain of his prize bookkeeper. Mr. A. L. English, the manager of the Gas and Electric Company, was very surprised and exceedingly sorry to see young Bullis go. Bullis, in order not to spend any time working after hours, had devised new ways and means to accomplish his work and had set an accelerated pace for the other staff members. Obviously, Mr. English valued his services and would wonder at his decision to sacrifice a good job for a diploma that might not get him any farther ahead than he already was.

Nevertheless, typical of some men of his day, when faced with the choice between risk and security, Bullis chose risk. To him the stakes were right.

Farther along in Harry's life there was a whimsical reunion with Mr. English of the Council Bluffs Gas and Electric Company.

The aspiring young man was not exactly setting out for the ends of the earth when he said goodbye to his parents, and Roe and little Jennie, and left Council Bluffs in the fall of 1911. Still, it was "a pretty far piece up the road" to Indianola, and he was burning several bridges behind him. A robust young man, six-feet-two, with a fine mixture of pluck, bravado and common sense, he did not stop to ask himself why he, Harry Bullis, should respond so heartily to these unorthodox ambitions stirring in his mind. His good, honest father had only finished the eighth grade, and a high school education was considered a very respectable achievement at that time. And here this Bullis boy had a notion to aim at college, too!

Undoubtedly his mother, who was a friend of the high school mathematics teacher in Council Bluffs, encouraged him and cheered him on. Still, it was a giant step forward, under the circumstances, and history sits in awe of the Yankee derring-do that sometimes causes one man to plunge ahead out of the crowd in spite of all the factors that should have made him content with his normal heritage.

Harry Bullis' faith in the immeasurable power of education never diminished. Education, he believed, can elevate the soul of man. Education can raise living standards of nations over the earth. Education can promote understanding among people and advance the cause of ultimate world peace.

The new student from Council Bluffs did not intend to spend four years getting that diploma at Simpson College Academy. He went there with the precise purpose of graduating and securing his diploma at the end of two years. This would have been appalling news to the unsuspecting faculty, so he broke it gently and gradually. He knew perfectly well that Simpson had never changed its graduation requirements of four years of English and three years of Latin.

Harry Bullis did not want to discourage other

bright students who might feel abashed about frittering away three or four whole years in high school. He made a strong point of reminding them that he had already accumulated all of his mathematics credits by studying in the evening.

Bullis had set his goal, and he began aiming straight at it. During his first year at Simpson, he secured a job firing the furnace for Professor Ruggles, the principal of the Academy. Since the Ruggles furnace needed attention in the morning and throughout the day, he became well acquainted with Professor and Mrs. Ruggles, and they came to know him as an industrious young man who was handy with a shovel. He also signed up for many more courses than necessary during that first year, made excellent grades in all of them, and laid the foundation for his "bombshell announcement" about wanting to be a senior in his sophomore year at Simpson.

During the summer he hired out to a farmer in southwestern Iowa. With practice, he had become so adept at handling more than one job at a time that he studied several courses while he was cultivating corn under the hot summer sky and doing other farm chores. He also had a couple of ladies named Mrs. McLaughlin and Mrs. Cupp on his mind. Before leaving Indianola at the end of the first year, he had arranged to manage the Mac-Cupp boarding club which was operated in the home of Mrs. Cupp.

While he was going about his farm chores that summer, he conceived a "packaging" idea to fill up and sell his boarding club. Never a man to accept a trite adage at its face value, Bullis decided that the way to a man's stomach might very well be through his heart. In the late summer, he wrote to five of the most popular girls on the campus and offered each of them a week's free board at the Mac-Cupp Club. Each of the five eagerly accepted.

Bullis then proceeded to ride the train between Des Moines and Indianola, talking with various students about his boarding club. He adroitly emphasized the fact that he had already signed up the five outstanding belles on the campus, and it was not long before Bullis had filled up his club of twenty-six members.

In a big room in the Cupp house, Bullis constructed a large round table with a seating capacity of twenty-six. There were moments of intrigue over the kitchen stove as Bullis and the two cooks quietly decided which man should sit next to which girl. In cases of incompatibility, Bullis changed the seating arrangements. All this—and food too! As a result of Cupid Bullis' match-making talents, several romances developed and marriages ultimately occurred. His deep, intuitive understanding of human nature has contributed immensely to Harry Bullis' success.

By signing up some important members of the faculty, the astute manager of the Mac-Cupp house added an air of prestige and academic dignity to the round table. Three faculty members of the club were Professor (Miss) Bunning who taught Latin, Professor (Miss) Baker who taught history, and Professor Robbins who taught science.

On Monday morning, after the club had been operating for a week, Bullis arose and made an announcement that proved he was fast becoming a polished and forceful speaker. He said, "The meals here cost three dollars a week. Every Monday morning after breakfast I will be in the parlor to receive payments. Remember, meet me Monday mornings in the parlor."

Business was as simple and direct as that for Bullis. "Meet me Monday mornings in the parlor" became a byword for all concerned, to be remembered in later years with appreciative laughter.

Meanwhile, there was that little business about intending to be graduated at the end of the spring term that year. When Bullis let his unprecedented intentions be known, there was astonishment and disbelief that anyone should consider such a thing possible. He was taking Caesar, which has always been widely recognized as second year Latin, and Miss Bunning said he had to complete third year Cicero. He told her he would take that on the side. After several weeks, this state of affairs resulted in much confusion, and Miss Bunning relaxed and told him she would accept two years of Latin for her requirement.

Miss Baker, who taught history, was not so easily confused. She was merely dumbfounded when she learned about Harry's attitude toward Meyer's Ancient History—a required course that wasn't even on his schedule for that year. "What," he asked her, "do I have to do to get that year's credit without going to your class?"

In the first place, she told him, he would have to read about twenty-five history books and take full notes on them. Then he would have to take a complete examination on Meyer's Ancient History.

Bullis assured her, with true Jack Armstrong spirit, that he would be ready for that examination ten days from that date.

Horrified, she asked, "How can you ever accomplish that?"

The picture was clear in his mind. He said, "I will go to all of my other classes, but I will not do any studying for them. I will spend all of my time analyzing Meyer's Ancient History and ten days from now I will be ready for your examination." He did just that, and she gave him a year's credit in ancient history.

Respecting his admirable ambition to move forward into college as soon as possible and taking note of his remarkable ability to "Drive Straight Ahead with a Positive Mental Attitude," the various members of the faculty at the Academy assisted him in every way possible to achieve his objective.

While he was at Simpson College Academy, Bullis participated actively in the Lowell Literary Society, taking advantage of every opportunity to improve his public speaking proficiency. That was an era when debating was a popular "spectator sport" and drew large audiences. In a 1912 scrapbook clipping from those days of yester-year, bold-face type heralds the announcement: "Literary Societies Clash in Debate."

Harry's scholarly aptitude is apparent on some old report cards which are liberally sprinkled with 97's and 98's, with no grades below 90. Bless Miss Bunning's understanding heart and Harry's dauntless determination, there is a handsome 99 in Latin. Harry took Caesar like Caesar took Gaul, and never mind Cicero!

Here also is the commencement program of the Simpson College Academy, dated June 9, 1913. The president of the class was Harry A. Bullis. He must have been instrumental in choosing the class motto: "Why Stay in the Lowlands; the Highlands are Calling."

At commencement time the president of the Indianola Academy class of 1913 won the oratorical contest with his talk, "The Power of a Purpose," in which he pointed out that our goverment was founded upon two fundamental ideas — the ideas of human liberty and justice. "When our forefathers created this nation, their thoughts were definitely directed toward these two fundamental ideas, and acting in the same principles, and thinking the same things, they were able to build up a strong, democratic state. Although they were but three million weak and untrained people, they won out against a larger force of trained and disciplined men because they were dominated by a master purpose which drove them ever onward toward their goal. The point is, the founding of our nation was not a matter of chance or luck—it was simply the expression of the power of a purpose.

"Some people always live down in the valley of life; they never climb to the hilltops; they never see beyond the crossroads. It seems to me if one ever wishes to get any place, he must see beyond the things of the present to the things of the past and to the things of the future; he must look beyond the apparent effect and result of the cause to the very cause itself. If we analyze the primary basic things that underlie all great world movements, we find that every such movement has been started and carried on by organized human effort, by a definitely directed train of thought; in other words, by a purpose . . ."

The gifted young orator was presented with a nineteen-volume set of The Hudson Shakespeare, bound in leather. This was the boy who had started life as "stammering Harry Bullis," who had sweated the battle for clear articulation while he was delivering papers and cultivating corn.

Harry and another senior tied for top grades in the class. The diploma he got from Simpson College Academy, he notes, was the largest diploma he ever received!

Bullis had entered the race late, he had broken a speed record and a precedent, and he had crossed the finish line like a champion!

Two years after he was graduated from the Simpson College Academy, the Academy—but not the college—ceased to exist. He always jokingly said that he had put it into discard because he insisted on shortening the curriculum. It may never have recovered from the "cyclone" that whizzed through it. At any rate, the institution provided a most convenient way for the young man from Council Bluffs to obtain his preparatory education before going to the University of Wisconsin.

Packing up his "Positive Mental Attitude," Bullis wasted no time heading for Madison, Wisconsin, the university city which is slightly more than three hundred and fifty miles northeast of Council Bluffs.

Chapter Three

The Highlands Are Calling

As a student from Iowa, Harry Bullis would ordinarily be required to pay out-of-state tuition, so he wanted to establish legal residence in Wisconsin as soon as possible. The recent graduate of Simpson College Academy obtained a job as one of the assistant University electricians and spent the summer "wiring in" buildings on the University of Wisconsin campus.

Bullis became so well acquainted with the janitors all over the campus that they gave him excellent service in any of the laboratories in which he was taking courses as a student. They took personal pride in seeing one of their fellow workmen going through the University of Wisconsin.

A month after Harry Bullis began work at the University that summer, he felt the crushing impact of the first great tragedy in his life. He was notified that his mother had died. It was a tremendous shock because Bullis had always planned to provide his mother with a very comfortable home in her later years and do his utmost to repay her for all of her loving affection and encouragement. He attended the funeral at Council Bluffs, Iowa. The next day he was back on his job at Madison.

Harry's little sister, Jennie Gould Bullis, was eleven years old at the time of their mother's death. Her father immediately arranged to have her enrolled in a Protestant boarding school, All-Saints College, at Sioux Falls, South Dakota. The All-Saints School, which at that time had turned out many distinguished alumnae, has since become an elementary school.

After her graduation from the Sioux Falls school, Jennie Bullis went back to Council Bluffs to be a loyal companion and housekeeper to her father for all the years of his long life. When Harry Bullis' father retired, about 1925, the son supported them until his father's death, in 1957, at the venerable age of eighty-nine. After George Bullis died, Jennie Bullis married William F. Peacock, who had been devoted to her for many years, and they continue to live in the old Bullis home in Council Bluffs.

Back at the University of Wisconsin, during that first summer of 1913, Bullis was eating his meals at Fluker's Boarding Club. Because the regular school year was not in session, business was slack at Fluker's, with only four men at the table. Harry Bullis relished the stimulating conversations that developed, because each man was very much an individual in his own right. Although he didn't realize it at the time, he discovered later in the fall that one of his table companions was the eminent statistician and economist, Dr. Willford I. King. Another fellow diner was a student who was taking a postgraduate course. The third member of the quartet was a union man. The union man and Bullis both appeared at their three meals a day in their working uniforms—overalls.

There were many discussions, particularly after the evening meal, with the union man upholding his belief in labor unions and Bullis endeavoring to present the viewpoint of the businessman. "The distinguished economist and the postgraduate student," Bullis recalled, "sent both of us back to our corners once in awhile with a lot of highgrade economics."

Intensely serious moments were interspersed with spoofing—a normal requisite in any civilized conversation. Bullis considered those lively sessions at Fluker's Boarding Club, informal though they were, as part of his education. He referred to them as "seminars in Arts and Sciences and in Labor Relations and Economics." He was never doggedly biased in favor of one group or another. There is a wealth of evidence to show that he always considered himself part of the working team and, as he climbed the ladder to even greater responsibilities, he never changed his psychic identification with manual and office workers. In turn, the workers in ordinary posts never lost their respect for the big man with the friendly grin who knew how other working people feel.

Bullis had a surprise in store for him when school began in the fall and he matriculated at the university. Imagine his astonishment when he learned that Dr. Willford I. King, his erstwhile table companion, was one of the most distinguished members of the economics faculty and that he had just written and published a book on "statistics"!

Bullis took Dr. King's course in statistics. The first half year was an undergraduate course and Bullis found King just as uncompromising with him as with all the other students. Their mealtime camaraderie during the summer of 1913 had no effect on their relations as professor and student. The second half of the statistics course which Bullis took was a graduate course, and he found Dr. King's approach to the advanced students entirely different. He asked Dr. King one day why his manner toward undergraduate and graduate students varied so much. King said he treated graduate students differently because they had learned the fundamentals and had completed their undergraduate work. He had a healthy respect for their advanced knowledge.

Bullis appreciated the manner in which the distinguished economics instructor brought the "statistics" material to life. Bullis admired King because he was a perfectionist and a disciplinarian, and because he forced his students—especially the undergraduates—to become thoroughly familiar with all the subjects he was attempting to teach them.

Over the years, Dr. King kept up a steady flow of correspondence with Bullis. The former teacher died at the ample age of ninety-two on October 21, 1962.

In order to accomplish his goal of completing an engineering management course at the University of Wisconsin, Bullis enrolled as a freshman in the electrical engineering course of the Engineering College, perhaps the toughest and most challenging course on the campus.

Here was the great test of a determined young

man's ability to accumulate knowledge outside the schoolroom. Harry had never studied mathematics in school. Would those nights of intensive application, back in Council Bluffs, prove to be enough? Harry was disturbed that he might be "conned out" of the Electrical Engineering College because he could not meet the mathematics requirements.

All of the freshmen in the section were given a two-weeks' course in algebra and related mathematics. Then came the examination that would determine which students would be eligible to go ahead. Again Bullis turned in a championship performance. Although he had gotten his mathematics by himself, he found that he knew more about the subject than if he had taken it in school. It is a widely accepted fact that an avid reader can learn more about literature outside the classroom than in it. With a subject like mathematics, this feat is generally considered almost impossible.

As a student who had to work his way through school, Bullis had little time or money for frills, formals and foibles. He thought social activities and fraternities were fine for students who could afford them, and he wasted no precious energy being envious of classmates who had greater financial advantages than he. Hard-working Harry Bullis thoroughly appreciated the fact that he was a student at Wisconsin, with the right and freedom "to drive ahead with a positive mental attitude."

With time for only one outside activity, he made the same choice as he had made at Simpson College Academy. He joined one of the three debating societies, the Philomathia Literary Society, and participated enthusiastically in the debates of that group. In his sophomore year he was chosen captain of the Philomathia debating team which triumphed over Hesperia, a victory to be remembered with satisfaction through the years.

When Bullis was attending Wisconsin U, debating was one of the great arts, ranking almost with sports. The top honor for a debater in his senior year was to be selected as a member of the Joint Debating Team, in which two of the literary societies always participated. In Bullis' junior year he was selected to be a member of the Philomathia Joint Debating team, an honor that relieved him from writing a thesis.

"I have always thought that it is unfortunate that educational institutions do not emphasize the importance of debating as they did in past years," Harry Bullis declared. "Graduates, whatever they go into, must talk and present their cases. They should have training in debating."

Incidentally, Bullis always thought it unfortunate that educational institutions do not compel their students to take more English courses. "English is the language they must speak and write, and many college graduates are not proficient in the language of their country."

At the end of his first year, Bullis was tied with two other members of his class for first place in scholastic standing. Those grades were vitally necessary to help him obtain the chief immediate objective in his academic life. Now he had the ammunition he needed.

At the beginning of his sophomore year, just before school started, he finally succeeded in being allowed an interview with the great Dr. Richard Ely who was head of the graduate courses in economics.

As he had suspected, Dr. Ely wanted to know why a sophomore was anxious to see him. He said to the tall young man, "I suppose you are one of those engineering students who 'can't take it' and who now wants to go over to the easier letters and arts course."

Bullis showed him the record of his scholastic work during his freshman year and asked him to read two or three letters congratulating him on his high achievement.

Dr. Ely nodded. "All right, young man, what can I do for you?"

"Dr. Ely, I want to take an engineering management course, something no one has ever taken and probably no one else will ever take," Bullis announced. "I want you to assign an adviser for me who will let me take any course I wish during the remaining three years I will be at Wisconsin. I want to complete my mathematics and scientific studies in the Engineering College. I want to take many economics courses, and I want to take some courses in the School of Business. I also want to be given the authority to audit some of your graduate courses and those of Professor Commons." That's what the young man wanted!

Impressed with the mature poise of this student who knew where he wanted to go and how he wanted to get there—even to the point of forsaking respected academic routes and routines—Dr. Ely did appoint an adviser who allowed Bullis to follow the program he requested. He received permission to audit some of the graduate courses. As a result, the College of Engineering at the University of Wisconsin for years classed Bullis as one of its alumni. The School of Commerce also claimed him. He could have majored in mathematics by writing a thesis. However, he did major in economics. Standing on the pinnacle of academic accomplishment, he knew that he had achieved his goal of obtaining the Engineering Management Course he had carefully drafted for himself years before when he was a young bookkeeper in Council Bluffs, Iowa.

Harry's name appeared regularly on the published honors lists at the University of Wisconsin. He was a reporter on the senior paper staff. One of the highlights of his college life was the announcement of his election to Phi Beta Kappa.

An important milestone in the college career of Harry Bullis was the securing of fourth place in the final oratorical contest on March 10, 1916. The title, "The Power of a Purpose," had served him well at Simpson Academy, but he dealt with sizzling contemporary events in the Wisconsin oration. Bullis pointed out that America was the one great nation not involved in the major conflict raging on the other side of the Atlantic. Of her unique position, he said:

"She leads all the other nations in wealth, commerce and industry. Into the hands of her present population is placed the most momentous problem of all her history—the problem of deciding the fate of international ideals of human liberty and justice . . ." His thesis in his oration was the blunt statement that the

United States should get into World War I and that it should not stand aloof from what was going on in Europe.

That was a shocking statement for a student to make at the University of Wisconsin with its predominantly German population. One of the five judges was so impressed with Bullis' courage that he awarded first place to him. Of significance here is the fact that Harry Bullis—a year or two before the United States became embroiled in World War I—predicted that this country would become engaged in that war.

At the commencement of his class at the University of Wisconsin in late May, 1917, the student from Iowa who had "made good" at Wisconsin presented the class gift of two thousand dollars in Liberty Loan Bonds to the University of Wisconsin to initiate a fund for the construction of a tower on the highest point on the campus. It was specified that clarion bells should be installed in the belfry. During the ensuing decade, various classes contributed their funds to the project. Now the tower crowns the highest elevation on the campus, complete with a set of melodious bells from Switzerland.

The student from Council Bluffs had strained and struggled for a college education. With intensive practice he had achieved the ability "to speak and read perfectly and easily and well." He had chosen to tackle an unfamiliar and difficult course of study, and he had reached his goal in triumph, with a Phi Beta Kappa key as his badge of exceptional merit.

Did the University of Wisconsin mean anything else to him? Many years later, as the speaker at an annual banquet of the Wisconsin Alumni Association, he would recall his undergraduate experiences with lyrical delight:

"Four of the happiest years of my life were spent on this beautiful campus, and I am happy to be back at homecoming time. This visit recalls many fond memories: the moon over Mendota . . . canoes riding rippling water . . . soft shadows on the Hill . . . couples strolling arm in arm . . . hours of earnest quest of knowledge . . . the soul-stirring pictures of thousands of loyal Badgers, bareheaded, erect, with their hearts swelling to 'Varsity' . . . then graduation and a fond farewell to Wisconsin."

But he neglected to mention his sometimes "soul-stirring" adventures as an intrepid sewing machine salesman! Although the extra-curricular vocation furnished the financial support that enabled him to stay in college, it was a summertime activity.

After his freshman year at Wisconsin, Bullis, with the assistance of his father, secured employment for the summer as a wholesale salesman for the New Home Sewing Machine Company. His territory included the western half of Iowa and the entire state of South Dakota.

When Harry Bullis became associated with anything he wanted to know how it operated—backward and forward, inside and outside. While his father had been a sewing machine man all his life, Harry knew practically nothing about repairing the intricate mechanisms of the sewing machine—a skill which he suspected might be slightly necessary in that job.

The Chicago office of the New Home Sewing Machine Company invited him to attend a two-day briefing session in Chicago. His expectations were modest enough. "I had expected that some of those two days would be spent in learning how to repair the machine. But no, I was passed from one executive to another, each telling, in his own way, the history of the company and its policies."

With the last afternoon of his "briefing session" flitting past, Bullis became alarmed and asked the sales manager, "What am I supposed to do if I am asked to repair a machine?" Someone in the office loaned him a beaten-up, dog-eared, typewritten statement, with the admonition that it be returned promptly. Evidently this material was considered a rare and valuable document. Bullis copied "How to Get the Best Results from Your Sewing Machine" into a little notebook which he carried in his pocket as he set forth to do battle with the unknown.

During the next day or two, he went north on the train from Council Bluffs, Iowa, to a town on the Missouri River where he was to call on his first customer. Getting off the train with the other salesmen at that stop, he went in and introduced himself to the proprietor of the General Merchandising Store which sold New Home Sewing Machines.

The man greeted him too enthusiastically for comfort. "I am glad to see you!" he assured the new salesman with hearty good cheer. "I have been waiting to see you for several months, because I have three machines that need fixing. We will just hitch up the old horse and call on each of these three customers and you can repair these machines."

Bullis figured the storekeeper was getting pretty far ahead of himself with that sweeping statement. He tried to squirm out of the trip but to no avail.

At the first farm home, they were led to an upstairs sewing room by the huffing-puffing farmwife. She explained what she thought was wrong with her sewing machine, and then she visited with the storekeeper. Bullis, in the corner with the sewing machine, got out his little notebook and read the instructions dealing with that particular problem. Miracle of miracles, he was able to correct the trouble and get the machine whirring merrily again.

His self-confidence took a nosedive at the second and third stops, where the machines stubbornly refused to co-operate with Bullis or his little notebook. In desperation, the baffled salesman suggested that the storekeeper send the sewing machine heads back to the factory. The storekeeper looked as though he would just as soon send Bullis' head back to the factory. The neophyte salesman didn't blame the storekeeper for being "utterly disgusted," and he was not too surprised when the man refused to order any sewing machines from him. Bullis remembered that the dealer did business in a town that "used to be called Ottawa," but he wasn't going to let that place become his Waterloo!

On the return trip to town behind the dealer's good old horse, Bullis frankly confessed that this was his first trip and that he really did not know anything about repairing sewing machines. "But," he declared,

"I will arrange to meet with an old sewing machine operator over the next weekend. During the following week, I will come back and repair those sewing machines if it's the last thing I do." He did just that, and the storekeeper ordered some sewing machines from him. It was a sale he never forgot.

By a strange quirk of fate, that was the last time—during the three summers that he wholesaled sewing machines—that anyone ever asked him to repair one!

Naturally, Bullis was new at the job of selling, which usually requires even more technique than repairing. While his father had always been a great salesman, no one credited Harry with having any attributes along those lines.

The Wisconsin University man had devised a sewing machine sales story which took him about ten minutes to deliver to his poker-faced rural "audiences." "These old time proprietors of general merchandise stores in the various towns in which I called during the first two or three weeks would just sit and listen to my whole speech while they were smoking their pipes, and then I would have to start all over again." In the days before radio and TV, this was probably the best entertainment those dealers had. About that time, Bullis would thump down his case in exasperation and say, "Now listen, Mister, I am working my way through the University of Wisconsin by attempting to wholesale these machines. I'll admit that I know nothing about the job. However, within a month or so, I will know something about it." Taking a deep breath, he continued, "Now the company is not going to keep me out here very long if I don't turn in some sales and you just have to buy one of these machines." About half the time, according to Bullis, that frank argument worked. He had a healthy respect for the persuasive powers of frankness.

There was a spirit of boisterous informality to salesmanship in the prairie country in those days. In the state of Iowa there is a town about every seven or eight miles, and salesmen working the stores would ride in the cabooses of freight trains, leaving early in the morning and making seven or eight towns that day, stopping at each town for fifteen or twenty minutes. Bullis joined that stalwart group of salesmen riding the caboose, the traditional wooden car that writes finis to the rear end of a freight train. The salesmen would give cigars to the engineer to put him in a good mood to blow the whistle five minutes before he was ready to leave.

When the train stopped at each little town, Bullis would sprint up the hill, or the most convenient street, to his customer's shop and present his case "perfectly and easily and well,'" always keeping his ears perked for that whistle. When the whistle sounded, the patient salesman often would put on his "desperate act," delivering a final ultimatum: "Now listen, I will give you a discount if you will order the machines. Take it or leave it!" Half the time the stunt would work and he would sell some machines. Then he would dash down to the moving train, toss his sales case on the front platform of the caboose and swing himself up on the second platform with a long-legged flourish.

Salesmen had various modes and methods for solving their transportation problems. In South Dakota, about fifty years ago, there were few roads and numerous little communities consisting mainly of one large mercantile store set down in the middle of almost nowhere. Only the farmers in the encircling area might have names for those places. Bullis would team up with candy salesmen who had Model T Ford cars, paying them three dollars a day to ride along with them to the small communities. Many times they would take down fences to drive across the lone prairies and pasture lands on their business trips. When Bullis handed in sales from those remote localities, the sales manager would wire back, "We never even heard of the place. It is not even on the map."

During that first summer, Bullis very shortly learned that his customers could ask him only fifty questions, so he developed model answers to fit them. Just as soon as the customer would ask a question or give the impression that he was not yet ready to buy, Bullis shot back an appropriate answer or comment. This method, he discovered, developed his own confidence, and he surely impressed his customers with his mental dexterity. His college record shows that it probably helped to make an excellent debater of the tall, energetic fellow from Council Bluffs.

At the end of the third summer, Bullis wound up his final sales trip in scenic Rapid City, South Dakota, on the western side of the state. The sales manager, pleased with his fine performance as an enterprising sewing machine salesman, wired him to take off a week at the company's expense and tour the awe-inspiring Black Hills country. Bullis accepted the offer with enthusiasm. Even though it would be a decade and a half before Gutzon Borglum would carve those sculptured heads on Mount Rushmore, the scenery was magnificent, and Bullis remembered that Black Hills vacation as one of his greatest experiences.

Whether it was scholarship or salesmanship, Harry Bullis always believed that the basic requirements are determination to work hard, plus a thorough knowledge of all the elements and details involved, including the human factors. Then an individual is equipped to take off in the direction which will lead to the peak of achievement. He always thought that the three summers he spent as a sewing machine salesman were of major value in the development of his personality. He had no one to lean upon. He made his own success or his own failure. With a natural interest in people, he learned to approach new customers with his hand outthrust and the greeting that was spoken with increasing self-confidence, "I'm Bullis of the New Home Sewing Machine Company."

Whether he was loping up the hill from a caboose, or jouncing across the prairie in a Model T Ford, he was always striving to "drive straight ahead with a positive mental attitude"—even if it meant taking down a few fences on the way.

Chapter Four

Bullis Tackles New York

"Get thee behind me, Satan!" retorted Harry Bullis when he received some mighty alluring job offers during his senior year at Wisconsin. His background of five years of experience with the Gas and Electric Company and his high scholastic record made him a man to be sought after, even without a diploma. Any average man, tired of being poor most of his life, would have been sorely tempted by the salaries that were dangled before him.

"If it's the last thing I do," Bullis kept telling himself, "I'm going to get that diploma from the University of Wisconsin!" And he didn't relax until he got it.

He did take time out for a trip during that spring of his senior year. Realizing that he must secure employment after graduation, he selected five of the most promising offers and notified them that he would divide the expense of the trip equally between the five companies.

The last prospect on the list was The Chase National Bank of New York City. Mr. Gerald Dahl, a distinguished New York lawyer and an alumnus of the University of Wisconsin, was looking for a young man to become his assistant. Bullis had been recommended to him by one of his professors, and Dahl and he had carried on a quite extensive correspondence.

Bullis ended his tour of the five companies by calling on Mr. Dahl. It was the grand finale of the trip. Like every other Midwestern boy who had never been to New York City, Harry Bullis was tremendously impressed with the importance of the metropolis.

The office of The Chase National Bank at that time was at 165 West Broadway. Promptly at the hour of his appointment he gave his name to Mr. Dahl's secretary.

He felt very jittery because he wanted to make the best impression possible. Imagine his surprise when Jerry Dahl walked out of his office, grasped his hand and greeted him, "Bullis, how the dickens are you?"

All of Bullis' nervousness evaporated. He felt as though Mr. Dahl were an old friend.

Feeling secure about obtaining employment because he already held a handful of aces—four other job offers—Bullis talked very frankly to Mr. Dahl. He even had the brash audacity to ask, "Mr. Dahl, what do you have to do to advance in The Chase National Bank? Do you have to marry the president's daughter?"

Dahl said, "Bullis, I can't answer that question, but I will take you in to see the man who can." He escorted Bullis straight to the office of Mr. Albert Wiggen, president of the bank. He undoubtedly winked at the president as he explained, "Bullis doesn't know whether to take a chance with The Chase National Bank or not. He wants to know if the only way to advance in this institution is to marry the president's daughter. You are the president. What are you going to answer him?"

President Wiggen leaned back in his chair and said, "Bullis, I have two daughters. The oldest one has been married for several years and the younger one told me just last week that she was engaged. Therefore, all avenues of advancement in the bank along that line are closed. However, let me tell you how I started out as a messenger boy in a bank in Boston and worked my way up to the position which I now hold." Bullis proceeded to be a good listener for the next half hour while Mr. Wiggen told the story of his brave struggles up the ladder of success.

Even though the compensation offered by the bank was less than any of his other four offers, Bullis was so impressed with the institution, and with the opportunity to work and live in the stupendous City of New York, that he agreed to enter the services of The Chase National Bank. Feeling pleasantly secure about his immediate future, Bullis returned to Wisconsin and the graduation exercises that he has never forgotten.

Doffing his cap and gown, he went back to New York and explained to Mr. Dahl that he would like to spend the next six months going through all the departments of the bank. Here was Bullis, the "measuring man" again, wanting to know how everything in this banking institution added up.

Dahl asked him, "What do you think I hired you for?"

Bullis answered, "I thought you employed me to become your assistant."

"Yes," Dahl agreed, "but why do you have to spend the next six months going through the bank?"

Bullis, aware that Dahl had recently come into the firm too, asked, "What do you know about this bank?"

"Not a confounded thing!"

"Well, don't you think one of us should know something about it?" He told Mr. Dahl that he was willing to devote much excess time to studying The Chase National Bank, which operated on a twenty-four-hour basis. He would like to talk to the chief clerk and arrange first to go out with the messenger boys, and then start at the note teller's department and proceed through the bank.

Somehow, this twenty-five-year-old fellow, born in a rural community in Nebraska, had conceived the notion that the improvement of a business institution would benefit everyone concerned with its operation, from the top executive behind his spacious desk to the janitor in his broom closet. Any strides toward greater efficiency would, like ripples spreading out in every direction, ultimately benefit the nation and even the world. But, some human beings are creatures of habit, Harry Bullis knew, and they are inclined to turn defensive at any hint that they are not performing with absolutely top-notch efficiency. Hauteur and a cold glare will greet any suggestions about turning over a new leaf.

It would be most diplomatic, Bullis told Dahl, if he were not known as his assistant around The Chase National Bank. He wanted to study the operations of the bank as a completely free agent. His attachment to Mr. Dahl's office would label him as a sort of early-day "efficiency expert," often caricatured as a tight-lipped, frugal-eyed fellow who pussy-foots around corners, counting paper clips. Harry Bullis was too big in every way to be a proper pussy-footer. On top of all that, he had this weakness—he liked people and he hated to make them uncomfortable.

Nevertheless, his engineering management course had provided him with a mental treasure trove of theories that needed testing out, and this was the prime place to do it. In Bullis' mind was a picture of an ideally-conducted business operation, profitably and conscientiously balanced in terms of management, workers, and consumers. Putting it quite simply at a later date, he said: "The search for profits fortunately improves the standard of living for all groups in our society."

Somehow this alien Midwesterner had been born knowing that a business is only as strong as the people who work in it. To succeed in discovering whether a large, distinguished New York firm was performing to the height of its ability, he would need to take his case directly to its employees.

All of his life, Harry Bullis had been starting at the bottom and working up. He went to Mr. Schweppes, an old German, who was the chief clerk and office manager and confided his plans.

The old fellow told him gruffly, "Now listen. You

may be a college graduate but believe me, you are not going to advance very fast here in the Chase Bank. It has taken me forty years to get where I am right now."

Bullis speedily dismissed a mental picture of himself sitting in Mr. Schweppes' place forty years from that moment. Seeing the "undaunted look" in the newcomer's eyes, Herr Schweppes agreed to let him go out with the various messenger boys. That day the tall University of Wisconsin graduate found himself treading the fabulous Wall Street thoroughfares, thrilled at the opportunity to enter the estimable banking establishments whose operation he had studied in economics courses in college.

When he was a teen-age bookkeeper, Bullis had been a jealous guardian of his overtime minutes because he wanted to study. He still wanted to study, but his classroom had become The Chase National Bank. At the end of the first shift, after he had accompanied the messenger boys on their rounds all day, Harry went to Mr. Schweppes and said, "I have nothing to do in the evening. Is there any way I can assist you? I have had a lot of experience in office work."

Mr. Schweppes might have raised a bristling eyebrow, but he consulted his schedule and said that the cashier could use some help. At that time the Chase Bank, which had not yet begun to modernize, and whose offices were out of date, had only one cashier's cage where the money was deposited. Bullis joined that staff of six or seven men.

Everything was going along smoothly until the cashier suddenly made a shattering announcement.

"We are six thousand dollars short in cash! No one leaves this cage until we find it." Bullis, the new man, got his particularly sharp scrutiny. The staff worked until midnight before they located the error.

When Bullis walked across the Brooklyn Bridge that night to Flatbush Avenue where he had a small room at the Brooklyn YMCA, he thought to himself, "Well, this is some first day at the bank!"

Bullis told Mr. Dahl where he was staying and that he would be available if Mr. Dahl ever wanted to talk to him on a Sunday. After about three weeks had passed, Jerry Dahl rolled up to the YMCA one Sunday morning in a big car with a chauffeur at the wheel.

Evidently Harry Bullis' presence had not gone unnoticed, as he had made his resolute way through one department of the bank after another. Mr. Dahl had been hearing about his activities and was anxious to know what conclusions Harry had reached.

Bullis proceeded to tell him, in characteristically pithy terms, what was wrong with The Chase National Bank. The employees in the various departments in which he had served had not been reluctant to talk to the big Midwesterner who showed so much interest in procedures.

At the end of Bullis' dissertation there at the Flatbush YMCA, Mr. Dahl said, "That is very interesting. Put it in the form of a memorandum. I want to send it to the president of the bank."

When he finally drew up the memorandum, Bullis recalled that it was in a much more conservative form than he had presented it orally to Mr. Dahl.

Mr. Wiggen and Mr. Dahl then requested the discerning young fellow to write a weekly appraisal on the state of the bank. If there was anything wrong with the Chase National they wanted to be enlightened about it.

High on Bullis' list of shortcomings and bottlenecks was an inflexible Mr. Miller, a vice president who was in charge of all office operations of the Chase Bank. Miller prepared Bullis for an encounter, in later years, with a rigid disciplinarian named Benjamin S. Bull in the Washburn Crosby Company. No form or method could be changed in the bank without the authority of Miller. This, of course, resulted in a status quo for the bank; and the employees had no incentive to suggest improved methods. Bullis disclosed this state of affairs in his weekly reports to the president and vice president.

Four months after Harry Bullis became a Chase "employee-at-large," the United States fulfilled his earlier prediction. The World War was on, and Bullis decided to enter military service.

Harry Bullis had known, for several years, what this war was about. Hopefully, it would be a "war to end war"; and equitable peace terms would halt the gangrenous spread of nationalistic power gluttony. Hopefully, it would teach Kaiser William of Germany and Emperor Francis Joseph of Austria-Hungary, and any other conniving monarchs and nations on either side, to reject Europe's heritage of fears and jealousies left over from old wars and backed up for decades by the bristling power of oversized armies and navies. There had been many wars, and every time the pie had been sliced differently at the treaty table, with hungry resentment burning in the eyes of those who had gotten the leanest portions.

One morning Harry went out and enlisted in the United States Army as a private. On the afternoon of the same day, Mr. Dahl called him into his office and said that the Chase Bank had just secured an ensign commission for him in the United States Navy. "Mr. Dahl," Bullis said, "you are just a few hours too late."

Dahl then asked Bullis to assemble a final report before he left the bank. Almost on the verge of marching off to make the world "safe for democracy," Bullis devoted much time and attention to compiling the material. He divided it into seven points, or seven major changes, that he thought should be adopted by The Chase National Bank, some of which would plow straight through the roadblock-authority of any obstinate vice presidents. To drive straight ahead with a positive mental attitude—sweeping aside outmoded, musty, tradition-sacred impediments to progress as though they were cobwebs—had already become second nature to Harry Bullis. It would be reflected all his life, in his valiant approach to his work, his country, the people and products of the planet on which he lived, and the vast universe which housed his Boundless Faith.

The young man who had "nothing to do in the evening" in the Big City actually did meet a lovely, very intelligent young lady. While he was at the University of Wisconsin, he had worked so industriously that he had lacked the time to become friendly with girls, although he did enter into more social life in his senior year when he saw commencement rushing toward him almost too soon.

After he entered the service of The Chase National Bank, his old teacher, Willford I. King, wrote Harry that there was a young lady named Irma Alexander with whom he should become acquainted. This would be no problem; she was a "fellow-banker" in The Chase National Bank.

The fact that Miss Alexander was also a fellow-alumnus of the University of Wisconsin would make her especially attractive to Harry Bullis. One of the top students in Dr. King's class, she had been graduated from Wisconsin in 1915, two years ahead of Harry's class of 1917. During those four months with The Chase National Bank, Harry sought Irma out and became well acquainted with her.

Dampness, autumn, and New York scenes that would soon become memories—there is a rain-scent of nostalgia in Harry Bullis' recollections of the day he joined up with Uncle Sam's forces. "It was a cold, rainy afternoon in the early fall of 1917 when I journeyed to Camp Upton, New York, to be enrolled as a private in the United States Army."

Chapter Five

Yankee in Paris and London

The camp facilities were just being constructed and most of the barracks were only half completed. If they had asked Bullis, those barracks at Camp Upton would have been finished a year earlier. He had known this war was coming.

Nobody was asking Bullis anything. He was packed into a barracks with a large group of other privates. "Being a lowly private," he recalled, "I couldn't even kick a dog around!" This is purely a figure of speech; Harry Bullis loved dogs.

Here he was, hoisting himself by his bootstraps again. Sometimes he would get discouraged as he thought to himself, "After all these years of securing a formal education, I am forced to start at the very bottom." He had need of one of his favorite prayers:

"O God, give me sympathy and strength
And keep my courage high,
God, give me calmness and confidence,
And please, a twinkle in the eye."

He resorted to that prayer, he said, many times in his career.

On the second day of his service as a private, a captain in the Engineering Corps visited the group and called out the name "Private Bullis." Bullis, who had drilled his way through two years of military training at the land-grant University of Wisconsin, drew himself up to his erect, formidable height, saluted the captain smartly, and answered, "Yes, sir!" It was obvious that the University of Wisconsin had equipped Bullis for almost anything.

The officer explained that he was a professional engineer and that he had just been commissioned a captain in the Engineering Corps. He had immediately encountered one difficulty—he knew nothing about military training or discipline. He was looking for a soldier who was actively familiar with the manual of arms and would be capable of becoming sergeant of the engineering company he was forming. After examining the records of the privates at Camp Upton, he had selected Bullis as the man best qualified to whip the company into shape—which is just about what Bullis had to do.

In the late afternoon, the captain escorted Bullis to the barracks where about one hundred and twenty-five members of his company—which at full strength would number two hundred and fifty men—were already quartered. These men were from the East Side of New York City, and Bullis measured them hopefully with his eyes. Apparently most of them only took baths once a month, and none of them knew anything about military discipline.

The next morning at reveille, Bullis addressed his group of one hundred and twenty-five raw privates on the drill grounds in front of the barracks. He explained politely that they were all now in the United States Army and that someone had to give orders. "Since I have had two years of military training at my university, the captain selected me to train you," Bullis announced. With typical Bullis optimism, he said that he was now going to teach the group how to execute some fundamental orders.

The first of these, he explained, was to form a straight line and then look to the right at the command "Right dress" — but not a man of the motley group stirred. Bullis saw that further cajoling would be of little avail.

With a prayer on his lips, Bullis shouted, "You s.o.b.'s, either I'm your leader or I'm not!" As might be expected, Bullis had also taken two years of boxing instruction at the University of Wisconsin. With an attitude that he described as "just plain scared," he bellowed at his sullen group, "I'm going back of the barracks and I'll take you s.o.b.'s on, one at a time! If you don't want to tackle me, then I'm your leader."

Bullis strode to the back of the barracks and waited, shaking slightly in his puttees. Almost anyone would figure that Harry could give a thumping good account of himself, as long as they came one at a time. Not a man of the company showed up. "That," Bullis said, "is how I became leader of that group."

During the ensuing days he built the company up to its full strength of two hundred and fifty possible soldiers. He was made sergeant, and everything seemed to be progressing in an auspicious manner. Bullis had reason to feel optimistic.

Then came a new jolt. One day, just as he was completing the job of turning out a well-disciplined company, he received orders to proceed to Fort Jay on Governor's Island in the Bay of New York and join a company which was being formed there and which would be an essential part of the Chief Surgeon's office in France. He was stripped of his rank of sergeant and became a lowly private again.

With "Jack Armstrong Bullis," this type of catastrophe would not be permanent. He was soon advanced again to the rank of sergeant. The company was composed mainly of college graduates, and Bullis became assistant top sergeant during its formation. Then the old army top sergeant was having difficulties with the men in the newly-formed company, so the colonel removed him and promoted Bullis to that position.

Like a terse tribute to the dreary, chill bitterness of that period, Harry said, "The men were living in barracks on Governor's Island. A cold wind swept over the island. Two of the boys died."

In the late fall of 1917, Bullis was given instructions to escort the company—at three in the morning—to Hoboken, New Jersey, where they were shuffled down into the hold of an old German coal boat that some jester had re-christened the "Mercury."

The amusing event of that embarkation reveals how truly optimistic Bullis could be. Having become an expert on army rules and regulations, he was aware that a top sergeant was entitled to a cabin. "Where," he inquired of the commanding officer of the Mercury, "is my cabin?"

"Cabin, hell!" the officer barked. "You are to go down in the hold with your troops." In wartime a sergeant isn't any more private than a private, but it was a good try. Bullis organized bucket squads down in the hold and prepared for a rough voyage.

The good ship Mercury had as its convoy an American cruiser. Halfway across the Atlantic, the Mercury lost the cruiser, and it was nineteen days before the vessel landed at St. Nazaire, France.

Under orders, Bullis conducted his company to the Chief Surgeon's office at Tours. It was not many days before one of the top officers in the headquarters of Colonel Charles Dawes, Chief Purchasing Agent for the American Expeditionary Force in France, arranged for Bullis to be transferred to Paris as a member of his Bureau of Accounts.

A picture of Sergeant Harry A. Bullis, taken on April 15, 1918, shows him as a fine upstanding young soldier, chin up, chest out, looking very reliable in his World War I uniform. By May 22, 1918, he had taken a searching look at the city on the Seine, and he wrote to G. M. Dahl, back at Chase National:

"I have been in Paris for almost five weeks. It is indeed a most wonderful city. . . . Paris has an excellent subway system. . . . One of the most enjoyable features about Paris is that the people take time to eat, drink and sleep. The Frenchman likes to promenade slowly along the beautiful boulevards, or sit in front of a cafe and sip his drink while he watches the people go by. . . . The French are becoming accustomed to the strenuous Americans, yet at times we shock them by our pace. . . .

"I do not believe that the Germans will ever take Paris. Paris is the heart of France. . . . It seems to me that this war will be won only after America has placed several million troops in France. America must not underestimate the strength of the Central Powers. She must throw her maximum resources into Europe and play the game to the finish. . . . I called at the American University Union here last week, and had the pleasure of seeing about two hundred signatures of the University of Wisconsin graduates who are in France and have registered at the Union. About fifteen of these are members of my class. . . ."

In the light of future developments in the life of Harry A. Bullis, one sentence takes on special significance. He commented, "I understand that the government forecasts an excellent wheat crop for America this year. That is very good news."

Bullis' military training at Wisconsin continued to prove a valuable asset in the A.E.F. Now he was asked to train the lieutenants and captains who were being added to the staff of Colonel Dawes without previous military training. It was just as well that Bullis was undismayed by opposition, because the new officers objected vigorously to being given orders by a mere sergeant.

It wouldn't be appropriate to invite these fellows out behind the barracks, but there was another way to break the deadlock. Bullis could become an officer too. An application, supported by excellent letters of recommendation, was submitted by Sergeant Bullis. One day he was notified that within three hours he was to be examined for a commission by three officers, which allowed him only enough time to get his suit pressed and his shoes shined.

Many college men who were inducted into the army as privates kept saying, "Oh, well, what's the use?"—and they remained privates until the end of the war. Bullis did not share their indifference. He was genuinely interested in the challenge ahead.

Fortunately Bullis had tackled the army rules and regulations with the same spirit that he had displayed in all of his former endeavors. He had decided, at the time he was inducted into the United States Army as a private, that he would become thoroughly knowledgeable in all things having to do with his branch of the service. When he was summoned for the examination, he hoped that he had prepared himself well.

His appearance before the three examining officers was backed up by letters of recommendation describing him as "one of the finest young fellows I have ever known . . . enthusiastic for his work, conscientious and persistent"—"reliable and accurate, possessing a personality which gains him friends at every stage of life"—and other highly laudatory comments on his habits and character.

Bullis answered the first three questions correctly. After that, he recalled, the examination was rather easy. A few weeks later he received his commission as first lieutenant in the Sanitary Corps of the United States Army. He took it upon himself, from the wealth of knowledge that he had accumulated, to develop a manual of rules and regulations of the American Expeditionary Forces, and he was admitted to many of the confidential conference meetings over which Colonel Dawes presided.

Colonel Dawes had been given his position as the Chief Purchasing Agent of the A.E.F. in France because, as a young banker in Lincoln, Nebraska, he had become a great friend of General Pershing when Pershing was the commandant at the University of Nebraska. Dawes was later given the rank of general. His name should ring a bell with students of history and with adults who were old enough to vote in 1925 —Charles G. Dawes served as vice president during the administration of President Calvin Coolidge. Dawes also shared the Nobel Peace Prize with Sir Austen Chamberlain in 1925, and he was the author of several books on banking and finance.

In Harry Bullis' scrapbooks are pictures of his brother Roe and other A.E.F. men in their jaunty overseas caps, knee length uniform coats and puttees— those long strips of khaki cloth that World War I servicemen learned to wind expertly around their legs, from knee to shoe-top.

Bullis' older brother was fighting in the Marine Corps on the front, in the French lines. Roe's company participated in the memorable engagement at Chateau-Thierry, not many miles from Paris, in which the German advance was decisively halted. Harry Bullis could hear the crackling and booming of the guns, but he did not know until late one night that half of the men in Roe's Marine Company were killed at Chateau-Thierry. Roe woke Harry up when he brought the remaining members of his company down to Paris to get cleaned up. Harry Bullis provided baths for all of them and they returned to their company at Chateau-Thierry the next day. After Roe explained what had happened, the commanding general forgave the remaining men for being "absent without leave" for a few hours out of all those gory, filthy weeks in the trenches.

Harry was seldom in close contact with Roe, but he thought about him often. In a letter to Professor Gilman at the University of Wisconsin, Harry wrote:

"I have a brother in France of whom I am justly proud. He is one year older than I am and is the only brother I have. His company is the United States Marine Gun Battery, which has been at the front for nearly three months, and which has been doing much gallant work both during the first offensive and during the present offensive. I haven't heard from him for over two months. Wherever he is, or whatever has happened, I take off my hat to my brother who has given all that he is and all that he has to his country. . . ."

Harry's impressions of Paris were vividly described in another paragraph of the letter to Professor Gilman:

"The offices of the Bureau of Accounts are located in what is reported to have been the finest hotel in France. (The Kaiser had planned to eat his Christmas dinner here last year.) This Palace Hotel, which is situated in the most aristocratic section of Paris, is in the shadow of the Arch of Triumph on the most famous avenue of Paris. Along this avenue, kings and queens have paraded with their victorious armies under the Arch of Triumph. Within the next two or three years, the victorious armies of France and her

Allies will march up this avenue and under the great Arch, as all of the other victorious armies of France and her allies have done. . ."

Harry saw his brother several times after the battle of Chateau-Thierry, the final time at Limoges in the southern part of France. Roe Bullis, with three remaining members of his depleted outfit, was in the hospital. Harry gave his brother all the French francs he had, and Roe proved himself an able businessman. He took the money, bought out the inventory of the Red Cross stand and retailed it at a profit. With the proceeds, he bought sets of precious Limoges procelain china for sister Jennie and their aunt.

A year or so later, Roe Bullis died of wounds he had sustained in World War I. As Harry had said, his brother had given all that he had to his country. Roe was honored with an impressive American Legion funeral in Council Bluffs, Iowa, the town that the young Bullis brothers had called "the capital of the world."

Some time after Harry Bullis had arrived in France during World War I, Miss Irma Alexander left her job at Chase National Bank to serve her country. She was appointed financial secretary of the Young Women's Christian Association with headquarters in Paris, where Harry was stationed. Lieutenant Bullis occasionally found his way to the Paris YWCA, and he and Irma became engaged. They agreed to wait until World War I was over to be married.

Irma Alexander's responsibilities were neither casual nor trivial. Because of her experience with Chase National Bank, she had been requested to take charge of the YWCA's banking business with the Army of Occupation. She learned all the banking laws and regulations, most of them different in each bank, and handled the overseas operations efficiently for many months.

Miss Alexander was also delegated to act as hostess for visiting American celebrities in France and Germany during her tour of foreign service. Later she recalled having studied the French titles and their pronunciations very carefully so she could speak them fluently when she introduced Mrs. Woodrow Wilson and other American dignitaries to French nobility.

Paris was a fascinating place to be, when the bugles sounded cease fire at eleven in the morning on November 11, 1918. Harry Bullis remembers that day as though it were a scene from "What Price Glory!" The streets of Paris were so tightly packed with squeezing, shoving, deliriously joyous, hoarsely cheering people, that each individual was forced to move in the same direction as the ecstatic celebrants, sometimes with feet lifted right off the ground for several steps.

Frenchmen were laughing through their tears, clasping strangers to their bosoms, waving wine bottles, tossing flowers. It had been another hideous, exhausting war; and many of them could remember when they had needed to rush troops to the first battle of the Marne in Paris taxicabs, which is considered just about as dangerous to the passengers as being in the thick of battle. But their beautiful, beloved city had survived, even though the Germans had been so close they could almost hear them belch. Naturally the Yanks were happy to help the Parisians celebrate the victory in which they had shared.

After the Armistice, President Wilson was scheduled to arrive in Paris, and Bullis was appointed a member of his staff. When President Wilson rode down the Champs Elysees in a triumphal victory parade with his Secretary of State, Robert Lansing, in the automobile behind him, Bullis—who was standing on the curb of the Champs Elysees with two other officers—remarked to his companions, "The President of the United States is sitting on top of the world. He will not be there very long."

Looking back on that victory parade and the Versailles Treaty, what conclusion had been drawn by the seriously perceptive student of economics, engineering, mathematics—and the history of the human race? "The peace terms of World War I," he noted, "were arranged by the leaders of four nations: Woodrow Wilson, President of the United States of America; Lloyd George, Prime Minister of Great Britain; Georges Clemenceau, the Premier of France, and Vittorio Orlando, the Prime Minister of Italy. At that time these four nations were the leading powers of the world. The nations who arranged the peace treaty in World War II were entirely different. Now Italy is a third rate power. One hundred years from now, the United States of America will probably be a second or third rate power. At that time China will probably be one of the leading nations of the world."

Paris, during the early winter of 1918, was warmed by memories of victory gained and peace restored. One day, when Harry Bullis met his fiancee, he told her that he had been ordered to Great Britain to attend one of the English universities for four months. It looked as though the young couple's theme song would be "There's a Long, Long Trail A-Winding," because Irma had news too—she explained that she had just been ordered to go to Germany with the troops.

Bullis suggested with typical American impetuosity, "Let's get married right away. Then, when you become ready to leave Germany, all I will have to do is ask you to join me in Great Britain.'"

Harry and Irma had only about four breathless days in which to get married. The dashing young officer had not reckoned with the fact that French regulations insist on publication of the banns for two weeks before a wedding. Living up to his capacity for driving ahead with a positive mental attitude, Harry spent three feverish days busily bribing various French officials. At last he and Irma were given permission to have a French wedding, and the momentous day arrived.

Still slightly shaken from the ordeal of one wedding service that day, the new bridegroom was surprised to discover that his fiancee's friends in the Young Women's Christian Association and the Red Cross unit had arranged an American wedding that evening in the apartment of Mrs. Fowler, a friend of Irma's. Bullis gulped when he saw the large group of American girls and officers in their uniforms, and he said he completely lost his nerve. However, when the soloist sang "Oh, Promise Me" in a pure, beautiful voice, his courage came flooding back and he went gallantly through the second ceremony.

Within a day or two, Irma Alexander Bullis went to Germany with the troops, and Harry journeyed to England with about one hundred and twenty-five other American officers. The future students from the A.E.F. arrived first at Notting Ash Camp at Liverpool, England.

With one exception, every American officer in the group was anxious to enroll at Oxford University so he could say in later years that he was an Oxford man. During the rough crossing of the English Channel with the other officers, Bullis had resolved that he would devote himself to obtaining the utmost benefit from this four months' opportunity that the United States government was giving him to further his education in England. He had examined the various universities in Great Britain with typical thoroughness and had determined that he wanted to attend the London School of Economics of the University of London, because the faculty of that school had many distinguished professors who taught economics and business subjects. As a student at Wisconsin, Bullis had become familiar with the books of many of those eminent professors, and he was eager to hear their lectures.

On his arrival at Notting Ash Camp in Liverpool, Bullis was startled to find that his name led all the rest on the list of men destined for Oxford University at Cambridge. Wasting no time on ceremony, he climbed up on that panel, crossed out his name, and signed it with a flourish under "The London School of Economics, London, England."

Bullis did not know that the man who had allocated the American officers to the various universities was his old professor of history at Wisconsin. Professor Fish was extremely disturbed when Bullis indicated a strong preference for the London University School of Economics over proud Oxford.

Harry Bullis knew what he wanted, and he lived up to his pledge to glean all the knowledge possible, while he had such a valuable opportunity. He became well acquainted with many of the famous faculty members of the distinguished school and absorbed as much information as he could. In a letter to Professor S. W. Gilman, dated May 6, 1918, First Lieutenant H. A. Bullis wrote:

"I am getting a great deal out of my accounting and business organization work under Professor Lawrence R. Dicksee and of my statistical work under Professor A. L. Bowley at the University of London, London School of Economics. The more that I study accounting, statistics, and graphic presentation of facts, the more I am convinced that there is a wonderful field open in the commercial world for intelligent men equipped with a combination of accounting and statistics." (How true this statement has proved to be!) "If you know of any other company requiring the services of a statistician having a knowledge of accounting and of the art of graphically interpreting facts, I shall be pleased to negotiate with that company and to call upon its executives in July or August."

Harry was still climbing that Army promotion ladder and leaving the bottom rung far behind. Shortly after he started studying at the London School of Economics, he was advanced to captain in the Sanitary Corps of the United States Army.

Evidently Harry Bullis did not mope around, feeling completely crushed because Irma was separated from him by the English Channel and many kilometers of land. He was concentrating hard on the economics course. On Sundays he would study religion and history by attending the services of three or four churches in Great Britain.

There is mute testimony that he must have had his lonely moments. Among his scrapbook souvenirs is an empty envelope with the return address, "Mrs. H. A. Bullis, American YWCA Hostess House, Paris." It is addressed to "First Lieutenant Harry A. Bullis, American Officers' Inn, 5 Cavendish Square, London."

The hospitable British did not neglect the American strangers in their midst. One of Bullis' "outstanding memories" during his sojourn in London, was having tea at Lady Astor's beautiful home on many a Thursday afternoon. Each week, Lady Astor invited a different group of distinguished leaders from England, Scotland and Ireland to her Thursday teas. Invariably one of the guests was the Prince of Wales, who later became King of England and now bears the title of Duke of Windsor. Mentioning that Harry Bullis became well acquainted with the Prince of Wales at Lady Astor's home might conjure up an intriguing mental picture of the slightly-built heir to the British throne and the very tall Captain Bullis, chatting over their teacups.

While he was at the London School of Economics, Bullis began to concentrate on the progress of the League of Nations which was then just being formed.

He wrote many letters regarding the League to several individuals in the United States.

In these letters he put his finger on a weakness in the League, a failure with regard to the false sense of national sovereignty from which the United Nations suffers today. He observed that the League of Nations was actually only a treaty, even in President Wilson's plan, among individual nations determined to keep as much sovereignty as ever. Bullis argued in his letters for a parliament or congress with authority to legislate for international co-operation.

"The League," Bullis said, "would serve only when there was unanimity. War would still be the recourse when the powers disagreed." He pointed out that armament was left to the discretion of each nation, as was conscription for war. He said, "Unless the nations arrange for more co-ordination than this, there will be another war in twenty years."

During some of Bullis' addresses two or three years before his death he said that the only enforceable arms control system in a nuclear age will be an authority higher and more powerful than its parts. He thought that a world order organization with a world constabulary to police the peace is now demanded because of the terrific spectacle of one hundred and twenty nations as members of the United Nations in our electronic, fast communications and nuclear weapon age.

In his letters in 1919 from London, Bullis deplored the post-war class consciousness throughout Europe and warned that "Our own legislation is showing that its influence is being felt in America." It was his contention that "the science of self-management, which is the science of life itself, should be taught in every country of the world. This was his definition of self-development education which should stimulate every individual to be concerned about his own welfare.

In a letter of May 28, 1919, to one of the officials of The Chase National Bank, Bullis looked beyond the muddled map of Europe and the League of Nations to the weaknesses of a potentially dynamic nation, his own homeland: ". . . We must develop to a greater degree the human efficiency of the individual man, or the manpower of our country. The power of money was amply demonstrated in the Great War just finished, but no one knows what manpower may do yet. We Americans must achieve greater things out of ourselves. That nation will build up the most which is the greatest man builder. The society of a nation is merely an extension of the individuals comprising that nation, and if we expect to make the next Great War—in which I firmly believe that America will play one of the major roles—a short and decisive one, we must develop to a greater degree our manpower—the personal element in business and in all activities."

In 1919 while Bullis was still at the University of London, he wrote an article pleading for the union of the universities of the world. "It would strengthen the League of Nations," he argued, "and increase the chances of peace." In this article he was a quarter of a century ahead of UNESCO.

After Harry Bullis had been attending the London University School of Economics for two months, he wrote to Irma asking her to leave Germany and join him in London. Reunited again, they spent delightful weekends in the English countryside, visiting Stratford-on-Avon and many historically significant English villages and towns.

History and its famous names still live in Harry Bullis' scrapbooks. There is a handsome admittance card to the Officers Club at 9 Chesterfield Gardens in London. The privileges of the club were extended to First Lieutenant Harry Bullis for the duration by Major General Biddle, the president; Field Marshal H. R. H. The Duke of Connaught, and the executive committee.

A night to remember was the War Anniversary Dinner which was celebrated at the Connaught Rooms, Great Queen Street, off Kingsway, on Tuesday, April 8, 1919. The London Daily News reported that the spontaneous college yells, starting with a U. of Wisconsin "locomotive" astonished Lord Birkenhead and Lord Bryce. "Mr. Davis, the American ambassador, was too much at home for surprise. But Englishmen are not familiar with college yells, and the dinner had not reached the second course before a group of 500 American khaki boys leaped to its feet and nearly blew the roof off with what proved to be the yell of Wisconsin University. . . . Wisconsin's example was speedily followed by Harvard, Yale, Pennsylvania, Columbia, Michigan," and many other American institutions of higher learning.

Toasts to His Majesty the King and to His Excellency, the President of the United States, were proposed, and American Ambassador John W. Davis referred to the group as "the vanguard of a great army of

American students that would visit the ancient seats of learning in Great Britain, and that there would be a reciprocal response by a like army of Britons visiting the United States. (Hear, hear.) He would like to see the exchange of professorships multiplying and re-multiplying." In other words, Oxford, Cambridge and London, would be replacing Bonn, Heidelburg and Berlin as centers of academic prestige in the decades ahead.

In one of Harry Bullis' scrapbooks is an application that was approved by the army authorities. Captain Bullis had requested that his wife be allowed to return to the United States in the same boat that carried him. He didn't know that the commanding officer would shortly provide him with plenty of company.

With the four months' course at the University of London terminated, Harry and Irma prepared to board ship at Liverpool for the return trip to the United States. The day before the ship sailed, Bullis was informed that he would be in command of two casual companies, composed of former convicts, on the voyage home.

He had no trouble with those men on the return trip to the United States, all of which gives a great deal of insight into the character of Captain Harry Amos Bullis of the A.E.F.

Chapter Six

Men to Match Her Mills

During his eighteen months overseas, Bullis had been applying his "mental measuring stick" to prospects for a future business career. In many letters which top officials in The Chase National Bank had written to him, he had been asked to return to the bank upon completion of his military service. He had also received a number of letters offering him attractive positions in other companies in New York City.

Writing from London on May 6, 1919, he told Professor S. W. Gilman, "I have just received a letter from Mr. Malcolm C. Rorty, statistician for the American Telephone and Telegraph Company." He was considering the offer, Bullis said, and would arrange for an interview with Rorty on his return to the States. He had recently been offered another job that would involve too much traveling, "a condition of living that doesn't interest me much now"—which is understandable.

Bullis' job-hunting attitude was like a blueprint for success in the hands of anyone who has determination, intelligence, and the gumption to work hard. He was not interested in slumping down into the first good offer that came along and vegetating there for the rest of his life. It was still a case of "The Highlands are Calling," and Bullis was getting the message loud and clear.

While his wife liked New York City and would have preferred to remain there, Harry's four months of experience with The Chase National Bank had convinced him that New York was no place for a young man to start at the bottom and attempt to work himself up. He had noted that the heads of practically all financial institutions and corporations in New York City were men who had become successful in other parts of the country and who had been called to their New York posts after they had attained positions of leadership elsewhere. With due regard for his wife's feelings, Captain Bullis of the A.E.F. was determined that they would not live in New York City.

The captain, like other Americans still in khaki, went on his quest for a future—a future that the war had delayed for some men and completely denied to others. He called on Vice President Dahl and President Wiggen of The Chase National Bank, and both of them urged him to resume his connections with the bank. He was told that six of his seven "improvement points" had already been put into operation. In spite of this cheering vote of confidence, Bullis indicated that The Chase National Bank was not quite what he wanted.

"Well," Mr. Dahl asked, "have you ever heard of James F. Bell?"

Bullis said, "No."

"Have you ever heard of Washburn Crosby Company and Gold Medal Flour?" Mr. Dahl wanted to know.

In his memory, Harry Bullis carried a treasured picture of his mother kneading bread dough and baking cakes and cookies in the old kitchen at home. His answer sounds like an inspired slogan for an advertising campaign. "Yes," he said, "my mother always used Gold Medal Flour."

Dahl explained that James F. Bell, who had just left the service of the War Production Board of the United States Government, was looking for young men to enter the services of Washburn Crosby Company. "I would advise you to call on him in Minneapolis," Mr. Dahl told Bullis.

Bullis shook hands with Mr. Dahl and Mr. Wiggen and told them he would contact James F. Bell when he and Irma went to the Middle West to visit their relatives in the immediate future.

Leaving the conference at The Chase National Bank, Harry and Irma strolled thoughtfully along for a block until they came to historic old Trinity Church yard where the gravestones of the makers of America date back to the late 1600's. Seated on a stone bench in the cemetery, they took stock of their situation. For a moment, Harry might almost have been tempted to dash back and tell Dahl and Wiggen he wanted that job after all. Practically all of their money had been spent while they were in Great Britain. They had just made a decision to decline the offers of employment in New York City and start all over again.

Presently they looked at each other and laughed as Harry reminded his wife of Horace Greeley's admonition, "Go West, young man, go West." Years ago, Harry had startled his boss, Mr. English, when he left his good, safe bookkeeper's job in Council Bluffs to set out for Simpson Academy. Again, he was choosing risk instead of a mediocre sort of security.

When the young couple left historical Trinity Church yard behind them that day, Harry was on his way to making history elsewhere. He would never again be the same man when he came back to New York, but he would remember. Years later, the president of the mighty General Mills organization would call on Henry S. Sturgis, vice president of the First National Bank of New York and a director of General Mills. The illustrious visitor from Minneapolis would stand at the window of Sturgis' second floor office, immediately opposite Trinity Church yard, and muse down on that same stone bench where he and Irma, many years before, had made one of the major decisions of their lives.

Harry Bullis recalls the midsummer heat that greeted them when they arrived in Minneapolis in 1919. He parked Irma in a small room at the Dyckman Hotel and set out for the Washburn Crosby Company to seek his fortune. Still wearing his uniform, Captain Bullis was interviewed for two and one-half days by James F. Bell and his associates—John Crosby, Charles C. Bovey, Frederick Atkinson, Guy Thomas and others. Looking at these men, Bullis must have wondered if he would get to know them better or if this would only be a terminal point in his quest.

One of the youngest of these top executives was James Ford Bell who was rapidly becoming the guiding genius of the Washburn Crosby Company. Bell was a tall man too, almost eye-to-eye with Bullis. He was a worthy son of his remarkable father, James Stroud Bell—the descendant of a long line of Quaker millers, who had ventured out from Philadelphia to become a managing partner in the firm as it was constituted in 1888. In his 1919 conferences with James Ford Bell, could Bullis have begun to imagine the tremendous part that this vice president of Washburn Crosby Company would play in his future?

Around Bullis were men who walked in an inherited aura of Minnesota history. President of the company at that time was John Crosby whose Washburn Crosby connections dated back to the shrewd, witty John Crosby who had moved from Bangor, Maine, to Minneapolis in 1877 to manage the early milling empire which had been established by spectacular soldier-statesman-businessman Cadwallader Washburn in the lusty post-Civil War years.

Minnesota had not asked for "men to match her mountains." Her mountains were her towering mills and elevators, and she had been richly endowed with generations of men to match them. Here, in 1919, were descendants of the colorful, farsighted early milling heroes—the efficiently daring pioneers who had needed to build their own ladders before they could set foot on the bottom rung.

If "blood will tell," Bullis was talking to men whose ears still throbbed to the distant, untamed roar of St. Anthony Falls on the Mississippi, and to the rasp of heavy millstones and the clank of porcelain and marble rollers, during the dawn of Minnesota's commercial history. Bullis could not go back into the late 1800's to join the ranks of Cadwallader Washburn, William Dunwoody, John Crosby, James Stroud Bell, Charles Bovey, and other earlier stalwarts, but he would do his pioneering in modern style, from a modern point of view.

There was one early stalwart who was too stalwart to suit Bullis. He referred to Benjamin S. Bull as "the great man" in deference to his undoubted ability.

They saved Mr. Bull until the afternoon of the second day of Bullis' round of interviews at Washburn Crosby. When he was ushered into the great man's office, Bullis failed to hear the name correctly, and he said politely, "I did not quite understand your name."

The thick-necked man bellowed, "B. S. Bull!"

Bullis, who wanted to be diplomatic and friendly, said, "That is interesting. One of the students I met at Wisconsin is a Benjamin S. Bull, who has since become a distinguished lawyer and has an office in Madison."

The shiny-domed man, thinking that Bullis was "kidding" him, looked as though he would turn purple.

When Bullis saw his wife that night, he told her, "If I am ever employed by Washburn Crosby Company, there is one officer who certainly is not going to like me. His name is B. S. Bull."

Harry Bullis uttered another fateful comment that night. If Mr. Bell did not make him an offer by noon of the third day, he said, they were going to move on to some other place because he certainly needed to secure employment soon.

As though he were a mind reader, James F. Bell told Harry Bullis at noon the next day, "Captain, we have decided that we want you to enter the service of Washburn Crosby Company. We want you to set your own salary."

Mr. Bell doubtless expected Bullis to put a fairly high premium on his services, especially when the young man resorted to some verbal hedging. Bullis said, "I do not think that is very fair, Mr. Bell. You know that I have just recently been married, and my furlough from the United States Army is practically finished, and I must secure employment. You also know that there is inflation rampant in this post-war period and that it is going to cost something for a young couple to live."

"Never mind, Captain," Bell said encouragingly. "You are to set your own figure.'"

Taking a deep breath, Bullis fixed his "inward eye" on the bottom rung of the ladder again. It looked comfortably familiar, and he was not afraid of it or the hard work that went with it. "If you will allow me to do what I want to do the first year, I will accept a salary that I consider suitable at this time."

Bell was startled when Bullis named a figure that would be fairly adequate for an unmarried, semi-skilled laborer. Bullis realized later that it was much too low; but he was not too proud to think of himself as starting at the very bottom, in the salary as well as the labor bracket. He believed that good men sometimes are ruined by allowing themselves to be kicked up the ladder too fast and being afraid to admit that they have developed bad cases of acrophobia when they are unable to cope with a multitude of unfamiliar problems and responsibilities.

Bell saw that this man knew his own mind. "You are employed. What do you want to do?"

Bullis surprised him again. "I want to spend the next year at the Minneapolis plant of Washburn Crosby Company learning the business—because if I am to advance in this company, I want to first know all about its production facilities."

Bell was absolutely taken aback by this proposal; but he must have thought, as he studied the tall, resolute young man before him, that this indeed might be "a man to match our mills."

Bullis wasted no time starting out on that year of employment in the Minneapolis plant of Washburn Crosby Company. At that time, in the summer of 1919, the plant was producing a peak of thirty thousand barrels of flour a day, a record production. Bullis went right to work packing flour and tackling other manual jobs. The general superintendent, W. H. Bovey, gave him permission to browse around the place so he could become thoroughly familiar with its operation.

The history of the company showed that the growth of "Patriarch" Cadwallader Washburn's flour empire had been more than just a matter of building mills and rolling out the barrels of flour. Many years of experimentation and improvement of milling methods—of benefit to the entire industry—had been necessary before the gluten-rich hard spring wheat of the Northwest was recognized as a fine product that would yield higher baking returns than the old king of the flour industry, soft winter wheat.

However, in Benjamin Bull's department, the accounting methods had remained solidly antiquated, and there were several other conditions that had prevailed for so long that they were accepted as "gospel."

There were some people who agreed too wholeheartedly with Bullis about the dangers of kicking a man up the ladder too fast, and they applied them to Bullis. The head millers formed a small, compact group who kept their sacred knowledge to themselves. All of them felt that they had labored diligently to attain their positions as head millers, and they were not going to allow any upstart young man to advance to their own heights of achievement very fast. Bullis had only been at the plant for a few weeks before he became aware, one day, that the head millers were grinding out rumors as well as flour. That fellow Bullis, the story went, had been placed in the plant to change its methods of operation, but they would defend the good old ways to the bitter end! Bullis recalled that almost everyone in the plant viewed him with suspicion.

That same evening, when the ex-captain returned to their one-room apartment with the bed in the wall and a kitchenette and bath, he said to his wife, "Well, Irma, I guess it is a good thing I was in the army for eighteen months, because I certainly am in a war at the Minneapolis flour mill!"

The only man who didn't regard Bullis with distrust was Chris V. Nelson, the foreman of the sack department. Progressive-minded Nelson was glad to adopt Bullis' suggestion for a more efficient way of performing his operations. Incidentally, after Bullis was transferred to the Minneapolis office a year later, he arranged for Chris Nelson to be transferred to the purchasing staff. In 1943, one of the first acts of a newly elected president of General Mills was the appointment of Chris Nelson as head of the purchasing department. Nelson, who had revealed his worth by being receptive to new ideas, held that important position for many years.

In "Business Without Boundary — The Story of General Mills," James Gray describes Harry Bullis at that time as "a young man in a hurry." From all the evidence, it is clear that Bullis carried in his mind a picture of progress in motion; it was a part of his personality and it kept spurring him on. Oddly enough, he was never in too much of a hurry to see where he was going.

Gradually Harry Bullis did win the favor of some of the executives in the plant by "selling" them on more efficient approaches to their work. It was difficult to remain antagonistic toward the friendly, optimistic, new employee who was eager to be helpful, as much for their benefit as for his own satisfaction. There was nothing arrogant about this hard worker. He lived with his wife in a tiny apartment, in a row of apartment houses packed together along a very ordinary street—they are still standing there—and he walked almost a mile to the mill every day.

Naturally the former student of the London University School of Economics was keenly interested in the bookkeeping and accounting systems, but he found out that nothing in the way of forms or methods could be changed at the Minneapolis mill without the approval of Mr. B. S. Bull. Therefore, nothing had been changed for years. In Mr. Bull he encountered a situation similar to the one he had found in The Chase National Bank before he went overseas.

After much deliberation, Bullis concocted an efficient method of performing certain accounting operations at the Minneapolis plant. Since these innovations could not be installed without the approval of Mr. B. S. Bull, he determined to confront the great man in his office and he asked for an appointment.

When the brave Mr. Bullis came striding into the general office, the Negro porter, Will Moden—who afterwards became a great friend of Harry's — almost turned white at the thought of Bullis' invading the bastion of B. S. Bull.

Mr. McCarthy, secretary to B. S. Bull, came running nervously down the corridor to meet the caller and usher him into the great man's presence. There the mill employee proceeded to present his case clearly and distinctly to the awesome individual behind the desk.

Mr. Benjamin S. Bull said, "That looks good to me. Put it in."

No one fainted, but the episode surely amazed everyone at the Minneapolis plant.

During his first year in the mill, Bullis convinced Mr. W. H. Bovey, the plant superintendent, that a cafeteria was vital to the welfare of the employees. Mr. Bovey appointed the alert Mr. Bullis and the assistant general superintendent, Dwight Bell, to select a place and install the modern eating facilities. In line with his active concern for the health of the American worker, Bullis also organized baseball and basketball teams.

Bullis seemed to have an endless chain of ideas for showing the employees that their activities were good news. He convinced Mr. Bovey that the mill should have a plant publication. Serving on the committee to choose an editor, he was instrumental in picking Earl Gammons who was a reporter on the Minneapolis papers at that time, and who eventually became manager of radio station WCCO.

Mr. Bull put his seal of approval on the long-enduring weekly publication by christening it "The Eventually News." He is credited with being the originator of the still-famous slogan, "Eventually—Why not Now?" which used to decorate bags of Gold Medal flour and scores of billboard advertisements. The catchy phrase was rumored to have been inspired by Mr. Bull's devotion to brevity, while he was hacking away at some wordy advertising copy.

The Gold Medal emblem on sacks of Gold Medal Flour will probably never be discarded. Its magnificent history can be traced back to 1880, when Washburn Crosby's three superior brands of flour were awarded the gold, silver and bronze medals at the Millers' International Exhibition in Cincinnati.

Washburn Crosby had been making a wide variety of news even before the 1880's. According to a story in the Northwestern Miller, "An old timer hath it that in the Washburn Crosby & Company exhibit at the Minnesota State Fair in 1880 was the main shaft of the Washburn 'A' water wheel salvaged from the explosion and fire that destroyed a large part of the Minneapolis milling establishment in 1878. The shaft was warped and bent, and gave dramatic indication of how hot was the fire and how thorough the destruction . . ." One of the terrifying disasters of that period, the explosion occurred early in the evening of May 2, 1878. It was a fire and brimstone holocaust with all the drama of Doomsday. Onlookers reported that the great roof of Cadwallader Washburn's "A" Mill arose to a height of five hundred feet and poising for an instant in mid-air, hurtled with a crash into the crater of seething flame where the mill had stood. As though set off by chain reaction, nearby structures along St. Anthony Falls exploded and collapsed, and the air seethed and churned with debris from three large mills—the Washburn, Humboldt and Diamond. It was noted that even after the explosion, the waterwheel of the "A" mill kept revolving steadily, as though determined to triumph over the surrounding ruins.

"That was the way things were in those days," the Northwestern Miller pointed out, "for the great Cadwallader C. Washburn, too, was determined to carry on, planning a new mill with his feet in the ashes of the old." He planned for his people too, immediately arranging to take care of the families of the men who had been killed in the 1878 explosion.

Washburn, of course, enlisted the aid of science to seek the cause of the explosion — it was determined that the slightest spark could make an explosive combustible of the fine haze of flour dust always present in the air. The hazardous condition was corrected by installing the Behrn exhaust to provide for ventilation of the millstones.

Harry Bullis appreciated learning about Cadwallader Washburn, the "father" of the company, who had been magnificent in times of disaster and stress, and who had remained aware of human values when it really hadn't been considered necessary. Articles and newspaper clippings in his scrapbook vouch for Bullis' abiding interest in Washburn Crosby traditions.

During that first year in the Minneapolis mill, a figure out of his own past re-entered Bullis' life. In 1919, Mr. A. L. English, the manager of the Council Bluffs Gas and Electric Light Company who had employed him as a teen-age bookkeeper, heard that the ambitious young man had entered the service of the Washburn Crosby Company. He knew that Bullis had graduated from Simpson College Academy with high honors, that he was graduated from the University of Wisconsin with honors and a Phi Beta Kappa key, that he had spent four months in the service of The Chase National Bank, after which he had enlisted in the army and risen from a private to a captain in eighteen months overseas. So Mr. English said to Mrs. English, "Let's go up to Minneapolis and call on this remarkable fellow."

Naturally Mr. English expected Bullis to have a high executive office. He called at the General Office Building of the Washburn Crosby Company and asked to be shown to Harry Bullis' office. This was news to the office staff. Mr. English had difficulty finding anyone who knew Bullis, but he finally was told that he could locate his former bookkeeper at the Minneapolis mill.

Down to the Minneapolis mill went Mr. English, and there he discovered a jolly miller named Bullis in overalls festooned with flour dust. Instead of a white collar position, this was a white overall job. "He was virtually shocked," Bullis recalled.

With a valiant effort, English managed to conceal part of his amazement. He told Harry that he and Mrs. English would like to have the Bullises for dinner that night at the Radisson Hotel, and the invitation was accepted with pleasure.

During the course of the dinner, Mr. English said, "Now, Harry, tomorrow night we want to come out to your home and have dinner."

Into Harry's mind leaped an alarming picture of their tiny quarters, that one-room kitchenette and bath with a bed in the wall. Bullis called that type of apartment "Picking-them-up-and-setting-them-down," because when you picked something up, you had to find a place to set it down and that was mighty difficult.

Harry exchanged desperate glances with Irma and then tried to convince the Englishes that it would be much better if the Bullises could give them dinner at a hotel.

"Oh, no," insisted Mr. English, "we want to come out to your home!"

Returning to their apartment that night, the Bullises took inventory in the twinkling of an eye. They only had a table and two dining room chairs. "What are we going to do about it?" Irma asked.

Harry said, "I will go down to the corner grocery and get two cracker boxes that you and I can sit on tomorrow night."

They had discovered, the night before, that Mr. English had to be careful about his diet. Irma learned that lamb chops were permitted. In her chafing dish, she cooked up a tasty dinner of lamb chops and set it on the table. Again the Englishes were shocked, but a jolly good time was had by all.

Even though he didn't say it, Mr. English might have thought that Harry Bullis would have been smarter to sit tight on that bookkeeper's stool in Council Bluffs. Unfortunately, Mr. English did not live long enough to see that his former employee, Harry A. Bullis, finally reached a point where he and his wife lived in a beautiful home with a full set of dining room chairs and that Harry even had an office of his own.

Chapter Seven

The "Measuring Man"

From some of his remarks, it is apparent that Harry Bullis never considered himself a shining jewel among men. A diamond in the rough—an ungilded lily, perhaps — he radiated the comfortable humility that arouses affection as well as admiration. He sought success with unabashed fervor, he set his goals, and he kept achieving—but every now and then he would pause and ask himself, "Is this really happening to me, to this fellow Bullis from Council Bluffs, Iowa?"

Because he never lost touch with the awkward, stoop-shouldered, stammering boy that he had been, he saw that same boy in the other strugglers around him, and it enlarged his capacity to understand and encourage those who lacked his self-determination.

Capacity — that is the expansive quality that was most noticeable in Harry Bullis' personality. While he was disposing of one challenge, he was looking forward to the next one. It was not enough to concentrate on cultivating corn—he also disciplined himself to speak perfectly and easily and well. It was not enough to work a six-day week as a bookkeeper—he taught himself mathematics at night. It was not enough to accept the four-year high school curriculum as it was—he reduced it to two. It was not enough to be a perfectly good private in the United States Army—Harry became a captain, and maybe he would have ended up a general if the war had lasted long enough!

Here he was, choosing to spend a year in a Washburn Crosby mill in 1919 and 1920. Again, a long day of manual labor was not enough. He was staying over for the second shift, so he could study the flour milling process from every angle.

The flour milling process—just a few simple words to describe the mighty enterprise from which America would often feed the war-ravaged and famine-torn nations of Europe, pouring out a vast flood of rich, white abundance! Post-Civil War immigrants would remember the daily black bread of their Old Country homelands. Their children would remember fine, white Gold Medal flour in the familiar bag. About the time that a boy named Harry Bullis was delivering the Council Bluffs **Nonpareil,** William C. Edgar, the editor of The Northwestern Miller was writing a book entitled "The Story of a Grain of Wheat." Poised on the rim of a great new century in 1903, Mr. Edgar rhapsodized prophetically on the future of wheat, flour and bread, in this great new land:

"The chapter on America, still open and continuing, tells of the march of the pioneer from east to west, always accompanied by a larger expanse of wheatfields; of records made in wheat production only to be broken by other and still greater ones; of a new nation reaching out to feed an older world; of vast systems of railway and steamship transportation created in response to an increasing demand for bread abroad and a steadily growing production of wheat at home."

Bullis was an avid student in the "flour milling classroom." He could see that Washburn Crosby was a great, far-sighted, dynamic company, and he chose to look at it from the best vantage point. There on the lower rung of the ladder it was not enough for him to collapse in an apathetic heap. He disapproved of apathy for himself and for the people around him. Instead of lunch buckets, he said, let's get some hot cafeteria food into these workers! How about promoting company spirit and healthful exercise by lining up some ball teams! How about a plant publication, so the employees can keep informed on activities inside the company! Bullis' capacity for improvement had height, depth, and unlimited breadth.

Did he feel that he was achieving enough, even then? Oh, no! During 1919 and 1920, Harry Bullis went over to the University of Minnesota and earned two semester credits, with a grade of A, in industrial accounting. Irma went with him. "She was more than a wife—she was a partner who took those University night courses with me," Harry remembered with fond affection.

On Armistice Day, in 1920, the first convention of the American Legion was held in Minneapolis, and Bullis organized all the ex-soldiers of World War I who were employed at the Minneapolis plant into a company and led them smartly up Nicollet Avenue. In 1920, many spectators must have wondered about that tall, erect captain marching at the head of his company. Many years later, when he participated in another parade in Minneapolis, there would be no question about his identity.

When Bullis took part in the 1920 American Legion parade, he had recently become a member of the Washburn Crosby accounting department. Just as he was completing his first year in the mill, in the midsummer of 1920, Mr. Benjamin S. Bull died of a heart attack. "There was confusion in the general office!" Bullis recalled. While Mr. Bull bore the title of "Chief Financial Officer" of the company, he had really dominated many of its operations. He had not developed a successor to head the accounting and financial operations.

James F. Bell's responsibilities already ranged over a vast and versatile area, but he was one of the milling giants who refused to dodge a fresh challenge. Although he admitted that he knew little about accounting, Mr. Bell said he would become head of the accounting department in addition to his other activities. He appointed an accounting committee of six executives, five of whom were present office executives of Washburn Crosby Company.

Who would be the sixth man in this select sextet? Big Harry Bullis washed the flour dust off his hands, combed his wavy hair, and answered the summons with alacrity. His year of "Mill apprenticeship" was finished, and he was ready.

In the allocation of office departments, three were assigned to Bullis. His description of one of them reveals the famous Bullis sense of humor. "One," he said, "was the statistical department which had a reputation that if you ever reached that department, it was the lowest place you could go in the company." Another department was labeled the "Profit and Loss Department" since it dealt with the profit and loss of various branch offices. Inside a week, Bullis had eliminated that relic of B. S. Bull's administration. By streamlining and merging operations, and slashing through miles of hallowed old red tape, Bullis emerged with one clean-cut area of supervision, the statistical department.

To Bullis, statistics was a lively and fascinating art. You could draw pictures and patterns with figures. With the proper explanations and diagrams, you could show where you had been, where you stood right now, and where you wanted to go. Even while he was in the mill, he had found time to draft an elaborately detailed report entitled "Motor Truck Cost Accounting," which would give "the best possible service to the customer at the least possible cost." His charts took everything into consideration, from barrel-mile costs to the placing of transportation equipment—both horse and truck—in the service for which it was best suited, "not for sentimental but for economical reasons." He pointed an accusing finger at "hidden" items of expense and depreciation that were not taken into account. He recommended that trucks be repaired at night and that interchangeable bodies be used for loading, so the drivers could facilitate deliveries.

As for the truck drivers, a bonus system should be instituted to encourage them to keep down repair costs on trucks and tires. Bullis also suggested giving an extra bonus to the driver with the best public relations record. "In a sense, he is Washburn Crosby's representative and can do much toward building up or destroying good will. Furnishing courteous service to the customer should be rewarded the same as giving cheapness per mile and carrying greater volume." The system, supported by so much logic and practical wisdom, was installed at the Minneapolis mill.

Figures, to Bullis, were never just cold numbers. They always represented people, products, and labor, and the personal and commercial profits thereof. You could put them all together, and they usually added up to something mighty tremendous. If they didn't, somebody had better start measuring again and planning some improvements.

Measuring the fruits of man's toil, as related to his personal condition and welfare, is a comparatively recent science. When he started worrying about cafeteria meals and recreational exercise for the workers in the Minneapolis mill, Harry Bullis was relating the efficiency-producing health of the worker to the number of barrels of flour he helped to process. When you want to build something, you start to measure. As he had noted in a letter from overseas in 1919, before he identified himself with the Washburn Crosby Company, Harry Bullis was vigorously in favor of building a bigger and better American worker. Harry would always be conscientious about the well-being of "the rest of the poor devils" around him. It apparently didn't occur to him that he often worked much harder and longer than those other "poor devils." He was not only ambitious for himself; he wanted everyone else to be enthusiastic about work and physical and mental improvement—to be vibrantly eager to promote the higher standard of living that was looming huge on the American horizon.

Harry's pleasant attitude toward his fellow men ran smack into a cold reception when he first started work in the financial department. The other "Old Guard" members of the accounting committee resented Bullis' having been brought up from the mill so quickly to become an accounting executive. They insisted on keeping a sternly possessive clutch on all the experienced personnel, although it was obvious that Bullis needed some assistants. The new young executive did not mope around, groveling for favors. He began to select and employ a number of young college graduates whom he believed had great potentialities. One of these was Gordon C. Ballhorn whom Bullis later appointed comptroller of General Mills. Ballhorn occupied that office for many years.

Bullis deployed his young men among the various departments to analyze procedures and operations. When all the material was assembled, he would prepare a new accounting system with a revised classification of accounts, tailored to the industry. By that time, Bullis realized that Washburn Crosby was operating under an obsolete accounting system.

The preparation of the new system was an ambitious, exhilarating project for him, and it took two years to complete. In the meantime, the new head of the Washburn Crosby statistical department became a member of the National Association of Cost Accountants and gave the group so much enthusiastic "Bullis support" that he later landed in the president's chair.

Bullis recalled the N.A.C.A. meetings as a source of instruction, diversion and sincere pleasure for him. Early in the 1920's he also became enrolled as a senior member of the Society of Industrial Engineers and was elected to serve as chairman of the Manufacturers' Club of Minneapolis.

Professor Gilman, at the University of Wisconsin, was quite impressed with an offer that his former student received from the Brooklyn Manhattan Transit Company in 1924. His starting salary would have been a substantial amount more than he was then receiving. But Professor Gilman was pleased when Harry wrote that he would remain with Washburn Crosby. Bullis believed there was a "real opportunity" right where he was. "The modernization of the accounting system of this organization is almost completed, and I am just now combining, with the analysis and interpretation of the comparative figures thus made available, a study of the economic factors involved in not only the operation of this company but in the entire flour milling industry. This, together with closer contact with the merchandising division of our company, should give me a good, practical, bird's-eye view of the business. Again, the officers of Washburn Crosby Company are keen, live-wire businessmen, and they are backing me up in wonderful fashion."

Bullis was confident that Karl Pearson had captured a high moment of truth in one short sentence when he wrote in his famous Grammar of Science, "If you can't measure a thing, you really don't know much about it." Applying Pearson to the Minneapolis concern, Bullis and his staff developed a revised accounting system and classification of accounts which would correctly measure the operations of Washburn Crosby Company so that they could be most easily interpreted to the operating executives. To Bullis, it was a masterpiece of practical logic, but he encountered one slight hindrance. Mr. Bell had admitted that he knew nothing about accounting procedures, and he was hesitant about giving Bullis the final authority to install the new system.

About this time, Mr. Bell invited Donald D. Davis, who was a banking executive in New York, to enter the service of Washburn Crosby. Mr. Davis had been chief assistant to Mr. Bell when he was in the War Production Board in Washington during World War I.

Feeling the need to refer the question to someone else, James F. Bell sent Mr. Davis all of the reports and surveys that Bullis and his staff had prepared, including the data on the new accounting system. In his office in the east, Mr. Davis studied the reports thoroughly and became convinced that the new accounting system should be installed.

When Donald Davis was elected secretary of Washburn Crosby Company, he summoned Bullis and told him to install the new accounting system because he was thoroughly sold on its merits and advantages. Necessary improvements were made as time went on.

Bullis no longer experienced any difficulty in expressing himself. In 1925, he wrote an article entitled "Opportunities for College Graduates in the Milling Industry" for the November issue of the Ronald Forum. At the midsummer meeting of the American Home Economics Association in Minneapolis in 1926, he told the institution section about "Some Shortcuts to Good Management." Included in his speech were such gems as, "You must come close to the appetite of each customer. . . . You can create and build value in your customers' minds by giving your foods a personality and making them stand out. . . . You should sell the end and not the means. Sell what your food will do for your customers; sell them healthy, satisfied bodies." The "Measuring Man" touched on budgeting —in which "you visualize your future operations and make a picture of what you are apt to meet."

In 1925, John Crosby, as chairman of the board, elevated James F. Bell to the presidency of Washburn Crosby. Bullis was getting a fine panoramic view of the company from the "summit point" of the central mills and offices in Minneapolis, but he knew that Washburn Crosby was a far-flung industrial empire with mills and food processing plants in other parts of the country, and a host of dealers and customers whose requirements were of basic importance. After several years as auditor of Washburn Crosby Company, Bullis became convinced that he should get closer to those dealers and customers and study the merchandising operations of the company, to round out his "practical, bird's-eye view."

After securing the permission of H. R. McLaughlin, general sales manager of the company, Bullis went to Mr. Bell with another of his unusual proposals. "For the next year," he explained, "I would like to leave my present position and become assistant to Mr. McLaughlin and spend most of my time in the field with the branch office managers."

Mr. Bell was becoming more accustomed to Bullis' bombshells, and this time he merely inquired, "And who is going to take your place as auditor of the company?"

Bullis explained that he always was developing men to take his place—he did not choose to be indispensable. It is apparent that Bullis disapproved most highly of men who keep an omnipotent clutch on their areas of authority, always making certain that no one poaches on their preserves.

When Bullis started climbing toward success, he did not choose a lonesome course. He did not hunt for a narrow ladder, so he could step on the fingers of anyone who wanted to climb in the same direction. "More than one can play at this game!" he said, and he chose a ladder that was high, wide and handsome, and he invited other men to share his ascent—if they also shared his belief in the merits of intelligent, hard work. Harry Bullis, the large-minded, wholehearted "builder of men," was still closely in touch with his God, and his religion gave him strength and fortitude in his daily dealings with his fellow men. Many years later, he would say in a radio interview:

"I am a man who believes in God. I believe that God is present in all of us, all of the time. Feeling this way it is impossible for me not to have the greatest respect for others, whatever their relationship to me, whether it's a member of my family, a business associate, or a stranger I pass on the street. I further feel a responsibility to my fellow beings, and I trust they feel the same responsibility to me."

The auditor-on-leave did spend most of the next

eighteen months in the field with Ray McLaughlin's managers and salesmen. One day when he was in New York, he telephoned Mr. James F. Bell and said that he would like to see him the next day in Minneapolis. When he went into Mr. Bell's office, he said he was convinced that what Washburn Crosby needed most of all was a comptroller who would be in charge of all accounting and statistical operations and who would be one of the chief assistants to the operating president of the company.

Some of the executives figured they probably had seen the last of that Bullis fellow around the place—with all his brainstorms for stirring up the comfortable old routine. That job in the field had appeared to be a demotion. Even though some of them were fairly disgruntled about it, Mr. Bell now bestowed upon Bullis the title of comptroller, and congratulations were in order. The former auditor was promoted to comptroller of the subsidiary companies.

Looking back over a significant decade in his life, Bullis recalled that the early part of the 1920's was a period of easy prosperity and rising prices. Any sensible business leader—knowing that "paper-profit manipulations" were running away with the stock market—realized that the boom could not last forever. "In 1927 and 1928," Bullis noted, "there was a great flurry of mergers between companies—with everyone concerned endeavoring to complete the mergers before the final crash occurred."

James F. Bell, as president of the company, was trying to decide whether the times were propitious for merging and expanding, or for retrenching. The idea of consolidating the Washburn Crosby Company with several other milling corporations had attracted him for a number of years, and he had been studying the situation.

Just about that time, a tempting plum appeared ready to drop into James Ford Bell's hand. Unlike the hectic September in 1889 when his father, James Stroud Bell, had fought off a British syndicate and triumphantly retained possession of the C. C. Washburn Company, this handsome offer of forty million cash dollars was too breathtaking to decline. It would mean the end of Bell's anxieties about the financial future of the company in those precarious times.

It turned out to be more than a case of accepting a check for forty million dollars with a hearty "Thank you!" to the eastern group of food products companies from which the offer had come. There was a bit of book work to be done first. Bell, Davis and Bullis went east and worked long weeks to effect the merger. Bullis, as comptroller of the Washburn Crosby Company, was the executive who often sat until midnight in a Wall Street office with representatives of the investing companies, analyzing the operations of Washburn Crosby Company.

It sounds as though it must have been a "spectacular production" as the transaction moved majestically forward, with all the documents being drafted and printed and on the verge of being signed, and all the business and social amenities being observed along the way. Finally, those weeks of strain in the realms of high finance appeared to be resolved. Before it was time to prepare the final documents, the eastern group withdrew their offer and the proposed merger was abandoned. However, the great benefit arising from this experience was the training in the entire field of mergers of Bell, Davis, and particularly Bullis because he had spent so much time answering the questions directed at him by a group of certified public accountants.

Chapter Eight

The Fifty-Million-Dollar Story

Early in the century, a Council Bluffs boy was jotting down a few figures about his newspaper route collections and his personal clothing expenditures. By the middle of the 1920's, he had become adept at evaluating mills and elevators, and compiling columns of figures that soared far up into the millions. By 1928, he knew how it felt to be involved in a forty-million dollar transaction. Soon after, a fifty-million dollar project would claim his figure-wise attention. It was a story that would become an epic of the modern business world.

When the Washburn Crosby gentlemen returned to their executive offices after the trip to New York, they were still the directors of a formidable chain of milling properties. There were the Minneapolis mills, rich in the traditions of Cadwallader Washburn and the men who had followed his lead. There were Washburn Crosby mills at Kansas City and Chicago, and at Louisville, Kentucky, and Buffalo, New York, each with its special reason for being where it was. The Chicago property included a corn meal mill and a cereal food plant.

Huge grain storage elevators, like "lighthouses" of the wheatlands, were a necessary part of the Washburn Crosby picture. In Duluth, Minnesota, on the shores of Lake Superior, the golden grain stored in elevators was shipped along the Great Lakes route to the plant at Buffalo, New York, for processing. Buffalo, strategically located, was fast supplanting Minneapolis as the greatest milling center of the world. Situated on "the Niagara frontier," wheat from the midwest and Canada could be shipped over the inland waterways, ground into flour in Buffalo, and exported with comparative economy and ease. James Stroud Bell had led the milling march to Buffalo in 1903; and other Minneapolis flour manufacturers would follow, often taking advantage of the "milling-in-bond privileges" which enabled them to import Canadian wheat duty-free, provided it was shipped out of the country as soon as it had been processed into flour so it would not compete on the domestic market. Frank Henry, who directed the original enterprise at Buffalo, had joined the Washburn Crosby ranks in 1893. Harry Bullis came to know Mr. Henry well in the years of his own association with the company. Gerald S. Kennedy, Mr. Henry's right-hand man, would have a congenial climb with Bullis on that wide ladder leading to the Highlands of American commerce.

Three affiliated companies, each boasting a history of struggle and success that might fill a book, swelled the Washburn Crosby roster. It was William Dunwoody who had founded the first small plant of the Royal Milling Company in the desolate "wilderness country" of Montana in 1892. By 1928, the Royal

Milling Company had mills at Great Falls, Montana; Ogden, Utah; and Pasco, Washington. There were also the grain elevators of The Rocky Mountain Elevator Company, located in the major wheat-producing section of Montana; and the Kalispell Flour Mills at Kalispell, Montana. Although each operated as an individual business unit, the Washburn Crosby directors supervised the affairs of the three associate companies.

James F. Bell, the president of Washburn Crosby, spent little time or energy brooding about the deal that hadn't quite come off. Growing stronger in his mind was the conviction that the facilities of Washburn Crosby should be expanded "to follow the golden grain" southward and westward into the sweeping wheat acreages of Kansas, Texas, Oklahoma, California and northward up the Pacific Coast. It was imperative, he believed, to secure mills between wheat producing areas and major markets.

Mr. Bell had laid some consolidation groundwork in previous discussions with Frank Kell, his "Southern counterpart in milling and other industrial enterprises. The Kell group of southwestern milling properties, spectacular in the grand Texas manner, included mills and some storage elevators at Wichita Falls, Amarillo, Vernon and Waco in Texas, and at Oklahoma City and Perry in Oklahoma. Although that section of the country had started later, it became an impressive challenger on the wheat and flour scene early in the century.

Roger Hurd of the Red Star Milling Company of Wichita, Kansas, seemed amenable to the idea of affiliating with Washburn Crosby in the best interests of his company, and James Ford Bell viewed several other milling enterprises with the keen-eyed regard of a man who realizes the advantages of expanding and streamlining an industry which is vital to the welfare of every family in the country, every day in the year.

Here was the place and the time when a completely reliable "measuring man" was a major asset to James F. Bell. Bullis hadn't looked into a crystal ball to get a glimpse of the future, but he had prepared himself. Confronted with millions of dollars on paper, he was not likely to get "buck fever." He knew his company, from the mill to the office, from the merchandiser to the consumer. He knew the feel of wheat and flour, and he knew how it stacked up in the ledger. He had been "through the mill" and had emerged with a complete miller's education. Bell recognized that Bullis, as the highly qualified comptroller of Washburn Crosby Company, would be faithful to his stewardship.

There was no doubt that Harry Bullis was superbly equipped for the 1928 mission into the Southwest. He examined several of the milling properties in minute detail. Seeking answers to questions that hadn't been invented yet, he counted the deuces as well as the aces. His expert grain man, Ralph Stiles, accompanied Bullis on two complete trips through the Kell plants at Wichita Falls, Oklahoma and Amarillo.

Although he tried to remain incognito, Bullis had difficulty impersonating "The Shadow." At Wichita Falls, Texas, he overwhelmed Mr. Kell and his associate, Mr. Thatcher, with questions about the Kell Mills. After they threw up their hands and said they would need to refer some of his inquiries to the Kell comptroller, Harry left Mr. Kell's office and went across the street to the Kell Hotel. Quite soon he received a telephone call. They had told the Kell comptroller that a representative of the Millers National Federation wanted to talk to him. When he heard that the Federation man was named "Bullis," the comptroller said, "Why, that's Harry Bullis. Is Washburn Crosby thinking of buying out the Kell Mills?"

Conjectures and rumors about a Washburn Crosby annexation of the Kell empire dogged his steps, but Bullis went systematically about his business.

Never a man whose head would "swim" after concentrating on pages of figures for several hours, Bullis stayed awake for two days and two nights until all necessary items and considerations had been properly listed. The height of his absorption in the project can be measured by the unwavering intensity of his forward drive. His attitude remained positive, night and day.

They gathered in Kansas City — those "milling greats" from the Upper Midwest and a vital section of the Southwest. John Crosby, chairman of the board, and James F. Bell, president of Washburn Crosby, were there, as well as Franklin Crosby, Bullis and Davis. Kell was there with his associates, and Roger Hurd was flanked by his colleagues in The Red Star Milling Company of Kansas City.

When Washburn Crosby had been on the brink of being sold, Harry Bullis—bolstered by a fine collection of charts and long columns of figures—had shared the table with some mighty sophisticated horse traders.

Again, it was time to wait and see what would happen. They all wanted consolidation, for the best interests of an expanding industry in a modern age, but Bullis knew from experience that strong men quail at the thought of making drastic changes in their lives.

Flour mills and elevators had been transformed into neat collections of comparative figures, laid out side by side on the conference table. Proposals were made and discussed in an atmosphere of equable rationality. Everyone agreed that the plan should be financed by an exchange of stock and that the associate companies should keep their corporate identities.

At the last minute, something chilled the ardor of seventy-year-old Frank Kell. Perhaps he could not bear the thought of an infiltration into his private domain. A brilliant and shrewd trader all his life, he may have hoped to drive a sharper bargain. When he walked out, he left a large gap in Bell's expansion pattern, but he did not tear it apart.

Roger Hurd and his Red Star Milling Company of Wichita, Kansas, did not swerve from the original plan. Any gain was a worthy step ahead for Washburn Crosby at that juncture. It was a stride in the direction of progress, Bell decided, and they would proceed as though Kell were still with them. Bullis, always ready to drive straight ahead with a positive mental attitude —and enthusiasm, too—packed up his accounting paraphernalia and prepared to set up shop again in New York.

Once more, the tussle with figures and evaluations was waged, and Harry Bullis stayed on duty night and day. When at last he signed his name to the imposing array of legal documents, it was as secretary of the new company. James Ford Bell, as the new president, stayed out of bed to sign. June 20, 1928, is the official date which marks the birth of General Mills.

Only nine summers before, a young captain of the A.E.F. had come to work in the Minneapolis mill of Washburn Crosby Company. Now he was secretary and comptroller of a fifty-million-dollar corporation, organized under the approving eyes of the First National Bank of New York and the National City Company. The consolidation was launched with an authorized capital of fifty million dollars of preferred stock and one million shares of no par value common stock, with authority to issue additional stock "for money, property, labor done, or services rendered as the board should determine."

Harry Bullis remembered the details of the "name choosing session" that was held in James F. Bell's parlor at the Ritz Carlton Hotel in June, 1928. Mr. Bell had emphasized that he did not want the new company always to be just a flour milling company so he suggested the first name of the company be "General."

There were three or four executives present, and each one started to suggest a second name. "I took the New York telephone book," Harry said. "As I recall it, there were about ten pages of companies whose first name was 'General.' When anyone made a suggestion for a second name, I checked with the telephone book, and usually found that some firm already had that name. However, at long last, we arrived at the name 'Mills' and I could not find any firm that was called 'General Mills' so the new baby was christened 'General Mills' right then and there."

John Crosby, chairman of the board of Washburn Crosby, was at home in Minneapolis when the tidings about the new company name reached him by telephone. James Gray, in "Business Without Boundary," tells of Crosby's typically droll comment. "Well, I'm glad you didn't name it General Miles, because General Miles didn't have much of a record in the Civil War."

The General Mills merger immediately inspired a deluge of newspaper stories which stirred the imaginations of a vast flour-consuming public. Feature articles were titled and sub-titled: $50,000,000 MILLING CORPORATION FORMED; JAMES FORD BELL HEADS BIG CONSOLIDATION; HEADQUARTERS TO BE SET UP IN MINNEAPOLIS; General Mills Comes Into Being As World's Greatest Milling Corporation — Takes Over Washburn Crosby and Four Other Concerns; Merger Acquires Mills in 9 States.

It was reported that the directors had set the corporation's capacity at 64,575 barrels of flour daily, from all mills. "The grain elevators have aggregate storage capacities of 18,470,000 bushels, of which about 4,000,000 is in Minneapolis." In addition, there were the flour mill and the cereal food plant in Chicago, and also the millfeed business which was distributed among the various flour mills.

The Minneapolis Journal for June 28, 1928, noted an announcement by Harry Bullis, secretary of General Mills. "The Washburn Crosby Company, recently merged with other large milling companies in General

Mills, Inc., . . . has been divided into three subsidiaries of General Mills." C. C. Bovey would be president of the new Minnesota division of Washburn Crosby, while James Ford Bell had been elected chairman of the board of the Minnesota company, as well as president of General Mills. Frank Henry became president of the Buffalo company, and H. G. Randall would head the Kansas City subsidiary organization.

Other officers of Washburn Crosby in Minneapolis were H. R. McLaughlin, vice president; F. M. Crosby, vice president; D. D. Davis, vice president and treasurer, and H. A. Bullis, secretary. All of the officers and F. J. Morley were directors. Presidents of all the companies included in the General Mills merger became members of the board of directors of that corporation.

In some of his statements to the press, James Ford Bell emphasized the advantages of the General Mills consolidation pattern in eliminating overlapping processes, expensive and wasteful sales methods, and duplications in the plants and in transportation, with the resultant economies being passed on to the consumer.

The demand for the first issue of General Mills stock was overwhelming. Subsequent General Mills stock offerings went into the eagerly outstretched hands of people who knew that flour is vividly important to the world's economy, whether it's in the kitchen or inscribed on gilt-edged certificates. The newspaper announcements were captioned: "These stocks having already been sold, this advertisement appears as a matter of record only."

In its first burst of acceleration, General Mills

common stock, issued at 65, climbed to a dazzling 86. The "success image" of the new organization became increasingly prominent on the financial scene.

James Ford Bell was not satisfied; General Mills had reached the gratifying heights of prestige, but the pattern was not complete.

Frank Kell, in his headquarters in Wichita Falls, Texas, watched the spectacular advance of the new corporation with special interest and respect. He still felt involved. When he indicated that he was ready to play "for keeps" this time, Bullis and his team were sent again to survey the Kell interests.

There were some routine legal skirmishes about the evaluation of the property and stock, but Bullis had been schooled on Wall Street. Serving as the chairman of the committee of the General Mills group, he could represent General Mills with poise and authority. On the final day of the Kell negotiation, Bullis recalled, Mr. Kell's three assistants wanted a figure which was quite substantially higher than the General Mills group had in mind. "I told Mr. Kell that if he did not use the General Mills figure, then I would have to tell Mr. Bell upon my return that I had failed. He said he did not want me to do that. To the utter amazement of his three associates, he accepted our figure." Mr. Frank Kell had demonstrated his "special interest and respect," and the handsome Texas-Oklahoma Kell Mills were shifted neatly into the General Mills pattern before the end of 1928.

Since low grades of wheat and by-products of flour milling are used as livestock and poultry feed, the Larrowe Milling Company of Detroit became another valuable consolidation asset during that period. The company had built up a fine record in the manufacture of Larro Dairy food and chicken mash, and the acquisition of the Larrowe organization provided for future expansion in that productive line and led to the founding of numerous retail outlets, popularly known as "farm stores" by the General Mills brethren.

James F. Bell had already turned his searching gaze farther westward, toward California and the Sperry empire which dated back to 1852, when Austin Sperry had set up a thriving flour mill to furnish sustenance for the Gold Rush prospectors in the Stockton, California, area. With the years, the original Sperry enterprises had moved both north and west, branching out along the Pacific Coast, and launching a prosperous flour trade on the high seas to the Orient. Sagas have been written about the picturesque ship captains and their brawny crewmen who sailed their heavy-laden ships across the Pacific to the land of the silken-robed Manchus and mandarins and the barefoot coolies.

In 1904, William C. Edgar spoke of the aspirations of James J. Hill, the master builder of early transportation facilities. "In his scheme of railway and ship building . . . he has said that five hundred millions of people in China will, he believes, become wheaten-bread eaters." Sperry was a notable part of that picture, shipping one-third of its flour across the Pacific until World War I interfered with normal trade activities. At home, Drifted Snow was Sperry's fine equivalent of Washburn Crosby's Gold Medal Flour.

In the latter part of 1928, Harry Bullis was one of

the leading members among the three or four officers who, with the company attorney, went to San Francisco to evaluate the Sperry operations for a period of about ten days. Because the Sperry Flour Company operated on a different accounting system than the newly formed General Mills corporation, Harry had requested the Sperry accounting staff to prepare a revised set of figures for him. The comptroller of Sperry Company protested the extra work. In fact, when the General Mills party arrived, the Sperry comptroller informed Harry that if the merger occurred, the president of Sperry Flour Company would have him discharged. Instead, when the merger was arranged after about a week and a half of negotiations, one of the first official acts was the discharging of the Sperry comptroller. He had made himself expendable.

James Bell's pattern for General Mills became basically complete with the addition of nine Sperry mills at Los Angeles and Vallejo, California; at Spokane, Tacoma and Pasco, Washington; and at Portland, Oregon, and Ogden, Utah.

Not only did Harry Bullis become familiar with the properties that were involved in the merger; during the lengthy inspection trips and conferences, he also became acquainted with individuals whose activities would be his intimate concern for many years to come. He might be described as "the perfect personnel man" —not because it was part of his job, but because he cared about people and their welfare in a progressive society.

The names of those early associates are woven into the records of Bullis' life—in letters in his scrapbooks and files, and in the diary he had kept so faithfully for thirty years. He was never too busy to send his colleagues—great and small—a note of appreciation for work well done and a word of encouragement when it might mean the difference between success and failure. In sickness and in health, they would be the recipients of his abiding interest and esteem. In the hours of their family tragedies he would mourn with them; and in the inevitable passage of time, he would sometimes stand with bowed head, mourning for them.

Harry Bullis wore no halo. He was a big, vivid, lusty fellow—surely not a "Pollyanna" of the ledger books. His vocabulary had been enlivened by some colorful words and phrases from his army days, but those "cuss words" did not seem to arise from the depths of his soul. They lost their impact because they lacked insolence and spite.

Bullis repeatedly mentioned the co-operation that he had received from various operating executives in the company. His was never "a one-man show." His attitude had seemed to be, "Come on, now—if I have succeeded, so can you. Let's get together on this!" Free enterprise, to Bullis, did not mean egotistical individual enterprise, in the old dog-eat-dog tradition. Because he had honestly endeavored to share the abundant rewards as well as the "intelligent hard work" with his associates on every level, his fellow-workers regarded him with more affection than awe. Often he had inspired them to perform better than they had thought they could, to live up to his evaluation. Over the years, Bullis had lived with the idea that "A leader is a man who surrounds himself with better specialists than himself and who makes them work as a team," and Bullis had doubled as a member of the squad and a buoyant cheerleader in project after project.

An old office worker himself, Bullis seemed to feel that secretaries, too, are "specialists" who deserve to be regarded with approval. He often mentioned Miss Helen Hansen who came to his office as an assistant secretary in the 1920's, after her graduation from high school. Miss Hansen became his secretary at the time of the formation of General Mills and made almost a lifetime career of it until she moved to California several years ago for reasons of health. Bullis would be the first to applaud a high school graduate whose increasing excellence could qualify her to become an executive secretary.

Every now and then, feature story writers wonder how the business world ever produced an optimistic, idealistic phenomenon like Harry Bullis. Did he get that way overnight? There are some rich clues in that essay from the 1929 N.A.C.A. book. "Cost data," Bullis wrote, "should be presented with accuracy and sincerity. . . . The art of presenting cost data is to place before the executive the truth in an orderly manner . . . he should be true to himself and present what he knows to be the truth, and not necessarily what others might desire or believe to be the truth."

Then the secretary and comptroller of General Mills proceeded to quote from Emerson's "Self-Reliance":

"The highest merit we ascribe to Moses, Plato and Milton is that they set at naught books and traditions, and spoke not what men, but what they, thought. A man should learn to detect and watch that gleam of light which flashes across his mind from within, more than the luster of the firmament of bards and sages. Yet he dismisses without notice his thought, because it is his. In every work of genius we recognize our own rejected thoughts; they come back to us with a certain alienated majesty. Great works of art have no more affecting lesson for us than this. They teach us to abide by our spontaneous impression with good-humored inflexibility the most when the whole cry of voices is on the other side. Else tomorrow a stranger will say with masterly good sense precisely what we have thought and felt all the time, and we shall be forced to take with shame our opinion from another."

After this classic utterance which is directly related to his lifelong philosophy, Bullis emphasized that cost data should be presented as promptly as possible —"served up hot, as news—not cold, as history," because the executive needs to see ahead.

In his summary, "the measuring man" declared that business is only about fifty per cent efficient. "Therefore, when we compare records of present performance with records of past performance, we are comparing what we are doing with a basis we know is inefficient. No management should be satisfied with its own past performance. The life of a business, like the life of an individual, should be dynamic—always moving forward." With "a positive mental attitude," he meant!

The following month, in July, 1929, The Northwestern Miller recorded his views on "The Common Sense of Cost Data" in which he said, "There never has been a time in history when accurate cost data, presented in the right way, and used with intelligence, were more valuable than they are today. The future holds still greater possibilities. The industrial development of the United States in the next twenty years will surpass anything in the nation's history. . . . One of the problems of American industry is to increase still further the purchasing power of consumers."

Bullis, the dauntless optimist, was largely correct in that prognostication; but his would be a lonely opinion. The nation, several months later, would be forced to take a "depression recess," and dazed consumers would wonder how their purchasing power could have evaporated overnight.

October 29, 1929, marked the most cataclysmic day for the New York Stock Exchange since its founding during George Washington's first administration. An era of pleasant post-war prosperity collapsed like a house of cards, with sixteen million shares of stock changing hands as frantic "stock-market players" tried to get out of the mess with their shirts still on their backs. Subsequent stock losses were estimated at fifty billion dollars, affecting the living standards of twenty-five million people, some of whom took the speediest route out of "this vale of tears" at the prospect of facing bankruptcy.

How would the far-ranging General Mills enterprise meet the dismay and apprehension of the "lean years" that were to come?

Chapter Nine

Champions in the Kitchen

General Mills suffered some of the widespread buffetings of the depression, but the ground did not quiver beneath the mighty organization. From the days of Cadwallader Washburn it had been built on a firm foundation of durable business principles, and faith in its survival was seldom in doubt.

The unyielding vigor of General Mills is best illustrated in a speech that Harry Bullis delivered at a convention of the National Federated Flour Clubs in Chicago on June 11, 1930, when the depression was becoming more and more alarming to the average American. After a sober discussion of all the factors involved in the expense of producing a barrel of flour and selling it at a profit, Mr. Bullis told a story about the two little frogs who jumped into a pitcher of cream:

"After they had drunk all the cream they wanted, they found that the pitcher was round and they couldn't get out. One frog gave up and sank to the bottom of the pitcher; but the other frog, who had the vision, courage, and the ability to work hard, thought he would kick as long as he could kick. So he kicked and kicked and kicked. He felt himself slipping, and he kicked still faster. Finally he felt something under his feet, kicked still harder, churned the cream into butter, stood on top of the lump of butter and jumped out. That frog—who had faith in himself—had the vision to see that he should kick, the courage to start kicking and the ability to continue to kick."

Bullis finished getting his point across in a concluding sentence, "Your costs will be all right and your profits will be satisfactory if you know the facts, have the right spirit, and the three qualities of vision, courage, and the ability to work hard."

Because he had those qualities himself, the man who stood before that audience had already become a member of the board of directors of General Mills. During a meeting on January 29, 1930, Mr. Bell stated that there was a vacancy on the board caused by the resignation of Mr. J. W. Sherwood. He presented the names of Putnam D. McMillan and Harry A. Bullis as candidates, and the board amended the by-laws to elect both Mr. McMillan and Mr. Bullis as directors at that time.

In 1930, Gold Medal Flour celebrated its fiftieth anniversary. It was a year of mixed blessings, because the business climate continued to languish. During those critical depression days, Harry's dedication to teamwork, leavened with friendly optimism, set many a fine example for his associates in the flour, feed, and cereal business. "The pathway of co-operation," he had always believed, "will lead to sound programs and progress. In nature, everything is co-operation and teamwork." He liked to paraphrase General Mills activities as an example:

"Back of the loaf is the snowy flour;
And back of the flour is the mill;
And back of the mill is the wheat and the shower
And the sun and the Father's Will."

Even though the time might not have seemed propitious, several General Mills "sleepers" were destined to start climbing into the "best seller lists" early in the Thirties. The acceleration came from many directions within the organization, proving that Bullis was correct about the advantages of teamwork. He spoke glowingly of the contributions that some early associates had made in the progress of the company. Among them were two zealous young men, Walter R. Barry, vice president and administrator of grocery products, affectionately known as "Mr. Grocery Products," and Samuel C. Gale, vice president and director of advertising, whom Bullis called "The greatest advertising executive I have ever known." Barry and Gale developed and introduced new merchandising and advertising methods which promoted and greatly expanded the sale of Wheaties, other cereals, cake mixes and Gold Medal Flour. These two major executives, along with Gerald S. Kennedy, vice president and administrator of flour and feed activities, and later chairman of the board, played a dominant role in the development of all operating activities. They were assisted by Leslie N. Perrin, authority on soybean research and executive vice president, who followed Bullis as president of the company.

Although their titles might not have been so impressive back in the 1920's and 1930's, their exuberance was fabulous.

It was Sam Gale who set out briskly to expand the Washburn Crosby Cooking School demonstrations into Wisconsin and other neighboring states in 1921. When a Gold Medal advertising stunt brought an unexpected flood of prize winners and recipe requests to the Home Service Department in Minneapolis, Gale took over the mammoth job of supplying both prizes and recipes. As an advertising man, he appreciated the value of establishing "a human contact" with all those ladies, near and far, who were baking bread and cakes with Gold Medal Flour in their home kitchens.

It seemed fitting and proper that this homemaking correspondence should be conducted on a lady-to-lady basis. The indefatigable Mr. Gale sought the co-operation of his home service colleagues in choosing a name with just the proper ring of authenticity to it. The surname "Crocker" was something of a memorial salute to a former secretary and director of Washburn Crosby Company who was remembered with affection. "Betty," of course, sounds like the name of any girl's best friend.

Betty Crocker became a homemaking institution, as human as the fragrance of cookies baking in the oven and dumplings bubbling in the stew. More "versatile" than many of her homemaking sisters, she became adept at concocting exotic delicacies when the drama of a special occasion demanded it, and she graciously shared her creations with Mrs. America.

"The First Lady of Food" had some predecessors in the Washburn Crosby Company. Even though commercial bakers use more flour than any other single group, ladies and "The Staff of Life" usually go best together in advertisements. At the turn of the century, the Gold Medal Homemaker was a long-aproned, full-skirted young woman with a ruffled white cap on her head, posing alongside a sack of Gold Medal Flour. "Very cleanly maid" was the caption on those ads. In the shocking era after World War I, the poster girl's ankles peeped out below her long skirt. She was holding up an empty Gold Medal Flour sack and saying cheerfully, "But the Grocer has more, Thank Goodness."

A picture of the Home Service kitchen in the early 1920's shows that it was neat but not gaudy. There was a checkered linoleum on the floor. The enameled stove had curved legs, and there was a medium-sized "kitchen cabinet." The staff wore long-sleeved white uniforms.

At first, the Home Service Department was too busy sponsoring Gold Medal Cooking Schools to appreciate Betty Crocker's possibilities. In the background, however, she was accumulating a large following of devoted homemakers who looked to her for domestic advice. Actually, this gracious and charming "composite creation" of many of the ladies in the Home Service Department was becoming very much alive. She was Florence Lindeberg's signature, and she was a picture painted by famous artist Neysa McMein. She began to speak with the voices of Marjorie Husted, Blanche Ingersoll, Betty Bucholtz, and a dozen other "Betty Crockers" on local radio stations across the country. Her voice was crisp and friendly, without affectation. She had a philosophy; she had standards and character. Early in the history of General Mills, she was receiving four thousand letters a day. She was, and still is, a homemaker without peer. Once she was voted the second best-known female personality in the country, after Eleanor Roosevelt!

Marjorie Child Husted, who joined the Washburn Crosby organization after World War I, was probably the most dedicated Betty Crocker of them all. She was the "central voice" emanating from the Minneapolis headquarters—not only preparing the scripts but delivering them into the microphone at WCCO after the station became affiliated with the Columbia Broadcasting System. Mrs. Husted spoke with the voice of inspiration and idealism, persuading housewives to become "artists of homemaking" on the highest level of which they were capable. That, she believed, should be the most stimulating career of all, and worthy of all dignity and respect.

Betty Crocker was most closely identified with Gold Medal Flour in her early years. The "Kitchen-Tested" phrase crowned both of them with fresh laurels in 1926.

Harry Bullis undoubtedly was close enough to the Home Service Kitchen to be an unofficial "tester" of succulent morsels fresh out of the oven. It is evident that he was generous with advice and encouragement. On one occasion, after he had given Marjorie Husted a "pep talk," she said in a grateful thank-you note, "This sounds like a fan letter—to Betty Crocker—but it is a deeply sincere tribute to you—for your understanding and strength. Don't ever underestimate your power for benefiting people—right here, in a business organization. For as an organization gets bigger, the need is far greater for executives of your vision and deep sympathy for human needs. . . ."

Although Betty Crocker's recipes ranged richly over the culinary world during the years of prosperity, her resourcefulness during the depression was of special note. She concentrated many of her programs on suggestions for low-cost meals that would be satisfying, attractive and uplifting to the spirit. Macaroni, of course, was one of the great "life-savers" during the depression. In 1925, Washburn Crosby had started to manufacture Gold Medal Semolina, made from durum wheat. It had led to the company's entrance into the macaroni field, with a fine amber product that would hold its shape while being cooked.

A multitude of entrancingly - illustrated Betty Crocker cookbooks have aimed to teach the public that bread is a great energy food, rich in carbohydrates. When General Mills was incorporated in 1928, the practice of putting recipes into sacks of Gold Medal Flour was inaugurated. In 1932, "silverware coupons" started a flood of activity that became virtually a separate business. As a result, Harry Bullis pointed out, General Mills became the top distributor of silverware in the world. Lives there a homemaker with soul so dead that she doesn't own a few of those early Medality teaspoons! Other attractive items in a variety of patterns have followed.

In a picture of the Home Service Kitchen during the Thirties, it is apparent that some remodeling and interior decorating had been done. There were ruffles on the shelves and ruffles on Harry Bullis. He and fellow-executives Leslie N. Perrin, Walter H. Barry and Samuel Gale were showing two of the lovely Home Service girls how to bake a very fine cake. All of the gentlemen looked like charming homemakers in their colorful aprons.

The development of Wheaties, like the creation of Betty Crocker, eventually sparked almost everyone in the company to attention. The Wheaties miracle shows what can be accomplished when enough imaginations are set ablaze in a worthy cause.

"The Breakfast of Champions" came out of the browning ovens of the Chicago plant in 1924. During many years of frustrating research and promotion, it scarcely seemed possible that Wheaties would ever be a universally popular "kitchen champion." However, there were vigorous champions in the company, and they refused to recognize failure in the Wheaties department. Wasn't wheat "the best food of man"? If only people would try Wheaties, they would know that those crisp brown flakes were enticingly tasty and flavorful!

There were several small radio stations in Minnesota, all of them struggling to stay in business in the early 1920's. When Donald Davis developed an interest in slowly expiring WLAG, the "Call of the North," which had been operated by The Minneapolis Journal, he arranged for it to have a mighty spectacular future in the Twin Cities area, and later on a national network. Financed jointly by Washburn Crosby, and Minneapolis and St. Paul, the new call letters of the station were the initials of Washburn Crosby

Company—WCCO. When WCCO brought the inauguration of Calvin Coolidge to the Upper Midwest in 1925, it made a definite impact on the life of the community, a condition that has prevailed through many years of radio and television.

The Wheaties message—the first singing commercial—burst out upon the air waves in 1926. Earl Gammons, who had been the first editor of The Eventually News, was the manager of WCCO, and he welcomed the challenge of the Wheaties campaign.

Still vivid in Bullis' mind was the memory of that original tune, sung with appealing sincerity and exactly the right amount of bounce:

"... So just buy Wheaties, try Wheaties—
The best breakfast food in the land!"

Bullis recalled that General Mills had recently been playing the old record, "Jack Armstrong, Jack Armstrong, the All-American Boy," on a five-minute spot program on radio. It was followed on the record by the singing of the Wheaties song, by the original Wheaties Quartet. Harry said, "Every time I heard that program in the early morning when I was shaving in my bathroom, it brought a touch of nostalgia and happy recollections to me." "All-American Boys" may grow up, but they still respond to echoes and visions of their younger days.

From crude crystal sets with one earphone to nationwide networks, from a few thousand packages to millions each year, radio and Wheaties paced each other from oblivion to the heights of popularity.

Bullis, who had nothing less than superlatives for

Samuel Gale and Walter R. Barry, referred to them as two of the most dynamic forces behind the national promotion of the Wheaties campaign. After Gale arranged for the Wheaties Quartet to perform a half hour of lively songs and Washburn Crosby commercials on a half-hour national network every week, the entire country became Wheaties-conscious.

The development of both the "Skippy" and "Jack Armstrong" series, Harry Bullis noted, was largely the work of Gale and Barry, but he and Donald Davis often became tremendously involved in the fascinating projects.

The "Skippy" scripts, written by Robert Andrews and featuring Percy Crosby's well-known cartoon character, began to carry the Wheaties message to the children of the land in 1930. In spite of the depression, sales spurted upward. Because of the increasing expense of the use of the name "Skippy" and because some of the episodes were considered a bit too hair-raising for the consumption of sheltered American youngsters, a fabulous character named "Jack Armstrong" was created out of the fertile minds of "The General Mills committee for the preservation and advancement of Wheaties."

Jack Armstrong was the model and idol of a whole generation of boys and girls who lived his adventures with him. Jack was intelligent, resourceful, and polite to his sister—without being a sissy. He managed to be all of the things that his fans would have liked to be—and if he got that way from eating Wheaties, then they would eat Wheaties too!

General Mills, with its Skippy and Jack Armstrong

programs, was probably the first company to carry its advertising messages straight to young consumers as they sat in front of the radio, vicariously identifying themselves with the exploits and accomplishments of their heroes. For ten years, "Jack Armstrong" was closely supervised by Dr. Martin Reymert, child psychologist and director of the Mooseheart Laboratory for Child Research. He joined groups of youngsters in front of the radio and studied their reactions. Dr. Reymert's standards were high. He stressed the need for sustained interest, educational and character building elements, and plenty of wholesome excitement.

Jack Armstrong was all the more plausible because he was allowed to keep growing older, with interests that would delight the maturing adolescent. After awhile he began to share his treasures with his listeners. Every mother can recall those precious box-tops that had to be removed carefully and the order blanks that needed to be filled out—and those suspenseful trips to the mailbox, until the Explorer Telescope, or the ring with its secret code in a hidden compartment, or the genuine Jack Armstrong "signal whistle" arrived safely.

When the men of General Mills began to ask each other why the men of the country shouldn't enjoy Wheaties too, a novel point in advertising history was reached. Sam Gale conceived the brilliant idea of having General Mills sponsor radio broadcasts of local baseball games, thereby linking Wheaties with health and physical fitness. Advertising man Knox Reeves came up with a slogan that was a "natural" to catch the eye of baseball fans: "Wheaties, Breakfast of Champions!" By using signed testimonials from sports stars in every field, Wheaties and the physical fitness program made championship history together. Noteworthy among public service contributions was a series of sports films, sponsored by Wheaties and the Wilson Sporting Goods Company, which has been available for showing in high schools and colleges.

The entire Wheaties story is characteristic of the zestful "championship spirit" of the great young executives in Washburn Crosby Company and General Mills. It is still a "serial" story, dedicated to the continued success of a cereal. Prolonged research testing produced "Radiant Crisp Wheaties" in 1957. In 1937 and 1941, two more ready-to-eat breakfast foods—Kix from corn, and Cheerios from oats—came "puffing" out of the General Mills food laboratories to join Wheaties. Just the mention of the word "Cheerios" evokes a provocative memory of "The Lone Ranger." His voice still echoes from beyond the distant hills, "Hi Ho, Silver—and away!"

Perhaps the most significant contribution to homemaking was the "discovery" of Bisquick in the early depression days. Carl Smith, a sales executive from the Sperry Division of General Mills, made himself immortal in the eyes of Betty Crocker and Mrs. America when he became inquisitive about a serving of fresh, hot biscuits that had been prepared in record time on a train to San Francisco. "How," he asked the Southern Pacific chef, "did you ever mix up that batch of biscuits so fast?"

The biscuit ingredients, Smith discovered, had been pre-mixed and stored in the refrigerator on the train.

Commenting on the incident in "Business Without Boundary," James Gray reveals his sensitive appreciation for creative talent in any area: "To have conceived this idea demonstrated in the Negro chef of the Southern Pacific lines possession of the kind of creative skill that gives human character its distinction. To have recognized the commercial possibilities of the idea demonstrated in Carl Smith a similar kind of insight. For it was an entirely new idea."

There were periods of research difficulty in the Sperry Division before the housewife was able to reach for the box of Bisquick on her grocer's shelf, confident that its leavening agent had not "gone flat" or that the fat content had not turned rancid. General Mills and Betty Crocker perfected, sponsored and launched the new product.

The debut of Bisquick was a revolutionary phenomenon in the kitchen cabinet department. As the drum major in the big parade of mixes that would follow, Bisquick was destined to activate a stepped-up rhythm in modern baking and cooking techniques. Betty Crocker and her girls began to stir and blend with even greater spirit—there were so many delicious tricks that could be done with a box of Bisquick, and so quickly and easily! Out of the Bisquick cornucopia tumbled desserts, meat pies, coffee cakes and dumplings, all possible in "jig time" with Bisquick. Gradually the Bisquick idea was extended to Betty Crocker's mouth-watering line of cake, cookie, and frosting mixes.

The life of the American homemaker would never be quite the same again. It was as though Carl Smith, teaming up with that Negro chef and Betty Crocker, had made her a present of extra minutes and hours in her housekeeping day. Betty Crocker had spoken of "dignifying" the role of the homemaker. With Bisquick and the procession of mixes that followed, she has done it. The life of almost every woman has been influenced, more or less, by the culinary short-cuts that have been introduced in the past thirty years. If a personal note might be injected, there is one housewife and mother who probably never would have found time to write one book—much less seven—if she had not had a generous "lift" from those colorful packages of "mix" on the shelf!

Bisquick was the pride of the men in the General Mills sales force. They could sell it with a confident grin, knowing that the grocer and his customers would welcome it. "It was a real morale builder," Harry Bullis recalled. Like the frog in the pitcher of cream, General Mills kept kicking away energetically through the depression years—completely aware of the depression, but too busy to be gloomy about it.

The depression seemed to interest, rather than frighten, a statistical-minded man like Harry Bullis. At so dire a period in history, he and Irma might have abandoned their cherished vision of owning their own home. Bullis and his wife had selected a lot on West Lake of the Isles Boulevard with the hope that they could some day purchase it and move out of their little apartment. At that time the Lake of the Isles Boulevard region was considered the most exclusive section in Minneapolis.

Could they go brashly ahead and build a home in

spite of the depression? Immediately after the stock market crash in 1929, individuals and leaders of corporations revised their plans for expenditures. No one wanted to spend money for anything.

True to his optimistic principles, Harry Bullis did not believe that Doomsday had come to stay. The week after the severe stock market crash, Harry and Irma bought the lot that they had been admiring for years. Of course Bullis did not dare to mention his purchase to his associates because they might have considered him most imprudent—or worse—for buying such a lot on a rapidly declining market.

With his intimate knowledge of the business cycle, he realized that even though it was a world depression, the state of business could not always remain at such a low level. The General Mills vice president also believed, contrary to most businessmen, that a depression is just the time to construct new plant facilities because the builder of such facilities could obtain the finest architects, artisans and builders—since they are most likely to be unemployed.

The Bullises hired one of the best architects in Minneapolis and also one of the best contractors. Each was delighted to have the assignment. Mrs. Bullis and architect Van Dycke then started drawing up the plans for the house that the Bullises had dreamed of for so many years. Now Irma would have space and scope to be "a champion Betty Crocker homemaker" in her own home.

Meanwhile, back at the office, Harry was getting some interesting mail from Colonel Carter of Westinghouse. In addition to besieging him with telegrams during February, 1930, the Westinghouse executive sent balance sheets filled with impressive figures. In a sprightly exchange of messages, Bullis was invited to attend a conference in Chicago, but he said he was practically on his way to Kansas City for a General Mills meeting and would try to visit Chicago afterward. Colonel Carter recalled that he had some business in Kansas City himself, so he suggested contacting Bullis there.

Harry had been nominated for a financial position in the great Westinghouse organization, but he declined without too many regrets. There was his loyalty to Bell, who had said that Bullis would be one of three men who would guide the destiny of General Mills in future years. Then there was the new home that Irma had designed and that they hoped to enjoy for a few years.

In his letter of farewell to the Westinghouse offer, Bullis proved himself a true philosopher, ". . . But the fact that you have sufficient belief in me to nominate me for such a position has increased my self-confidence and self-respect, and that is about all that a man has in this world anyway. I thank you."

Congratulatory telegrams were sent to him by many associates.

In his message to Harry, Donald Davis said, "Having nice visit Mr. Bell. Just learned exceptional tribute paid to your ability by large Eastern Interests . . . am glad of your final judgment."

Frank Burke, of the Sperry Division, set the wires humming from San Francisco. "Have just learned of the splendid compliment paid you in recognition of your ability, capacity and soundness of judgment through medium of the flattering offer put before you by an outstanding concern which is an endorsement of the recognition which we all hold for you but want to say I think your decision to stick with the old ship is courageous and commendable and indicates confidence and faith in our enterprise and its management. . . ."

About two months later, on May 24, 1931, laudatory messages started flowing in Harry's direction again. Excerpts from the minutes of a memorable board meeting tell the story:

"Thereupon Mr. Bell presented for the consideration of the Board present the name of Harry A. Bullis as a candidate for the office of Vice President of General Mills, Inc. Upon motion duly made by F. F. Henry, seconded by T. C. Thatcher and unanimously carried, Harry A. Bullis was duly elected Vice President of the corporation."

What a gratifying and thrilling day that must have been for the small town boy from Iowa! He was standing high on the ladder of success, but he was still the same Harry Bullis who could talk the language of porters and office workers and wheat farmers. No matter how high he climbed on that ladder, he could always stretch out an encouraging, comradely hand to those on the lower rungs.

In his old home town, the newspaper he had delivered as a boy took pride in saluting him. Large type in the Council Bluffs "Nonpareil" proclaimed: "BULLIS IS PROMOTED BY GENERAL MILLS; Former

Council Bluffs Boy is Vice President of Huge Company —Works His Way Upward."

Harry enjoyed sharing that precious moment of achievement with Irma, who had attended those night school classes at the university with him. She was deeply interested in all of his activities, assisting and inspiring him during the years when he probably received more titles than anyone else in the company. She was his "beloved wife Irma" in many of his references to her.

In addition to his heavy load of assignments within the General Mills organization in the Thirties, Bullis was increasingly active in the National Association of Cost Accountants, the National Association of Manufacturers, the University of Wisconsin Alumni Association, the United States Board of Trade, and numerous other business and civic groups. The boy who had struggled to teach himself "to speak perfectly and easily and well" now had a demanding schedule of speaking engagements.

When construction on the Bullis home was started, only one other house was being built in Minneapolis. Harry secured the architect's and contractor's promises to keep the project a secret; he knew that if any of his associates heard that he was building such a fine home at such a precarious time they would really think he was using poor judgment.

The house, on very secure foundations, slowly progressed upward until its skeleton form was visible and people started being curious about it. It is pretty hard to hide anything that size, but Harry was still trying to keep it a secret. While he was on a two weeks' trip to California, the temptation was too much for the architect and contractor. A picture of the handsome new home appeared in the Minneapolis Journal. According to the text, "It is of reinforced concrete, hollow tile and frame, the exterior being done in stone and stucco. The roof is of slate. A. R. Van Dycke was the architect and Danielson Brothers, the contractors." The caption above the picture said that it was "A $40,-000 Home." Since those were depression days, a slight adjustment in currency values should be made. Just as he had expected, Harry Bullis' colleagues expressed amazement that he would dare to build such a splendid home when business was so depressed.

After so many years in that cramped little apartment, he and Irma were enjoying their spacious new home. In the Bullis scrapbooks are many pictures of the house and grounds at West Lake of the Isles Boulevard, right across the road from the lakeshore. There was a lovely garden in the Bullis' back yard, with a profusion of flowers and shrubs to enhance the Minnesota "theater of seasons." In a marble fountain, two enchanting cupids seemed to giggle coyly. Prominent also was the miller's beloved trophy, a genuine massive millstone, its grooves revealing that it had been "dressed" and used for grinding wheat in the days before steel rollers.

Harry had always enjoyed being active. After they moved into their new home, he was able to indulge in one of his favorite hobbies—taking long walks. He used to walk three times around the Lake of the Isles on a Sunday afternoon. Since it was three miles around the lake, that "stroll" added up to a total of nine miles. Later he reduced his mileage, but the total was still impressive. Almost anyone who has ever lived in that section of Minneapolis remembers seeing the tall General Mills man taking those Sunday afternoon walks.

When Irma and Harry decided to give a party in their new home, it was the first of many. The invitation was a "partnership" affair:

> "I said to the wife the other night, sez I, let's have the old gang over to the new house some evening soon. 'That will be fine,' sez she, 'but the weather is very warm.' Let's have them anyway, sez I. So, Thursday, July 9, is the date. Seven P.M. is the time. 2116 West Lake of the Isles Boulevard is the place. (Bring your poems.) H. A. Bullis.
>
> "We shall be happy to have you. Irma Bullis."

Some jotted notes suggest that this was a well-planned party:

Program for evening—

7:00 to 7:30—look at house and grounds

7:30 to 8:15—movie pictures, refreshments, drinks, etc.

8:15 to 9:30—games, either cards or something else.

Refreshments—sandwiches, Cokes, ice cream

10:00—go home

That last item conjures up a highly unlikely picture of Harry Bullis swinging the front doors open wide at the stroke of ten!

Chapter Ten

Gallant Businessman

In 1932, Harry Bullis was flying even higher than the Highlands, and he became a vigorous advocate of plane travel. One of his "notes in flight" dated September 27, 1932, mentions that Humboldt, Kansas, was to the right, when the plane was halfway from Kansas City to Tulsa. The pilot's name was R. J. Dick. The altitude was forty-five hundred feet, and the speed was one hundred and fifty miles an hour. This was advertised as the "World's Fastest Airline."

There was a reason why it was necessary to cover a great deal of territory in the shortest space of time. In 1932, Bullis, with the titles "Vice President, Secretary and Comptroller," gladly relinquished the office of secretary of General Mills—after serving five years in that post—to Sydney Anderson who had been responsible for the operation of the company's Farm Service Stores.

Bullis, along with his other duties, took over the supervision of the Farm Service Stores, located in many states, and which at the time were reflecting a loss. He called the Farm Service managers together and thanked them for their efforts, but he said, "Knute Rockne once told a Notre Dame football star that while the lad was a great runner, he seemed to run too damn long in the same place!" In spite of the national depression of the 1930's, Bullis assured the managers, that kind of running had to be improved upon. Putting it on a partnership basis, he said, "Let's find a way to make some yardage. I am here as one of you. We'll do it together."

A letter to Frank Henry, from one of the company's old-time branch managers at Baltimore, gives a heartwarming picture of the spirit that Harry Bullis brought to his new endeavor:

"Mr. Magoon, of the Farm Service Stores, invited me to attend a dinner given last Saturday night for all of their employees. . . . I have known Harry Bullis practically ever since he came with the old Washburn Crosby Company and on several occasions have had the pleasure of hearing Harry deliver talks on different subjects, but I never heard him put over a message as he did last Saturday night."

Typical of Harry's regard for the human element is a true story told to the author by a former Farm Service Store operator: "There we were—two fellows running this little store down in Iowa. Business wasn't very good. Then along came Mr. Bullis—a big vice president and one of the top men in our company. He talked our situation over with us and gave our morale a boost. After he got home, he sent us a personally autographed picture, and we hung it on the wall in the store. Farmers would come in and say, 'Do you really know an important fellow like Bullis?' It surely made an impression and gave us a big boost!"

When he assumed the Farm Stores assignment, Bullis thought only in terms of hard work, leading inevitably to success. That his "Chief" was one of the prime rooters in his cheering section is apparent in a message he received from James F. Bell on June 24, 1933:

"Dear Harry—Thanks for your most interesting and comprehensive letter. In the action taken I see the results of your advice and sound judgment in which I repose great confidence. Needless to say I heartily endorse all action taken. . . . I think you have already accomplished wonders in cleaning up the rural store situation. . . ."

According to the minutes of a board of directors meeting on October 24, 1933, Harry Bullis was appointed as the executive officer responsible for the grain products operating activities, in addition to his General Mills divisional assignments. In 1934, when James F. Bell became chairman of the board and Donald D. Davis was named president of General Mills, Bullis became vice president in charge of operations. He continued pursuing his vigorous activities in the field.

During all his executive years with General Mills, Bullis traveled extensively on morale-building trips throughout the field. When James F. Bell was president, he considered Bullis "the most flexibly enthusiastic" of all General Mills executives.

In 1936, Walter Barry—"Mr. Grocery Products"

and in Mr. Bullis' opinion, the most outstanding merchandiser in the company's history—wrote an eloquent tribute to the "flexibly enthusiastic executive":

"You are the model for all of us, because of your human qualities, your optimistic spirit and your thoughtfulness. If being great is being big in small things, the kindly word and deed here and there, then your niche is already carved out."

It was this sensitive ability to make men and systems perform almost as though inspired that led the boy from Council Bluffs to the summit. He had stood alone — with no money, no influential relatives, no wily inclination to make "deals"—but sheer dedication and his own devotion to intelligent hard work kept him climbing toward the top in General Mills.

In his speeches inside and outside the company, Harry Bullis was a "business educator" dispensing valuable advice.

In his 1936 message to all General Mills salesmen, Bullis talked about the universal urge to achieve: "Most people want to do big things. They dream of the day when their real powers will blossom forth in all their glory, and something big will be done. The great trouble about waiting to do the big things is, the years are piling up.

"The day is not far away when one's powers to accomplish will be unequal to one's ambitions, and the dream will remain a dream unfulfilled and unattained. To sit by the dead embers of unrealized dreams is poor comfort for the years to come, and a sad commentary upon one's record of aspirations and achievements.

"The big things can be done by most of us who dream in terms of successful achievements. How? It doesn't take a prophet to disclose the secret. Just ordinary sense and understanding of life will point the way to big achievement—**do it today.** Do the little things that lie in our way and must be done—do them now, for the little things well done are the foundations of bigger things we crave to do. Success is but the accumulation of little things faithfully done. **Today** is the most momentous day in your history—it will not come back—when it goes its record of work goes with it. You cannot do tomorrow what should be done today. Tomorrow brings its own work. Give tomorrow a chance by doing today's work today."

During a meeting of the operating executives of Farm Service Stores, Inc. and the Howard Grain Company on April 10 and 11, 1936, Bullis presented a voluminous report on the financial status of the Farm Service Stores, division by division, all over the country. At the end of the meeting he again "expressed his enthusiasm for the future."

After extensive travels, during which he visited practically every dealer in approximately two hundred stores, Bullis got the stores functioning profitably, and then he turned them over to one of the other operating executives. It was another championship performance.

Even with a schedule that would leave two or three other men limp, Harry managed to get away with Irma for some delightful vacation trips. In July, 1932, they took a ten-day canoe trip, accompanied by two guides, down the Nipigon River in Canada. It was a fishing trip, and Harry caught the limit of brook trout every day.

When Mr. and Mrs. Harry Bullis were listed as passengers on the S. S. South American for a Great Lakes cruise in August 1933, they were initiated into the "Most Noble Fellowship of Ye Rollicking Rovers, by Proclamation to All Ye Inland Seas' Deities Great and Small." Harry still had the certificates of membership.

On December 12, 1934, the Minneapolis Journal noted that "Mr. and Mrs. Harry A. Bullis of 2116 West Lake of the Isles Boulevard sailed Saturday on the steamship Santa Paula for a holiday tour and a visit in California. They will stop in Havana, Cuba, and at points in the Panama Canal Zone, en route to Los Angeles, via the Panama Canal."

Part of one of their vacations was spent appraising the 13,500-acre, lavishly-appointed Circle M plantation at Macon, Georgia, which James Bell and six other men had purchased as a quail hunting preserve. Located on the property were more than one hundred tenant houses, seven cottages and one large house built around a central court. Harry noted that the operations concerned with the plantation included production of cotton and cottonseed, production of feed, ginning, and grist corn milling; and he suggested ways to put the place on a paying basis. Harry performed many services of this type for Mr. Bell.

In the process of rejuvenating the Farm Stores, Bullis also stirred up a great burst of enthusiasm for sales contests among the various divisions. Originally called "President's Contests," they somehow became dedicated to the vice president in charge of operations.

The Bullis Backbone Trophy Contest in 1935 was typical of the dramatic atmosphere which characterized the sales contests. Boisterous, bumptious, and crammed with tomfoolery were the spirit-rousing posters and circulars which were printed by all the competing divisions. Rivalry was fierce. Although it was fun to make a "game" of it, underneath all the "window-dressing" was sincere dedication to the attainment of higher sales figures for General Mills products.

In the announcement of the Backbone Contest, Harry Bullis was shown standing next to an almost Bullis-sized silver trophy, five and one-half feet tall, with a bag of Gold Medal Kitchen-Tested Flour in his hand. The original picture, Harry said, had been "rigged" by some of his playful colleagues, with a "blown-up trophy" superimposed in the space next to him on the photo. It appeared that there was a deplorable scarcity of trophies that size, so he had to have one made. It cost him a pretty penny, but it turned out to be great sport, and he enjoyed the excitement as much as the competing teams. The trophy would be awarded to the flour milling company showing the greatest increase in Gold Medal Kitchen-Tested Flour sales during February and March of 1935. The suspense mounted, with James F. Bell wiring, ". . . Makes me wish I was back selling in Michigan and having run for your cup." D. D. Davis, in a message from Chicago, said, "Final total figures reaching me here this morning are such that demonstrate better results when I am away than when I am home. If you can guarantee

March, April and May in equivalent amounts, will immediately sail for Europe."

Every unit all over the country strained to be "The Winnah," but the Royal Milling Company of Great Falls, Montana, walked away with the mammoth trophy. Both Bullis and Davis attended the victory banquet honoring the sales and office force at Great Falls. The cup, which was made by International Silver Company of Chicago, was the largest cup ever manufactured by that concern—and probably the largest ever made for trophy purposes in this country.

Harry Bullis' slogan in all the sales contests was "Take time to work." Bullis exemplified it, never pausing to ask himself if he were weary from the constant round of banquet speeches, meetings and evaluation reports. He shunned negative thinking, forging ahead with high spirits and the famous Bullis grin. All around the country General Mills associate companies applauded his stimulating addresses. Having a personal contact with this eloquent representative of their company exhilarated them.

On March 18, 1936, William R. Morris of Washburn Crosby in Buffalo, wrote D. D. Davis, "Harry makes a wonderful ambassador. He radiates good will and has the faculty of making everybody feel good."

In answer, President Davis wrote, ". . . You are right—he makes a wonderful ambassador—and at the same time he has a very keen appreciation of the fundamental nature of our many problems."

In promotion letters and speeches to sales groups, Harry constantly chose the invigorating, colorful theme. In his sales bulletin message of September,

1935, he emphasized the fact that "You Can't Score in the Locker Room After the Game." He said, "The chief 'pet peeve' of any football team is the 'locker room All-American.' The guy that 'thrills' his teammates with his verbal feats of daring after the battle is over —nine times out of ten this guy gets a loud birdie from the boys who were in there digging all afternoon. Remember this . . . touchdowns aren't made in BULL sessions after the game. Neither are sales touchdowns made from a sideline position. The only place to win games is on the field of battle . . . where you put your words and efforts into actual sales producing action!"

His letter of September 19, 1937, to the Sperry sales managers and bakery flour salesmen asked, "What is the Price of Success? When Greta Garbo first came to Hollywood, she had plenty of opportunity to be alone; nobody paid much attention to just another beautiful girl with ambitions to become a world-famous actress. Henry Ford, tinkering away on a strange mechanical contraption in his barn, was known only to his neighbors, and they were inclined to think he might be 'teched in the haid.' Even today, few people realize how many years of hard work and hard thinking are back of the success which put millions of Fords on the highways and projected their maker to world headlines. . . . There's lots of hard work and practice in achieving success."

Enthusiasm—the positive type of Bullis enthusiasm—glowed like a beacon light in the center of a whirling pinwheel of brisk activity, during all the sales award campaigns. Too numerous to be quoted at length here are the dozens of "splendid and truly inspiring" speeches of Harry Bullis that "left everyone bubbling with enthusiasm."

Bullis was not the sort of businessman to bury his head in the sand of company affairs and forget about the rest of the world. Even before he had become intimately concerned with World War I, he had made the whole wide world his business. With sharpened awareness of all the factors involved, he could see fresh war clouds gathering on the European horizon in the early Thirties. Gefreiter Schicklgruber, the obscure young Bavarian soldier in World War I, had become Adolph Hitler now; Bullis was keeping a wary eye on Der Fuehrer as he went about the monstrous business of inflaming the German people with promises to lift them — "the master race" — to the heights of world domination.

Before and during World War II, Bullis compiled about twenty war scrapbooks. He assembled the material because of his convictions that the United States would enter this war too. The scrapbooks contain newspaper clippings and magazine articles, starting with 1934 when Hitler was just attaining power in Germany. They illustrate the gradual change in public opinion that took place in the United States regarding our entry into World War II.

In the collection is the New York American story about Hitler's self-righteous pretexts for putting down the 1934 Monarchist revolt — "ruthlessly and with Prussian thoroughness. . . ."

The executive who had started at the bottom of the ladder himself took an almost "paternal pride" in the advancement of his colleagues and associates in the company.

Around 1930, a bright-eyed young man had entered the employ of General Mills. It was rumored that "Charlie" Bell was such a nice fellow to have around the mill that everybody forgot he was "the Big Boss' son." James Ford Bell had been exposed to a rigorous training period, with no special favors from his own father—it was a case of "sink or swim"—so it was family tradition for the third-generation Bell to learn how to keep himself afloat in rough waters, some of them far from home. Harry Bullis spoke admiringly of Charles H. Bell's service as a mill hand, accountant, salesman and promotion executive and of "the youthful vigor, vision and confidence which he brought to each of these activities" during his early years with the company.

Close to Bullis was Marc Stark, who held a cherished place in the Bullis book of memories. Marc apparently joined the Washburn Crosby Company shortly before Harry did. When Harry was transferred from the Minneapolis mill to the Minneapolis office late in 1920, Marc was an important part of Bullis' personal staff, doing much research work for him and acting as his assistant when he reached "the high executive stratosphere." Years later Marc Stark looked back with thankfulness over the long period of close association with the man who had "come up from the mill." Wrote Stark, "Everyone can see the tangible evidences of what you have accomplished, but I wonder how many fully appreciate the tremendous energy, the self-sacrifice, the honesty of purpose, and above all the open-minded human understanding which you have brought into the solution of the company's problems."

On a more recent occasion, Marc Stark noted that Harry Bullis had developed his sound philosophy while he was still a young man. "A basic part of that philosophy was always to help other people. Well over forty years ago, after completing some cost accounting assignments at the mill, he was made supervisor of several departments in the Washburn Crosby general office, including the statistical where I was working at the time. Very quickly Harry discovered that while I knew the mechanics of compiling data, I had no training in statistical theory and method. Soon he had me reading and studying the books which would help me, not only on statistics but cost accounting, budgeting and economics."

"This desire to help others," Stark noted, "was accompanied by an abiding faith in people. Bullis always tried to bring out the best in everyone. He frequently pointed out that each of us has within himself a 'big man' and a 'little man.' When the 'little man' gets control, we become impatient, angry and negative —then everything goes wrong. But if we are patient, swallow our pride and think in positive terms, we generally find a good solution for our problems and in any event we have retained our self-respect and the respect of those around us."

The "Bullis positive philosophy" did not waver in fair weather or foul, Stark says. It "touched the lives of many hundreds of employees. It built morale and kept it high. That kind of morale was a big asset during the dark days of the depression. It was characteristic of him that he tried to give a lift to all who came into his office. Even a reprimand was followed by positive suggestions which took out much of the sting and removed mental cobwebs."

Harry Bullis had always been a man with a clear-cut set of business principles. In 1931, he told the General Mills Field auditors, "Your work is worthy of the best you can give it. It is good mental discipline, because it provides the means and conditions for individual thinking, and allows you opportunity to express your judgment." Bullis always respected the man who wanted to succeed and who used imagination to "streamline" his job. Success, he declared, is doing your best work in the easiest way, while enjoying the greatest amount of happiness. He spoke to the field auditors about getting "an insight into the methods and personnel of business, thus providing excellent preparation for even greater responsibilities." Among the important principles to be kept in mind were: "Be thorough. . . . Be curious and alert. . . . Be accurate and sincere. . . . Be tactful. . . Be optimistic. . . . Be a doer, not merely a talker."

Harry referred to Charles "Chuck" Olson, who came to work at the Washburn Crosby office in the 1920's, as "one of my boys." In a letter to Harry, Olson wrote:

"No one in General Mills has done more to encourage and inspire young men than you have—you have left an indelible mark in the company and the things you have done and stood for will long be remembered."

Even when he was working in the mill in 1919, Bullis was taking appreciative notice of employees who were qualified to make more significant contributions to the progress of General Mills. As a young auditor in 1922, he began to employ and train men of high potential."

It might be said, jokingly, that there was a bit of guile in Harry's knack for hiring men who were as promotion prone as he was—he had to employ highly competent successors to step into his shoes! Harry had never believed in settling comfortably down in a job. "As soon as I got a job, I always began working out of it into a better one," he said. "To me, all jobs were temporary, simply leading to bigger jobs."

A stammering, stoop-shouldered boy learned how to build men by practicing on himself, but it is evident that Harry took more pride in his record as a builder of other men. The achievements of "his boys" continued to be a deeply personal source of gratification. As he moved up in the company, his dynamic spirit was reflected in the triumphs of the men he had developed, and many of them later reached the top echelons in the General Mills organization.

Among the first men in the galaxy of future management and executive stars whom Bullis employed was Gordon C. Ballhorn, another graduate of the University of Wisconsin, who became a vice president and was a long-time comptroller. Then there is James P. McFarland, vice president for consumer foods and a director of General Mills. William B. Cash, a vice president, is director of marketing, Grocery Products Division. Everett Andresen, vice president, is director of trade relations, Grocery Products Division. Dr. J. J. Shronts for many years has been medical director of

General Mills. Robert C. Wiper is commodity analyst of General Mills. D. H. Fuhriman was district office manager and district coordinator of the Oakland, California, branch office.

Those are only a few of the men whose lives were fruitfully affected by the Bullis "ladder-climbing philosophy." He built morale among his executives and employees by sponsoring their advancement if they paid the price in "intelligent hard work"—a trademark phrase with Bullis, which he used often in his speeches and writings. Deceptively brief and uncomplicated at first glance, it carries terrific impact as a soul-searching device. Bullis believed that the intelligent, hard-working employees deserved to be trained, encouraged, rewarded and assisted. He gave them responsibilities and permitted them to make the most of those responsibilities.

The men reaped benefits, and so did General Mills. Bullis took every opportunity to offer encouragement and to express his appreciation for worthwhile results which were achieved by his associates, especially by the men in the field. In building men, he taught them how to advance toward their goals and reach them successfully. An old hand at the business of setting goals for himself, he shared his formula of contagious confidence, imagination—and that most important of requisites, "intelligent hard work."

Later, Harry Bullis would say in a magazine article, "If personnel is the most difficult factor in business to regulate and control, it also returns the greatest dividends when the job of human relations is properly done. . . .

"Employees should not be treated merely as cogs in a machine. They must be accepted as associates who have self-respect and self-confidence. Each should be given an opportunity to advance if he or she is willing to pay the price in intelligent hard work."

General Mills has had a long and honorable record in the field of amicable labor relations. Cadwallader Washburn had demonstrated a healthy level of interest in the personal welfare of his employees. The first John Crosby, who had come out from Maine in 1877, refused to join other Minneapolis millers in a wage-cutting proposal. "I shall pay my men what they are worth to me," declared "Honest John." James Ford Bell, in 1918, originated the practice of guaranteeing a minimum number of working hours a year to workers who had been employed by Washburn Crosby for two years or more, and he instituted a workers' committee system to meet with management and discuss labor problems and wages.

General Mills pioneered many improvements in workers' benefits, but Bullis was slightly ahead of everybody in his belief that the employees deserved top consideration. A worker who feels properly rewarded, he knew, is more likely to perform as a "partner" than as a subordinate. He becomes part of the success pattern in his company because he feels successfully secure.

There were overtones of well-merited pride in Harry Bullis' voice when he mentioned the employees' pension plan that was inaugurated at General Mills in 1939. For years he had been chafing restlessly under the system which was haphazard in its loose application to each individual case. A uniform pension system, "the measuring man" declared at many an executive meeting, was what was needed. "Pensions," he said, "must be considered as an element of cost, a form of depreciation on men."

The opportunity he sought came when the Supreme Court declared the A.A.A. processing tax unconstitutional and General Mills received a windfall refund of $1,650,000. Before anyone else could suggest a better place to put it, Bullis pounced triumphantly on it. Now his long-advocated pension plan could become a reality! The officers and directors, who had gradually become convinced of the justice of his arguments, voted to match the sum of the refund, and the General Mills pension plan was launched with $3,300,000 in the bank. General Mills was the first milling company to create a retirement pension plan for its employees. The big man at the board of directors table was still watching out for the little fellows down in the mills and offices and out in the field.

Later, Bullis would originate an incentive program for management in which profits—above a predetermined level—would be distributed among the people whose leadership capabilities had made the gains possible. Many are the letters expressing pleasure and gratitude for those unique "awards of merit."

Looking back in 1944, Harry's great friend and cherished associate, Gerald "Spike" Kennedy, would write:

"Long after the mists of time have blanketed the memory of your personality—long after all of us have gone the way of all men, your name will be remembered for many things, but two in particular will stand out above all others: the retirement system and the incentive program. The first is now in operation; the second is in preparation. Both of these personalize the relationship of the employee with the company, and both reflect the emphasis on human values which has been the keynote of your every sentence since you 'joined up' twenty-five years ago.

"May continued success attend your administration, and may health and happiness keep pace with the long strides you are making in the achievement of a General Mills that truly serves the many."

Back in the 1930's Harry had already been making long strides and acquiring an awesome string of company titles. He was delivering an almost incalculable number of speeches as vice president in charge of operations, attending to General Mills business on many different levels, and becoming increasingly involved in industrial, fraternal and civic activities. He took some time off for walks and golf, and anyone could guess where to find him when the University of Wisconsin and the University of Minnesota had a date to play football. In Chicago, on June 22, 1937, he saw Joe Louis knock out Jim Braddock and win the heavyweight championship of the world. "I had a ringside seat," he remembered. He saw several of Louis' other matches. After having taken those two years of boxing at the University of Wisconsin, he had always been interested in heavyweight championship bouts.

Between 1935 and 1939, General Mills had continued its progressive march forward on the industrial scene. During this period the vacuum distillation process for vitamin E production had been announced. Company divisions had been established, with the subsidiaries losing their corporate identities. PurAsnow flour had been introduced. The employees' pension plan had been approved, and the first informal stockholders' meetings, pioneered by James F. Bell, were being held.

In January, 1939, an Arctic expedition reported that Gold Medal Flour, Wheaties and Bisquick had kept the expedition table well supplied with tasty, nourishing food during fifteen icy months "on top of the world."

Many new radio programs had been added to the General Mills roster, including such nostalgia provoking daytime serials as "Arnold Grimm's Daughter," "Valiant Lady," and "Betty and Bob." "Jack Armstrong" was still going strong all over the country, while Sperry Flour was broadcasting "Doctor Kate" and "Dangerous Road" for the edification of West Coast listeners. General Mills also presented "Grouch Club" on the Pacific Coast, and "Curtain Time" over WGN in Chicago. "Hymns of All Churches" was part of The General Mills Hour on the NBC network. In 1939, at a time when the world was seething with rumors of another era of bloodshed to come, General Mills sponsored the penetrating news programs of H. V. Kaltenborn, world traveler and top radio commentator.

On the eve of Harry Bullis' fiftieth birthday, the clumping of goose-stepping boots was echoing grimly from across the Atlantic, and Der Fuehrer's glory-goaded Luftwaffe was taking to the air to proclaim the invincibility of the Thousand Years' Reich. It mattered not that Poland—land of a host of enlightened patriots from Casimir III to Ignace Paderewski—longed for peace and security. Poland still shuddered in bleak remembrance of the violence she had suffered during World War I, ravaged between the jaws of Russia and Germany. It was the same harsh, bitter story again.

In mid-September 1939 the capital city of Warsaw was subjected to a period of merciless bombardment. Among the millions of Polish people whose lives were shattered was a titled gentlewoman named Countess Maria Smorczewska. There would be many years of privation and misery for her before the city of Minneapolis would begin to take the place of Warsaw in her life.

Chapter Eleven

A Big Man for the Highlands

"Mr. Bullis was extremely thoughtful about remembering the 'red-letter' days in the lives of his friends and associates," recalls Helen Hansen, his secretary for many years. He took impulsive pleasure in dispensing the "kindly word and deed here and there" to show his fellow wayfarers that he appreciated their company along the road of life.

Early in 1939, Glenn Krueger thanked his "Chief" for sending good wishes on the anniversary of his thirteenth year with the company. "You certainly never miss an opportunity to pass on a word of praise or appreciation. . . . You have accorded me finer treatment than any man with whom I have been privileged to be associated. . . ."

Sincere warmth is noted in the exchange of cards and letters between Harry Bullis and his correspondents. It was a case of friendly interest, not "politics."

The "reciprocal admiration society" became most ambitious when Mr. Bullis had a birthday. Commemorating the event are scores of enthusiastic greetings from executive branch officers, employees, and other friends. His "Old Gang"—Ralph Stiles, H. O. Frohback, M. P. Stark and G. C. Ballhorn—saluted him with a leather bound book which listed all his virtues and attributes: "To Harry Bullis, our friend and partner over the years. Your Honesty, Courage, Fair-mindedness, Resourcefulness, Application, Cooperation, Loyalty, Self-Discipline, Thoughtful Friendliness, and Love for Your Fellow Men Are an Inspiration to Your Associates . . ."

From J. S. Hargett and J. G. Schmitz, officers of the Southwestern Division, came a huge, handsome Proclamation inscribed on fine leather, appointing Harry Bullis an Honorary Colonel on the Executive Staff of the Southwestern Division.

Ray McLaughlin, president of the Central Division and a master of deft phrases, recalled admiring Harry's ability "to toil terribly" in the early years; later he had come to appreciate his "courageous soul." "You have that magnificent quality which will not admit or recognize defeat, and this will not only carry you far, but it will inspire those around you to do great things, things perhaps of which they did not think themselves capable. . . ."

On May 24, 1940, Donald D. Davis announced the election by the board of directors of H. A. Bullis to the new position of executive vice president of General Mills. According to "The Modern Millwheel" for June, 1940, "Mr. Bullis is perhaps the most popular man in General Mills. Following a brief announcement of his appointment to this new office, hundreds of congratulatory letters were delivered to his desk in Minneapolis, Minnesota. Harry Bullis' immense popularity with employees is due to the fact that he has spent most of his business life as one of them, and always thinks of himself first and foremost as an employee of General Mills. He understands their feelings and their problems from first-hand experience. . . ."

Among the many letters and wires was one from a former General Mills vice president who was astonished, back in 1919, when Captain Bullis of the A.E.F. wanted to start working in the mill. Now that same vice president, James Ford Bell, was chairman of the board, and Bullis had become executive vice president of General Mills. Perhaps Bell was thinking back with satisfaction to those early days when he wrote in 1940, "I do not know of anything that has given me as much pleasure and personal satisfaction as the recognition which the board accorded you at its last meeting. It is something you have earned through your own ability, perseverance and intelligence. You have taken your part in this organization in a splendid manner, one that has won admiration and respect from all. . . ."

Kermit Paulson of the Central Division of GMI in Cleveland recalled the days when he had been able to consult Bullis frequently. "That it has been wise for me to follow this advice is borne out on this happy occasion. . . . It certainly is an inspiration to me to be able to say, 'I knew him when' because it should prove to all . . . that in our grand Company one's ability is the only limit to progress."

Harry Bullis, in the pictures that accompanied the 1940 news stories, was a "fine, upstanding figure of a man," as they used to say. His eyes looked out with lively interest at the reader. Broad shouldered and erect, he weighed slightly over two hundred pounds. With his wavy, silvering hair and distinguished features, dressed in a handsomely tailored suit, Harry Bullis epitomized the Champion American Businessman. The scars of his early struggles were all on the inside where they would daily inspire him to temper "market-place justice" with mercy.

Among his many "extracurricular activities," the Millwheel noted that "Mr. Bullis is a National Vice President of the National Association of Manufacturers. . . . He is a past National President of the University of Wisconsin Alumni Association and a Past National President of the National Association of Cost Accountants."

For months, Bullis' "fellow partners" continued to bombard the new executive vice president with masterpieces of artistic ingenuity. The Sperry sales department published an enthralling booklet entitled "The Life of An Enthusiast." It was prophetically noted, below his baby picture, that small Harry had a turned-up toe—"an early sign of forward thinking and enthusiasm."

Success did not make Harry Bullis pompous. He still enjoyed being "one of the fellows" at the annual General Mills picnic at Excelsior Park. Under the pictures of the most photogenic Minnesota executive is the jovial comment, " 'Sitting Bull' standing up pitching horseshoes. Some pitch!"

On November 8, 1940, after the election of Franklin D. Roosevelt, Harry Bullis indicated the position he would take in relation to partisan politics. There is a unique quality about a Republican businessman who sends this type of message to his colleagues after a Democrat has been returned to the White House:

"Sixty million citizens told the world yesterday in no uncertain terms that Democracy is a vivid living force in America. More than half of all Americans are jubilant today and all are determined that nothing shall stop the progress of this country. We should remember that there is no law against initiative, no law against leadership and no law against expansion. We in America and in General Mills have the ingenuity and resourcefulness to meet any situation. We do not overcome anything by resisting it. We overcome most things by cooperation and helpfulness."

In the face of increased federal taxes, Bullis could still lift his head and advise his fellow-millers to "Meet the Challenge of This Difficult Year with Courage and Enterprise." In the Modern Miller for December 7, 1940, he said: "There are plenty of difficulties in the milling business this year, gentlemen, but our aim should be for a general stimulating, clear-minded drive straightforward on all fronts in an atmosphere of faith, confidence and courage. . . .

"We in the flour milling industry have made many blunders, but as long as we can keep the spirit of optimism, hope and positive clear thinking, as long as we think broadly and not narrowly, as long as we keep our feet on the ground and approach our problems with poise, balance and equilibrium, and above all, as long as we perform an economic service by giving the American public good food products, at reasonable prices—just so long as we do these things the flour industry will progress and go forward."

As early as May, 1939, Bullis was publicly predicting in many addresses that the United States would become engaged in World War II sooner than expected.

Bullis saw the conflict in Europe as a world challenge to men who believed "in the ultimate decency of things." Among his many speeches on the subject of preparedness was one he delivered as chairman of the Open Forum on Problems of Manufacture and National Defense at the Regional Business Conference of the United States Chamber of Commerce on January 27, 1941, in which he declared emphatically, "A world of people is in distress and the revolution does not fit into any known package. We are not sure when, where, and how it will end. This is a new war and a different world. . . . The main difficulty which faces us in our defense program is the psychological impediments which may prove to be very dangerous. We are attacking the problem of defense with all the enthusiasm of boy scouts but we are preparing for the last war, it seems to me, rather than this present war. The French were really fighting the last war. The Maginot Line was typical of the state of mind which believes you can meet challenges by sitting still and can keep what you have by building a strong fence around it."

On April 17, 1941, more than six months before Pearl Harbor, Bullis launched his own offensive during a visit to Atlanta, Georgia. He urged more power for the president. He said, "Hitler will be defeated through American efforts and industrial production, but in order to clear away the confusion and lack of understanding of the need to get started now, it may be necessary to knock together the heads of both business and labor. . . . The war is going to be won by American industry." Harry Bullis, like poet Carl Sandburg at that time, was asking his fellow citizens if this country should wait complacently until it saw the whites of the Nazis' eyes. Few were the discerning voices in this brave minority.

Ralph McGill, the progressive-minded editor of the Atlanta Constitution, appreciated Bullis' provocative view of contemporary history during his luncheon speech. "Harry A. Bullis of Minneapolis," McGill wrote, "commented on the five great leaders of the world today. 'A little more than twenty years ago—

" 'Joe Stalin, who holds the destinies of millions of Russians in his hands and brain, was a political terrorist, either getting out of jail or in. Or hiding from the police.

" 'Winston Churchill, ex-newspaperman and ex-member of the war cabinet in 1914-1918, was discredited because of his Dardanelles campaign.

" 'Benito Mussolini, ex-newspaper reporter and soldier, was organizing the discontented ex-soldiers and thugs always ready to join up where loot was in prospect.

" 'Adolph Hitler was a frustrated painter of pictures, house painter and ex-soldier. He was a small-time political agitator to whom a mere handful listened.

" 'Franklin D. Roosevelt was apparently hopelessly removed from active life because of his physical disabilities.

" 'Today the destinies of almost every living person on the globe are within the hands of these men, directly or indirectly. It is a mistake to say that any one of them did not achieve his position by the will of the people. In a sense, it was discontent which put each one in the position he holds.' "

Because he was Harry Bullis, the executive vice president of General Mills was not "just talking" during this period. Behind the scenes, he was "driving straight ahead with that positive mental attitude" for which he had become famous. On January 18, 1941, Donald Davis and Harry Bullis of General Mills completed negotiations for the purchase of the abandoned Minneapolis plant of the Northern Pump Company on Central Avenue. Back of that news item lies an almost legendary tale of imaginative minds at work in an unfamiliar field during a time of world peril.

As though the production of flour, grocery products and feed were not a gigantic enough project, Bullis started pushing General Mills into munitions work long before any mill-sized war contracts were in sight.

At that time, Arthur D. Hyde was in charge of the manufacturing operations of General Mills, under the direct supervision of Harry Bullis. In Bullis terminology, this meant that Hyde was free to use his own judgment and creative imagination to get the job done. In Hyde's department at the Minneapolis flour plant were an efficient, small research staff which had invented machinery to produce Wheaties, a group of machinists, and a large inventory of modern machine tools.

Hyde and Bullis agreed that the company must begin to use these men and modern machine tools; otherwise, when the United States became involved in actual warfare, the government would appropriate the company's machinists and machine tools and award them to a conventional producer of defense equipment. It may also be assumed that Bullis and Hyde welcomed this bold, patriotic challenge.

Who would ever suspect that a flour milling concern could become so versatile overnight? Bullis instructed Hyde to go confidentially to Washington, in the latter part of 1939, deal with the United States Navy, and obtain a simple mechanism or product that the company could produce. At first, Hyde had difficulty convincing Navy officials that the "General" in General Mills had put on his uniform and was ready to march to war, but at last he obtained an order to make counter-revil cylinders and plungers for naval guns. Then General Mills was awarded a prism order, which it ran off in record time by perfecting a device to grind fifty-four prisms simultaneously. "With this greyhound start," Bullis recalled, "the company decided to bid on bigger and more difficult things."

Eyes widened in amazement when the Minneapolis Journal announced on January 7, 1940: "General Mills, world's largest flour milling company, will enter the munitions business for national defense. The company has received an order from the Navy Department for the manufacture of parts for anti-aircraft gun assemblies in its machine research laboratory in Minneapolis."

Later that month came the purchase of the huge Northern Pump Company plant which had been abandoned when Northern Pump moved into its new plant outside of Minneapolis. Hyde transferred his machinists and equipment into the plant, and General Mills was in the business of producing fire control equipment and other complicated mechanisms for the United States Navy. From a description of some of the war-time projects, a large plant was necessary. Among the items produced there were huge, twenty-foot-high, eight-hundred-part gun sights, segments of which had to be machined to one ten-thousandth of an inch. Those precision gun sights, manufactured by a conventional flour company, were the most complex type of naval ordnance in production. General Mills multiplied its engineering-inventing staff from five to one hundred, and increased ordnance employment from fifty to fifteen hundred. The results were a sharp cut in gunsight building time. Ahead were commendations from the Navy and millions of dollars in orders for other precision instruments.

Thus, before and during World War II, General Mills made a tremendous contribution toward victory by successfully manufacturing equipment for the Navy. Harry Bullis referred admiringly to Art Hyde and his great war-time team of inventors and machinists.

Flour would always be first on the domestic and foreign fighting fronts during the war; but the General Mills pattern widened out in every direction to produce vitamins, alcohol, dehydrated soups, oat flour for D-rations, and even bags that could be used to construct sandbag fortifications.

General Mills was getting ready to "pass the ammunition" for almost a year before President Roosevelt declared a state of unlimited national emergency.

When major powers are at war, the world begins to shrink. Although Pearl Harbor was yet to come, the country stirred uneasily as the Atlantic Ocean seemed to grow narrower day by day. Now was the time to recall the warnings of alert Americans and to hope that the resources of a massive, productive democracy could tip the scales against Hitler's outrageous machine.

By contrast, the tone of Harry's letter, on his father's seventy-eighth birthday in 1941, is like a mellow breeze sifting down over the young wheatlands and dairy country of southern Minnesota to the old Bullis home in Council Bluffs, Iowa:

"Dear Dad: Happy Birthday, Dad, on June fourth. Seventy-eight years young, and when I say young I mean young. To me, Dad, you certainly are a young man—young in spirit, young in all your faculties. You are living in the present and the future and not too much in the past. You are a great dad, and I am proud of you. You have been a fine father to Jennie, Roe, and me. We cannot begin to tell you how much you mean to us. Attached is a little birthday present. I hope that if you have not already made your trip to Excelsior Springs that you will do so, and enjoy the baths and your old associates there whom you have seen annually for several years. The years have been kind to you, Dad, probably because you are still staying young and also because you have a loving daughter who keeps house for you. I am reminded of Browning's lines:

"Grow old along with me!
The best is yet to be,
The last of life, for which the first was made;
Our times are in His hand
Who saith, 'A whole I planned,
Youth shows but half;
Trust God, see all, nor be afraid.'"

Harry always spent Christmas with his father and Jennie, and George Bullis visited at his son's home in Minneapolis often during his lifetime.

During the summer of 1941, the average American was still trying to go about his business much as usual, even though the Swastika had darkened most of the map of Europe and "Defense" was a word that was being heard more frequently. On July 30, 1941, Governor Harold E. Stassen appointed Harry A. Bullis a member of the Minnesota Defense Council. About a week later, the Alameda Times, in California, saluted Harry Bullis in its "Builders of Defense" column.

During his college years at the University of Wisconsin, a tall young man from Council Bluffs, Iowa, had been elected to Phi Beta Kappa, the highest scholastic honor a student can achieve. In October, 1941, he was invited to become one of the distinguished Phi Beta Kappa Founders, with its select membership of two hundred. Early the next month, he was elected president of the Phi Beta Kappa Association in Minneapolis. His "Chief," James F. Bell, thought highly of the double endorsement. "This is a signal honor, but I know of no one who deserves it more than yourself. . . ."

With that twinkle in his eye that keeps a man forever young, Bullis recalled that he participated in several football rallies at Wisconsin. According to a newspaper clipping dated November 23, 1941, the speeches of Harry Stuhldreher, "Roundy" — a sports writer whose real name was Joseph Patrick Coughlin —and Harry Bullis, kindled so much enthusiasm that both the police and fire departments had to be summoned to keep the student body in order!

On December 11, 1941, Bullis sent his November operations letter to D. D. Davis, the president of General Mills. After he had finished expressing himself as an accountant, concerned mainly with company debits and credits, he became a man with a war weighing heavily on his mind. It was December 11, four days after Japanese bombs had rained down on serenely peaceful Hawaii, making shambles of the formidable American fleet resting in the harbor. It was three days since President Roosevelt had appeared before Congress calling for a formal declaration of war upon the nation that had launched the "unprovoked and dastardly attack" upon the United States on "a date that will live in infamy."

In that operations letter to Davis was the stern note of urgency regarding the threat to the remainder of the free world. "Our country is at war," Bullis wrote. "The call is 'All Out for Total War.'" Just as he had gone out to enlist in World War I, instead of waiting to be drafted, Harry was ready to march in the front lines of industry. "Those of us who were in the First World War . . . know that conditions are very different from conditions during times of peace. As President Roosevelt said in his last fireside chat, 'War is at best a dirty business.' We have before us a job that is going to test our citizenship. . . . Events have proved the folly of sitting still while all the rest of the world is changing."

A 1940 milestone was the inauguration of the General Mills Health Association. In 1941, General Mills purchased the Great Western Manufacturing Company of Leavenworth, Kansas. On the food front, the Buffalo Cereal Plant was completed in 1940, and Cheerios and Betty Crocker Vegetable Noodle Soup were introduced in 1941. During 1942, General Mills acquired a number of large storage elevators at Duluth, Minnesota.

The executive vice president of General Mills started the 1942 New Year by writing an article on behalf of the war effort. "Industry Masses Its Vast Power For Victory," published in the January 10 issue of "Commercial West," is rich in human interest observations. He pointed out that modern wars had ceased to be almost exclusively the business of fighting men. Industry must play a larger part than ever before, often under the critical handicap of a shortage of young manpower. Valuable machines, he said, must not be allowed to stand idle. The time had come when men must work harder and longer, increasing man-hour production.

Bullis never belonged to the shift that kept holiday. In the mill, he had stayed over to study the next shift in action. The constant glow of light burning in the window marked the place where Harry Bullis still worked at his desk when everyone except the night watchman had gone home. The business of General Mills was as much a part of him as each breath he drew into his lungs. Somehow he managed to take vacations with Irma, play golf, attend football games, and be active in a variety of organizations—but if General Mills needed him, he was present in every sense of the word.

Among the ladies who "also served" was Irma Bullis. After World War I, she had continued to be an active officer in the Women's Overseas Service League, officiating as vice president for Corps Area VII. On February 17, 1942, she "tried out" the Women's Overseas Service League stationery when she wrote to Harry; she told him she had attended a Wisconsin party, at which "everyone said it did not seem like a Wisconsin party without you." She was busy with the Red Cross Sewing Guild. Because Harry was in San Francisco, she warned him that it was ten below zero in his home country. "Take note of the temperature here in Minneapolis and bundle up when you come home. Well, I am waiting to welcome you."

March 23, 1941, was a momentous day in the World War history of General Mills. "First torpedo director shipped from our Defense Plant," Bullis noted in his diary.

Somehow Harry found time to take on another vital job. As chairman of the Minnesota Industrial Salvage Committee, he appealed for "Scrap for Victory" in the Northwest Miller for March 25, 1942—pointing his finger at billions of pounds of obsolete scrap metal lying idle all over Minnesota when they were desperately needed as war materials by our armed forces.

Never had scrap metal been appreciated as much —except by the junkman—as it was during the mechanized era of World War II. Harry Bullis was pictured in the Minneapolis Star Journal for August 1, 1942, with George Hess, comptroller of the Great Northern Railway, who was contributing nearly four hundred pounds of forgotten and useless corporate seals to the salvage drive.

The General Mills ranks were being thinned by many calls to war-time duty. The third-generation Bell, Charles, had joined the Civilian Production staff in Washington in January. In March, young Bell wrote to tell Harry that he had applied for a commission in the Army Air Corps. He was to be assigned to the staff of the colonel at Wright Field, Dayton, Ohio. The colonel was E. W. Rawlings, whose qualifications would later lead him to a top executive position in the General Mills organization.

When Bullis was asked to become a special part-time mediator of the National War Labor Board, he decided that there were limits to the number of hours in his day. In addition to his heavy company commitments, he was chairman of the Minnesota Industrial Salvage Committee, chairman of the Special Gifts Division of the 1942 Minneapolis War Chest, chairman of the Manufacturers' Section of the Industrial Resources and Production Division of the Minnesota Defense Council, senior vice president of the Minneapolis Civic and Commerce Association, and in three or four other activities connected with the war effort.

When American youngsters come home from school and bite hungrily into a slice of bread, they seldom realize that today's bread contains "guardian ingredients" to keep them buoyant and bouncing with good health. In promoting the development of "enriched" white flour, General Mills research played a "pioneering role" in one of the greatest contributions ever made to public health. Writers in The Modern Millwheel have called it "The Quiet Miracle"—the health-giving product of "a nutritional revolution."

As in the history of most scientific advances, countless nutritionists, doctors, and chemists labored in industrial and college laboratories for long periods of time, searching conscientiously for a process that would give white flour the same nutritional value as whole wheat flour. White flour was overwhelmingly popular; but whole wheat flour, which was darker and required refrigeration in warm climates, was far richer in thiamin, riboflavin, niacin and iron.

Among the dedicated General Mills research men who carried the early enrichment experiments forward, with the encouragement of James Ford Bell, were Dr. Alonzo Taylor, Dr. Harold M. Boyd, Dr. C. H. Bailey, and Dr. John S. Andrews. In 1936, Dr. Andrews and his staff started the experiments which, after thousands of tests and harassing complications, would prove that most of the vitamins were not concentrated in the wheat germ but were present in the "branny layers" that went into animal feeds. "Some of America's best food went to the pigs while some of the nation's children fell victim to pellagra," the researchers concluded. The experiments continued, with wheats of all types and varieties being analyzed and evaluated.

The formula for Vibic Flour, perfected in Dr. Andrew's laboratory in 1940, was the first "almost" white flour in which some vitamins and minerals had been "restored" in proper proportions. Vibic Flour was awarded the seal of acceptance of the American Medical Association.

In 1940, G. Cullen Thomas, who first headed the Products Control Department at Washburn Crosby in 1924, was instrumental in convincing national medical, food and research authorities that the enrichment program was possible, practical, and vitally necessary to the nation's health in combatting widespread vitamin deficiencies.

Dr. Andrews and Paul W. Salo, now General Mills Director of Food Engineering Research, have worked out the company's enrichment concentrates program and have developed methods for distributing vitamins and minerals in flour.

In "Business Without Boundary," James Gray reported, "By the close of the year 1942 there were few who held out against the policy which General Mills actually had inaugurated with its Vibic Flour. The company also had been the first to order the enrichment of all its family brands. This was done by Bullis, as president, against the advice of some of his associates. Some rival companies did not immediately put themselves to this expense, but Bullis, acting on principle, insisted that General Mills must do so voluntarily. . . ." Many are the people whose lives—and capacities for accomplishment — have been "enriched" by their association with Harry Bullis. Just as he had stumped for the Employees' Pension Plan, Bullis relentlessly upheld the proposition, throughout the industry, that all white flour should contain as many vitamins and minerals as whole wheat flour.

Bullis had always contended that profits are the result of performing an economic service and if any operation is not profitable over a series of months, it should be discontinued because some competitors can perform the economic service better. However, he always balanced profit-making with social consciousness. A practical businessman in every sense of the word, Bullis still seemed constantly aware that the most sublime profit and loss statement ever compiled is the one from St. Luke: "What shall it profit a man, if he shall gain the whole world, and lose his own soul?"

During the summer of 1942, Harry Bullis almost became a colonel in the United States Army. Much correspondence was exchanged, climaxed by a special trip to Washington and interviews with officials. On July 5, Harry sent a telegram to General Charles S. Chester of the Army Specialist Corps, thanking the general for the honor and saying that he had discussed the matter with his partners who agreed that he was making a greater contribution to the war in his present position. Later on, J. F. Bell put an even stronger value on Bullis' inexpendability, when the Ordnance Department in Washington wanted him. "Let me say at the outset that you could not have selected a better man, nor one of greater capabilities in any position of major responsibility. . . . But the successful conduct of the war is not alone in active war service, but also in the maintenance of the essential industries which are vitally needed for the preservation of a proper war economy. . . . Ours is an essential industry. Mr. Bullis is executive vice president. I consider his services essential to the conduct of the business. I do not know how I could replace him. . . ."

On July 18, 1942, the executive vice president spoke from his heart at the dedication of the General Mills Service Flag. The company, he noted, had four hundred and ninety-five men in the service at that time. Because he could remember the experiences of a young captain in the A.E.F., Bullis was qualified to say, "Our men in service have life—life at its warmest and fullest and freest, at its utmost vigor, at its cleanest and clearest—life unbounded in volume and scope, yet guided with a military discipline that will make each of them the captain of his soul. Every one of them is a great American, a patriot. General Mills is proud of its men in active service, and the list grows longer every day. . . . They will be welcomed back by a company grateful for what they have done for it and for their country."

In late September, the surge of war-time impulses suddenly shifted Harry A. Bullis into the position of acting president of General Mills. At a meeting of the board of directors of the company on September 25, 1942, the directors granted a three months' leave of absence to the president, Donald Davis, "to undertake certain activities in connection with the operation of the War Production Board at Washington, D. C." Harry Bullis would serve as acting president during the three months of Davis' absence.

On October 20, when Bullis addressed the highly active Gold Medal Men's Club which he had started back in 1932, he congratulated the organization on its phenomenal record of growth—from less than one hundred members to more than eleven hundred. Sam Gale, the president of the Men's Club, had asked him to speak about General Mills at war, and Bullis noted that "the dynamic president of our company, Donald D. Davis, is in Washington heading up the War Production Board's new Program Coordination Division. We are thrilled that our president is occupying such an important position in the war effort. We believe that both Mr. Davis and General Mills are making an important contribution to the war. . . ."

Speaking as a man whose experience deserves the biblical description, "good measure, pressed down, and shaken together, and running over," Bullis noted that many major operating executives in the company had climbed up the ladder of success over a long period of years. "Their progress at times has not been rapid, but it has been sure. They started from scratch. They did not get into a rut, and they did not stay on the beaten path that is for beaten men. Their motto is 'Forward.' Their careers with our company are a demonstration of what can be accomplished in America. . . . We have seen the great industrial corporations of Europe taken over by the dictators in power, and we realize how fortunate we are in America, where a man can still exercise the rights of free enterprise and individual initiative, and can ascend the ladder of success if he is willing to endure the pain of struggle for the satisfaction and the glory that go with achievement. And back of the success of any man in industry who has climbed up that ladder, are many nights when he has burned the midnight oil and many long and trying days when he has worked hard for his company."

As moving as poetry, as practical as the efficient throbbing of machinery on the assembly line, as American as the Bill of Rights—this was the voice of Harry Bullis speaking to men of many backgrounds whose lives have been enriched by his advice, his warmth and his deep understanding of their problems as individuals.

Bullis sponsored Men's Clubs in all the divisions of the company. The ladies were not neglected; Harry managed to attend many meetings of the General Mills Girls' Club as an honored guest speaker. The man who understood how all the workers felt was instrumental in starting the Twenty-Five Year Clubs. Each group held an annual meeting during which employees who had achieved twenty-five years of service with General Mills were inducted as new members and were presented with gold pins. An entry in Harry's diary told of his desire to award watches, but he was voted down.

There was an air of suspense in the upper echelons of General Mills during the closing days of 1942. Mr. Davis was trying to decide whether he would remain in Washington or return to General Mills. Late in November Mr. Bell wrote to Mr. Davis asking him to make an early determination about his future plans, so the morale of the company could be kept high.

At a board of directors meeting on December 29, 1942, Donald Davis decided to relinquish his duties as president of the company. As Chairman James F.

Bell pointed out, "Mr. Davis' conclusion had seemed inevitable from the time of his decision to undertake direct responsibilities with the War Production Board." Mr. Bell cited Mr. Davis' valuable achievements in the company, but he pointed out that under war conditions, changes take place with great rapidity and that the company must establish and maintain its organization with coordinate responsibilities and authority to move with equal speed. Being president of General Mills was a full-time job; the board was left with no alternative than that of accepting Mr. Davis' resignation as "a patriotic, courageous, and self-sacrificing one which the board must both respect and honor."

Chapter Twelve

Harry Bullis to High Command

When a former "Iowa country boy" went home from the board of directors meeting on December 29, 1942, he had been elected president of mighty General Mills, Inc. Irma Alexander Bullis, who had pondered Harry's future with him on that stone bench in Trinity Church yard could rejoice as she looked back with warm pride across the difficult but rewarding years.

At the time of his election to the major administrative position in General Mills, Harry Bullis was a man with a Ten-Point Creed which has often been published as an example of high idealism in the business world. Now, more than ever before, he would have the authority to put the following ten principles into action:

"I Will:

1. Build men—big men.
2. Give everyone on the pay roll an opportunity to advance if he is willing to pay the price in intelligent hard work.

3. Emphasize the human side of the organization and build morale in General Mills.

4. Have a socialized mind and spirit, and attempt to see modern business as a responsible public service, and profit making as the building of public good will, wider purchasing power, and general welfare.

5. Have a strong scientific spirit and outlook, using the research approach to every problem.

6. Follow the four R's of creative business thinking:

   Realism
   Research
   Resolute Reasoning
   Rigorous Common Sense

7. Have courage for change—daring in concept—boldness of imagination, and vigor of conviction.

8. Cooperate with government regulations. Do everything possible to maintain the American Way of Life.

9. Have high standards and no compromise with principle.

10. Have faith in God.

When "I Will" was published in Printers' Ink, Editor R. L. Pritchard noted that Mr. Bullis said he would **build** men, not **lead** men. "There are too many so-called leaders who are simply opportunists with their aims basically concentrated on personal gain and power. But a builder of men . . . men who in turn build other men . . . ah, indeed, that is a worthy cause . . . broadly constructive in the interest of wide progress."

Here was Harry Bullis, the boy from Council Bluffs who had started out with nothing except his own ability and determination. True to that prophetic class motto of his Simpson Academy days, he had achieved the Highlands.

As soon as the news began to circulate, spontaneous cheers greeted Harry Bullis' elevation to the presidency of General Mills. There were no lukewarm, formal messages of congratulations; they sounded more like firecrackers popping on the Fourth of July.

The Northwestern Miller, in an article entitled "Harry Bullis to High Command," explained the heartfelt elation of the people whose lives Bullis had touched with his consistent sense of justice and faith in the rightness of things:

"While the choice of Harry A. Bullis, executive vice president and acting president of General Mills, Inc., to succeed Donald D. Davis as president probably was in some sense mere order of succession, the implications of Mr. Bullis' exceptional fitness for the task are evident alike in the action of the board and in the knowledge of those who have observed Mr. Bullis' steady rise in the exercise of responsibilities through the years.

"It may safely be said that the choice of no other man from among the many in the organization qualified to head milling's greatest establishment would have been so cordially welcomed both by the company's own staff and by its customers and competitors.

This applies most particularly to the company's relations with other millers, an independent lot if ever there was such a thing as independence in this world. Yet, under the intelligent, fairminded and scrupulously straightforward handling of these relations by Mr. Bullis, General Mills has won and, particularly in recent years, retained the respect and confidence of its competitors to a degree quite exceptional in an industry in which to hate the biggest fellow is almost an article of faith."

Among the hundreds of enthusiastic letters that poured into Bullis' office were messages from people of high and low estate—from top executives in other companies as well as his own, to "little fellows" whose cause he had so often championed. Some were dictated and typed; some were telegraphed; others were handwritten. Many were the expressions of delight at this climax to "a magnificent and spectacular career."

George Cormak, the milling authority who perfected Wheaties, injected a homespun note into his message from the CX ranch at Sheridan, Wyoming: "Well, Harry, you sure are entitled to congratulations, and you know you have mine—warmed up good and hot on the CX cookstove, sparking and sputtering from mere joy. . . ."

The new president of General Mills continued somehow to make time for the human contacts that he considered essential to the morale of the company—and to the company wives at home. During his administration—two years as executive vice president and five years as president of General Mills—it was his custom, at the end of a particularly difficult and strenuous day when obstacles had to be met and overcome, to ask the three most important executives on his personal staff to meet in his office at the close of business at five o'clock.

Then Bullis would ask the executive who he knew had been in the most difficulty that day to tell the group the details of the battle he had been waging. At the end of his recitation, Bullis would lead in a general laugh. After the others had spoken their pieces, Bullis would usually lean forward and say, "You birds have really been in a pink tea party today. Let me tell you what I have been up against!" His salty vocabulary would set them whooping with laughter, as he gave a humorous, quick picture of some of the tricky conversations in which he had been involved that day. Along about 5:45, the party would break up and everyone would go home feeling much better.

"That," Bullis said, "was my psychological way of keeping the members of my personal staff from going home after office hours and 'beating up their wives'!"

Supervisory leadership in industry was important to the president of General Mills during World War II. In "The American Foreman's Contribution to Victory," he noted that the foreman must handle multiple responsibilities. He must efficiently execute plans of executives and engineers, train workers and serve as their leader, and be sympathetic to the problems of workers as individuals in order to keep morale high. He must also be able to handle organized labor contacts diplomatically.

On January 2, Mr. Bell approved Bullis' organization chart. He had recommended L. N. Perrin for the office of executive vice president, Walter Barry as a member of the executive committee; three new vice presidents, S. C. Gale, G. S. Kennedy, and Searle Mowat; and J. J. Selvage for president of the Southeastern Division. He also advocated "increased compensation" for various executives.

On January 20, when he addressed the joint Girls' and Men's Club Dinner, he made his first public announcement about the instruments being manufactured in the General Mills war plant.

From the Minneapolis Times of January 21 to TIME Magazine for January 25, 1943, the story was picked up and circulated all over the country. "Secret Naval Weapons Being Produced Here," said the Minneapolis paper. The news about "one of America's most unusual wartime conversions" was considered sensational. One or two of the weapons being produced in the new plant "promise such surprise for the enemy that it cannot even be stated at this time the kind of enemy warcraft against which they may be used—air, surface or under the sea."

"Miracle in Minneapolis" was the title of the TIME story, bursting forth with usual journalistic momentum: "It was mid-October off Guadalcanal. The Jap cruiser wheeled and turned like a crazed whale. On the pursuing U. S. destroyer Duncan nimble fingers adjusted a torpedo director, sent a tin fish on its way. Smoke and water geysered up. The Jap shuddered, rolled over, started towards the bottom.

"The maker of that Jap-killing torpedo director was no oldtime munitions outfit, no veteran precision manufacturer, no war-wise Naval ordnance plant. It was energetic, ingenious General Mills, Inc., which before the war was a peaceful flour miller (Gold Medal, Bisquick, Wheaties). But last week General Mills was running a huge Naval fire control plant, was hard at work turning out complicated gunsights, torpedo directors, smoke-screen gadgets, telescope and periscope prisms." The feature story did a brisk run-through on all the intriguing facets of the amazing venture and ended by saying, "For this fancy production record General Mills is modest, even refuses to say who gets the credit. But one man stands out—glad-handing Harry A. Bullis who started to learn the flour business as a mill laborer, in 20 years was auditor, comptroller, secretary and executive vice president. An amateur prophet, Orator Harry Bullis in May 1940 publicly predicted the U. S. would be at war sooner than expected, started pushing the world's largest flour miller into munitions work long before any mill-sized war contracts were in sight. . . ."

Speeches, chairmanships, interviews, conferences —all over the country—kept Harry's schedule brimming with activities. At the board of directors first meeting of the year, the new president's request for one million dollars for research and six hundred thousand dollars for institutional advertising was approved. Within the framework of industry, both might be classified as educational investments. Always during this period, the gospel of "enrichment" was at the top of Bullis' educational agenda; he did not relax his efforts until the entire milling and baking industry had been converted.

On February 12, Bullis addressed a full meeting of

the operating board and made a sincere plea for cooperation. That night he was host at a General Mills dinner for sixty-four guests at which John Crosby, F. M. Crosby and C. C. Bovey spoke. Harry gave his Ten-Point Code. He mentioned in his diary that John Crosby gave a wonderful talk. The next day Crosby called Bullis on the phone and said he was convinced that Bullis would be a great leader of General Mills and the equal of any of his predecessors. Harry appreciated that heart-warming tribute from a venerable patriarch of the company.

Most of the President's Annual Award Contests had been dedicated to Harry in previous years, so it was poetic justice that he should in actual fact become president. The 1943 award trips started in March, at a time when Harry was often anxious about Irma's continued illness. When Harry would take her on annual vacations for two or three weeks, in Arizona or Florida, he took a professional nurse along with her and wheeled her about in a wheel chair. After spending most of two months in the hospital, Irma could still write a cheerful letter to Harry on April 25, 1943: "On this beautiful Easter morning I have very much to make me rejoice. My greatest blessing is the love of my husband which he expresses in so many wonderful ways. I rejoice in the recognition that is coming to you, Harry, and that I can share so intimately in that acclaim. Few women have had such a privilege. . . ."

From Chicago to San Francisco to Tacoma to Atlanta to New York to Kansas City—and points in between and beyond—went Harry Bullis, the new president of General Mills during 1943. He addressed meetings, toured plants, shook hands with hundreds of employees, made optimistic, dynamic speeches in numerous banquet halls. Reporters sought interviews with him because the new president of General Mills was a tremendously newsworthy man. Hadn't this tall, genial fellow been instrumental in putting a flour milling concern into ordnance work? Wasn't he known as a humanitarian of the business world? He was a big man who wanted to build big men who would help to make a big country even bigger. With his wide knowledge of economic problems, he could furnish the press with some pertinent observations on future prospects for a war-torn world.

The Tacoma Times for March 29, 1943, titled a Bullis interview: "Head of General Mills Sees Unprecedented Prosperity at Close of World War II."

"General Mills Head Who Put Firm in Ordnance Looks Ahead" was the title of an impressive article in The Milwaukee Journal late in April. The Journal noted at length that Harry Bullis found a "creative attitude of mind" important and that he saw the business executive of the future as a man possessing "social consciousness."

During a visit to the Southeastern Division both the Atlanta Journal and the New South Baker headlined his predictions for "A Postwar Boom in Dixie." Among other statements, he asserted, "I'm an optimist. I can't agree with those who think the world is going to the dogs. Rather, I see a better world after the war —a world improved by the opening of new fields of endeavor, new products and a new conception of human rights. . . ."

On his president's award trips, Bullis addressed as many as eleven annual award dinners. A sample of his itinerary covering a two weeks' period is staggering. Visiting one or two plants a day in as many cities, he went from Minneapolis to Chicago, to Atlanta, to Memphis, to Oklahoma City, to Amarillo, to Kansas City, back to Chicago, to Louisville, back to Chicago again, and off to Detroit, then to New York, then Baltimore, then back to Chicago and finally home to Minneapolis. No wonder he valued his early training as a caboose-hopping sewing machine salesman out in South Dakota!

Creative talent of all types was characteristic of the "big men" Bullis kept building. Not only were they gifted in salesmanship and research, but they knew how to dress up their annual award brochures with sprightly drawings. Some of the rollicking literature proves beyond a doubt that enthusiasm ran pretty rampant in the company.

The text of the Victory brochure published by the Central Division during the "Picture Hanging Contest" in 1943 was unique in its theme. "In all reverence, we thank God: that we make up a company whose business is as good as we make it, whether we are operating under peace or war conditions—that we can use our ingenuity, initiative and determination for our own personal progress and security of our families—for the opportunity to use our ability to the fullest—that we are guided by and have the counsel of executives who take a personal interest in our welfare and who are true business leaders, consequently are leaders in peace, war and postwar planning . . .

that we have an opportunity to enjoy our duties and privileges as members of this great company, and pay tribute to the 'General' of General Mills—Mr. Harry Bullis!"

A delightful contest circular, originating in the Sperry Division in 1943, pictured the banquet for "The Man Who is Coming to Dinner." Harry is the only fellow with a face in this picture; he is seated at the center of the head table, smiling enthusiastically. Faceless guests, with question marks instead of features, occupy the other chairs in the banquet room.

The President's Annual Award Contest went into its third year with the fiscal year 1944-45. At one point, Bullis noted, "A busy trip—one dinner after another. It was like running for office!"

In addition to the award trips, the president of General Mills was "on the road" on numerous other missions. At the annual meeting in Wilmington, Delaware in the summer of 1943, he presented his detailed "Review of the Year's Work." Evaluating the progress of the company during the fiscal year 1942-1943, he noted that earnings before taxes were $14,883,000, or nearly $6,500,000 above the previous peak of 1941-42. In the accounting of his stewardship, he showed that General Mills had passed along most of its huge 1942-43 income of $217,000,000 to the farmer, to its employees and to the government. Salaries had increased, and there had been high war-time labor turnovers. The Employees' Retirement System and the Health Association were continuing to operate in a satisfactory manner, Bullis reported.

One of the items mentioned in that annual review

was the newly purchased Purity Oats Company in Keokuk, Iowa. The plant played a major part in producing large quantities of rolled oats for the army and navy, the oats flour for Cheerios, a special porridge for Lend-Lease, and flour for army K-rations. Entries in Bullis' diary show that he kept advocating the development of oats products. Clarence Hidding, general manager of Purity Oats at the time of its purchase, proved himself to be a valuable asset. Within a year, he was transferred to an executive position in Minneapolis. Hidding developed a popular dehydrated soup and arranged for the packaging of tin containers of quick cooking oats to be distributed to starving millions all over the world. After the war, he and his team operated as "big men" in expanding the foreign market for General Mills products.

On May 29, 1943, it was commencement day at the University of Wisconsin again, and Harry Bullis became one of those remarkable contradictions—a prophet with honor in his own country. It is significant that Bullis received his first honorary degree from the school he had selected so carefully, had worked so diligently to attend, and had esteemed so highly through many an alumni membership campaign and Saturday afternoon football game. A gentleman of consequence, he would receive many more accolades from various sources, but this honor marked a zenith point in his life:

> "Wholly self-supporting as a student, he was graduated from this University with highest academic honors. Enlisting as a private in the United States Army in the First World War, he

emerged from the A.E.F. as a captain. Beginning as an auditor practically unknown to anyone in the organization, he rose to the presidency of General Mills within the span of about a score of years. Distinguished both for his dynamic qualities in directing the business affairs of a basic industry, and his keen and sympathetic understanding of its human relations with labor and the public, he has become one of America's industrial leaders. Past president of the Alumni Association, he has never been too preoccupied with business to give to the University his enthusiastic and inspiring support.

"Upon recommendation of the faculty and by vote of the regents, I present to you, Mr. President, Harry Amos Bullis, to receive the honorary degree, Doctor of Laws." (Statement prepared by Professor William H. Kiekhofer, Chairman, Committee on Honorary Degrees.)

During that same visit to Madison, Wisconsin, Bullis was also inducted as an honorary member of Beta Gamma Sigma.

The very next day Harry Bullis attended the commencement exercises at another school that was dear to his heart because its academy had unlocked the doors to higher education for him. On May 30 he was awarded the honorary degree of Doctor of Business Administration at Simpson College in Indianola, Iowa.

Whimsical was Harry Bullis' comment about a Phi Beta Kappa Associates dinner which was held at the Coffman Memorial Union at the University of Minnesota on November 13, 1943: "Think of serving a dinner for ninety cents! Apparently the Union thought the intellectuals would not partake of much food. They were probably mistaken."

At that meeting Bullis reaffirmed his stand on the value of scholarship in a progressive world. "If the roots of liberty are to be maintained in America, we members of Phi Beta Kappa have a definite obligation to perform. We must be leaders who are helping to solve our current national and international problems. . . . Today, as we see the lights of learning fading one by one in the schools and universities of Europe while they become purveyors of organized propaganda for the dictators in power, we realize how fortunate we are in America, where scholars are still free to seek the truth and speak the truth as they see it, and we realize the debt we owe to scholars and to all persons who are furthering higher learning and intellectual pursuits. . ."

Bullis thought in terms of victory, in all his endeavors—which may have been a prime reason for his success. As chairman of the "A" List Division of the 1943 War Chest Campaign, he and his captains raised over half the quota, and sent the total budget over the top.

Point 8 of Harry Bullis' Creed is: "I Will—Cooperate with government regulations. Do everything possible to maintain the American Way of Life." He has always thought in terms of the constructive approach. When the question of government subsidies for flour millers came up in the fall of 1943, many of the millers took pride in their status as "an independent lot."

A November 9 entry in the Bullis diary mentions that Herman Fakler called "Spike" Kennedy and wanted him to serve on a flour subsidy committee. On November 10, Bullis wrote, "At the executive committee meeting this morning we debated whether or not to allow 'Spike' Kennedy to go to Washington as a member of a committee of five millers to meet with the RFC. Perrin opposed and at the start was backed by Mr. Bell. I was supported by Barry and Sydney Anderson (General Mills legal and legislative adviser). We won. 'Spike' is going tomorrow evening. It would have been a great mistake if we had not been represented at this conference." Bullis felt that the millers were operating under multiple wartime handicaps and that the government could help to promote the efficiency that was vital to victory.

Gerald "Spike" Kennedy had been transferred by Bullis from the Buffalo plant to Minneapolis in 1939, and appointed director of operations control. He represented General Mills in Washington during World War II—interpreting the subsidy program and helping to make it run smoothly. Actually, Kennedy performed the patriotic service of advising the entire milling industry. After two and one-half years the subsidy program, along with the rest of the Office of Price Control measures, was voted out of existence by Congress.

During the war years Bullis was occupied with countless activities inside and outside the company. There was one thing that he wasn't, and that was a director of the board of the Chicago Northwestern Railway. A 1944 memo to Mr. Bell noted that the chief executive officer and three separate groups had recommended him for the board position but that he had declined with thanks. Bell responded. "O.K. Good judgment. I knew this was coming and I felt sure you would refuse."

On May 17, 1944, the president of General Mills established a personnel department at Minneapolis covering the development and coordination of personnel policies for all divisions and departments of General Mills. He appointed a director of personnel responsible to the president. The primary purposes, which illustrate his creative approach to the human factor in the business world, were, "The greatest possible realization and utilization of the abilities of our employees . . . and the development and coordination of personnel policies."

On their company anniversaries, Harry had arranged for albums of congratulatory letters to be sent to Ray McLaughlin and John Crosby. Behind the scenes there was some surreptitious activity as his own twenty-fifth anniversary with Washburn Crosby and General Mills approached. The result probably has no parallel in the business world. There is a note of awe in the entry for August 15, 1944, in Harry's diary. "When I reached the office there were red roses and a beautiful album of two hundred and eighty-six letters."

Those letters could be the subject of an enthralling and instructive book, all by themselves. They tell the story of a man whose understanding, aggressiveness, wisdom and integrity have brought out similar qualities in those around him — a man who endeared himself to his associates both as a great "fellow human being" and as a great business administrator.

Lowry Crites remembered Harry's ". . . ability and desire to personalize and humanize ordinary business relationships. I know of no man who could have traveled a similar road for a similar time and made more friends." Mr. Crites is now a vice president of General Mills and general manager of the company's grocery products division.

The late Cliff Samuelson recalled being involved in a tragic and unforeseen accident when he was relatively new to the company. Even though he scarcely knew Bullis at the time, the busy executive called Cliff into his office and immediately "went to bat" with the General Mills legal counsel to avert serious repercussions that might have affected Samuelson's family. "This," Samuelson wrote, "is the kind of thing that goes beyond the realm of efficiency and makes for loyalties which have helped build the company. . . ."

Ruth G. Anderson, one of the home service executives, referred to an incident in the life of a young chemist who came to General Mills after he had lost interest in a previous job. "He had been working only a short time in our research laboratory on East Hennepin Avenue when one day a visitor stopped to chat with him. 'To think,' he said when telling about the incident later, 'of all the years I was with the Blank Company and hardly knew the president's name! And after only a few weeks at General Mills Mr. Bullis took time not only to stop and ask me what I was doing but to make me feel that what I was doing was a necessary and highly important part of the business success of General Mills.' "

Leslie Perrin, executive vice president, wrote, ". . .

General Mills is proud of its president, our men in the armed services are given hope for future security through the program you have encouraged for their benefit; and morale is high in our entire personnel largely because of your congenial influence."

There was a congratulatory message in fine script from Will Moden, the porter who had almost turned white at the thought of young Harry Bullis stalking into B. S. Bull's office, long years before; and another of the porters, Morton Lark, assured the president of General Mills, "Your friendship and kindness which I have enjoyed these past twenty-five years have meant much to me. . . ."

James Ford Bell had not forgotten 1919, when he had been looking for promising young men. He recalled in 1944, "I remember the day we first met. It did not take very many minutes for me to decide you were a man I wanted, a man of the type and caliber and ability that ranked with the standards of Washburn Crosby Company."

Distinguished people, whether they were company executives, clerks, or porters, wrote with charming candor to the man who had made them feel distinguished as individuals in a great business family. There were many Horatio Alger comparisons in those letters. Like Alger's heroes, Bullis had done everything except rescue the boss' daughter from dire peril. He was courageous, honest, industrious—he was the rural lad who had climbed a mighty steep ladder to success, without stepping on anyone else's fingers.

Chapter Thirteen

Bullis' "Declaration of Peace"

Although Harry Bullis often bowed graciously to James Bell's words of advice, he was not an acquiescent "yes-man" or a carbon copy of his "Chief." Bullis had his own ideas about policies and innovations, and occasionally the two big, dynamic executives would find themselves on opposite sides of the fence. Obviously Bell appreciated Harry's bull-dogged tenacity, since "yes-men" were likely to be a dime a dozen. There was deep respect between the two men. Bell knew that Bullis was uncompromisingly devoted to the welfare of the company. General Mills was his life; it was the country boy's dream of greatness realized. If he had been "born into the company," he would have been conscientious about its progress; but there was always that extra glow, that feeling of wonderment that he—stammering, stoop-shouldered Harry Bullis—should have come so far with so little assistance from anyone. Anyone except God. Where God was concerned, he was still a young lad standing on a wooded hilltop, awaiting the sublime Moment of Truth.

When "Fortune," the eminent business magazine, featured the General Mills story in its April 1945 issue, the company had been making industrial history in ordnance work, postwar planning, public relations, and research on almost every possible level. The article stressed the forward-propulsion spirit of the two tall men who were guiding the destinies of the company as it marched ahead in territory old and new. Of James F. Bell, chairman of the board, it said, "He has little interest in the past but a consuming curiosity about the future."

"Fortune" described Harry Bullis, president of General Mills, as a man who began to make friends as soon as he went to work for the company. "He rarely forgot the birthdays or anniversaries of his associates or the names of their children. In another man this might have been taken as shrewd politics. General Mills people insist Mr. Bullis does nice things only because he likes everybody."

The "Fortune" article, listing advances in the wartime "versatility" program under Bullis' first years as president, mentioned vitamins produced by a company owned jointly by General Mills and Eastman Kodak, electrical appliances, chemicals, and Navy fire control equipment.

When a flour miller turns out successful defense equipment during a war, the newspapers consider him more glamorous than a stack of "pin-up girls." More than a year after it was credited with the destruction of its first Japanese cruiser, Naval secrecy was lifted on the amazing exploits of the "jitterbug" torpedo, with its deceptive little device that could "figure its own angles." It operated, according to reports released late in 1943, "like a terrier attacking a bull." "The little American destroyer darted out of her smoke screen and closed in fast, shells spattering all around her. At two thousand yards, she fired her torpedoes and doubled back. For a moment, sailors on the Jap cruiser felt a frantic clutch of fear . . . then they relaxed, hissing disdainfully. . . ."

It was almost a joke to see the torpedoes skimming past, far wide of the mark, as though they had been fired by a nervous gunner with his eyes shut. But suddenly the Japs stiffened. Drawing abreast of their cruiser, the torpedoes acted as though they had just recalled their urgent mission. Making a smart right-angle turn, they headed straight for the Japanese cruiser. Three terrific explosions almost ripped the ship apart.

American destroyer commanders were able to set their torpedoes for any course—aiming them straight at target, or putting the enemy off guard by sending them swerving, curving, and even doubling back in a figure eight. According to the Minneapolis Times Tribune story of December 29, 1943, "No matter what the course, the torpedo will hit point X at the given time, and if Mr. Moto's there too, he will be 'so solly.'" The torpedo director that made these "trick shots" possible came out of the ordnance plant of a flour producing company, General Mills. A wartime wonder!

Then there was the "hedgehog" which the Navy credits with playing a dominant role in sinking some three hundred German submarines. The project was so secret that Harry Bullis released no information about it until November 16, 1945. "Only a handful of the one hundred and fifty precision instrument builders who worked on it knew what they were making," he said.

The intricate fire control instruments manufactured at the plant automatically enabled the "hedgehog" to keep its twenty-four rocket projectiles trained on the target regardless of the rolling of the ship or the movement of enemy submarines. The "hedgehog" was a revolutionary improvement over depth charges. The weapon successively fired all twenty-four projectiles within two and one-half seconds, hurling them in an elliptical pattern above the position of the submarine. The projectiles exploded on contact only, enabling the attacker to know when a hit had been scored.

While the war was still in progress, Bullis had his postwar planning group working on the problem of what the employees of the mechanical division might produce after the war. It was decided to start manufacturing household appliances on a small scale. The company first produced the General Mills electric iron. This was followed by several other household items. After several years, the company's appliance business was sold to a Chicago firm.

Because the current emphasis of General Mills is on consumer convenience foods and specialty chemical operations, General Mills has recently sold the assets and operations of its Aerospace Research and Engineering Departments of the Electronics Division to Litton Industries of Beverly Hills, California. While General Mills now believes it can no longer perform a sufficiently worth-while economic service by these facilities, this fact does not detract from the glory of its contributions to World War II victory, when it performed "above and beyond the call of duty" in turning out fine precision equipment for the United States Navy.

Praise and awards were earned by General Mills, "a formidable fighter on many fronts"—during World War II. On April 30, 1945, President Bullis was notified by the United States Navy that the mechanical division of General Mills was granted a third renewal of the Army-Navy "E" Award, and that he would receive a new flag with three stars which could fly proudly over the plant.

On June 27, 1945, Bullis accepted the War Food Administration "A" Award which honored the men and women of all the Minneapolis mills of General Mills. This was the Twin Cities' first "A" Award. Later six other General Mills plants in various cities received Achievement "A" Awards. Purity Oats was the first plant in Iowa to rate an "A." Tom Moore, president of the Coca-Cola Company, saluted the wartime achievements of General Mills on a coast-to-coast radio program featuring Lawrence Welk and his orchestra.

General Mills servicemen and women could look forward regularly to a letter from the president of their company with news about the activities inside the organization. There were also Christmas remembrances, mailed early. One of the finest Christmas presents of all—a promise for the future—was a small handbook entitled "Your Job with General Mills After the War." An accompanying letter, dated December 25, ended, "I wish you, personally, a victorious New Year." With two packs of playing cards went a message, "From my own experience in the last war, I know that these little pasteboards come in mighty handy now and then." At the high point, there were 2,824 General Mills men in service, and Harry Bullis kept assuring them that their company would welcome them home with jobs and hearty expressions of appreciation for their devotion and sacrifice.

In Harry Bullis' office was a plaque with the names of all the company employees who gave their lives in the service of their country. Believing fervently that every patriotic gesture counted, he sent an American flag to each executive in the organization with the request that it be displayed in their office or plant.

Bullis received many interesting letters from the boys in the service. Clark Madsen wrote: "When I was acting as Naval liaison officer on the staff of General Omar Bradley's 28th Division, I often told the army officers that General Bradley was very much like the president of our company because every man in his entire outfit—from all the buck privates to the chief of staff—liked him, respected him, and would do anything for him."

In a letter congratulating Bullis on his election to the presidency, Dean Latterell, Second Lieutenant in the Army Air Forces at Avon Park, Florida, wrote that his family had trouble understanding his fondness for the General Mills office. "The few times I managed to get back I have raced right down to the office to see the old 'gang'! And believe me—I've enjoyed every minute."

General Mills became the first industrial sponsor of a landing craft when Harry Bullis presented a three hundred dollar check to Ensign M. Friedman of the Navy to buy furniture and recreational equipment not included in regular naval commissioning.

Several days before D-Day, June 6, 1944, every plant, office and division of General Mills received the following telegram from Bullis:

"Amid history making Invasion Day, everyone should rise and join in silent prayer for the success of the invasion and the safety of the millions of men in the Allied Army. We are confident of success." Acting on this telegram, arrangements were made to notify every General Mills location by the blackout signal system when word of the European invasion was received.

The largest flour milling plant in the world, located at Buffalo, New York, was in darkness from 6:00 to 6:05 on D-Day, while everyone asked God's blessing on our men and women. At 11 a.m. that morning everyone in all General Mills offices stood in silent prayer for the success of the invasion.

On May 1, when the surrender of Germany was expected momentarily, Harry Bullis asked the organization to refrain from an all-out celebration. "Rather than an occasion for hilarity, the company believes that the surrender of Germany should be an occasion of thanksgiving and prayer. We owe it to the forty-four men of General Mills who have given their lives for the cause and to those in the service who may lose theirs in finishing the job."

On March 8, 1944, Harry Bullis was invited by Elmer Davis, director of the Office of War Information, to attend the conference of the Office of War Information and War Advertising Council in Washington. In a report to Mr. Bell, Bullis gave a lucid picture of the highlight of the conference—the meeting with President Roosevelt in his office at the White House during which the president spoke informally to approximately seventy-five of the group.

The main purpose of the conference was the education, through advertising, of the American people. Roosevelt expected victory, but he felt that it would be a long war and that it would require concentration of purpose and unified action on the part of the public.

"Before this group of industrialists and advertising executives," Bullis wrote, "the president turned on some of his famous personality. He looked a little tired." Bullis was amazed at the hodge-podge of nick-nacks—juvenile representations of zoo animals, etc.—on the president's desk.

As an active Republican, Bullis attended the Republican convention in 1944. On November 8, 1944, the day after Roosevelt defeated Dewey in the national election, Bullis did not prowl the halls forecasting doom. He wired his division presidents:

"The 1944 election is proof to the world that democracy functions in war as well as peace. We congratulate the winners and pledge them our united support. United we will win the war, keep it won and build constantly toward expanded service and opportunity. What remains is America. America is a great country. The watchword is 'forward.' "

There were no orders to refrain from jubilation when the Great Victory Day dawned at last. President Bullis sent out the glad tidings that V-J Day, marking the end of the war with Japan, would be celebrated in General Mills with a holiday for all the employees. "All plants and offices will be closed and remain closed on V-J Day, August 10, 1945. All wage employees will be paid a bonus equivalent to the regular hours which would normally be worked times their straight time hourly rate in lieu of payment for time normally worked."

Bullis saluted the termination of World War II with several inspiring statements. The widely quoted message to the company employees contained this moving paragraph: "Victory is a beginning, not an ending. It is the beginning of the huge task of reconstruction—of remaking the world in the pattern of permanent peace. At this historic moment we are confronted with two of the greatest challenges ever to face mankind. The first is to achieve in a rapid and orderly manner a level of production and distribution of goods and services in this country at least half again as high as has ever been achieved in peacetime in the past. The second is to build upon the first start of the San Francisco Charter a world organization for the preservation of peace."

Bullis' experiences during World War I, in which he lost his only brother, strengthened his disillusionment about world wars and his belief that world wars should be abolished. In a New Year's message to the General Mills organization in January, 1945, he said:

"The grim truth is that war cheats industry out of an incalculable quantity of human intelligence which normally would serve it. Dead men take out no patents. War destroys customers for all time. War piles up financial burdens which threaten solvency over the long range. To be sure, general contracts make business profits, while nobody cares in a war about mounting national debts. Industry realizes, however, that debt is but deferred taxes."

Bullis kept promoting numerous postwar programs for the benefit of veterans, including training programs designed to reduce the effect of the four to five-year gap in normal progress and business experience of service personnel. General Mills offered physical examinations to protect individual veterans against improper placement which might aggravate service connected disabilities. The company also broadened its retirement benefits for veterans who were members of the retirement system prior to military service.

In May, 1944, President Bullis of General Mills was appointed chairman of the Millers National Federation Committee on Postwar Planning for the Milling Industry. The committee, composed of twelve milling companies, developed and presented postwar plans of far-reaching importance for the entire milling industry.

In Bullis' attitude toward periodic labor and wage disputes, there was none of the bristling antagonism that often characterizes management-labor relations. He was firm in the face of demands that seemed unreasonable, but he was the first to accede to sensible requests. In the very early days of the company, "Honest John" Crosby had said, "I will pay my workers what they are worth to me." Harry Bullis went farther, saying in effect, "My 'fellow partners' should be paid all that they are worth to the company." Several strikes were nipped in the bud by the granting of bonuses of an extra month's salary. Some 1944 letters reveal that Bullis pulled an unprecedented "switch" when he arranged for a delegation to appear before the Wage Stabilization Board in Chicago on behalf of wage hikes for General Mills ordnance workers during the wartime period of "frozen" wage ceilings! Supported by the appeals of witnesses representing labor, industry and the public, Bullis presented a logical case for the workers and the extraordinary request for wage increases was granted.

As president of General Mills, a member of the National Association of Manufacturers Board, vice chairman of N.A.M.'s Postwar Committee, and vice chairman of N.A.M.'s Distribution Committee, Bullis was vigilantly aware that postwar planning should not be relegated to the things that we will do "when we have time." In addition to domestic problems ahead, the country needed leaders to formulate "a coherent international economic policy."

In 1945 Bullis lost his amateur standing as a writer. "We Can Have Better Food and More of It" appeared in the April 14 issue of Liberty Magazine and caused a wide stir. To his surprise, Bullis received a check for five hundred dollars from Liberty Magazine for authoring that article. In "We Can Have Better Food and

More of It" he attacked the popular premise that two thirds of the people in the world must go to sleep hungry every night, concluding with this sentence, "If the peace planners think of bread and butter as much as they think of guns and boundaries and the parliaments of the world, you and I may live to see the day when all peoples will have more and better food because we live in a world well organized for peace." The accompanying illustration is a pathetic picture of an emaciated young Chinese mother, trying to nurse her half-starved baby.

On October 13 another article, "Foreign Trade—and Your Job," was published in Liberty Magazine, with Bullis noting that "The United States has turned its back on isolation and embarked on a course of co-operation in world affairs. . . . Few of our citizens remain unsold on political co-operation with other nations, but many question the wisdom of economic co-operation. . . ." He expressed a point of view which at the time was not too popular with many American manufacturers. It is believed that they have largely come around to sharing his viewpoint now.

An ally of whom to be proud, back in 1945, was John Cowles, the distinguished president of the Minneapolis Star-Journal and Tribune. In a letter dated October 25, Mr. Cowles assured Harry Bullis: "Not only do I agree completely with the political and economic philosophy that you express so well in your article on foreign trade that appeared in Liberty, but I think it is a fine thing that you, as a leading industrialist, have publicly expressed your views in this way."

John Cowles also served as a director of General Mills, and he was one of the few who then agreed with Bullis' liberal ideas on foreign trade.

Throughout World War II, the Betty Crocker Kitchens continued issuing a series of publications to aid in conservation of food and keep American morale at a high point. In "War Work, a Daybook for the Home," Harry Bullis explained in the foreword that the material was assembled in collaboration with government officials responsible for general plans for civilian war activities. It was a basic outline from which every homemaker could make a contribution to victory. Almost two million copies of the booklet were distributed, mainly by request. Large Betty Crocker public service advertisements about food sharing and food rationing were published in newspapers. There were timely Food Sharing radio broadcasts.

On October 25, 1943, Betty Crocker and her staff invited the "bosses"—the board of directors—to lunch. On the menu was a choice of Betty Crocker soups, with buttered, salted Kix or Cheese Cheerios, braised sweetbreads on ham, mushrooms, sliced tomatoes, pickled peaches with spiced cherries, corn muffins made with New Mix, Bisquick biscuits, and cinnamon rolls and celery crescents made with Gold Medal Kitchen-Tested Flour. For dessert, there were Softasilk Cakes: cocoa divinity, golden layer, orange filling; and Wheaties Nut Crunch Ice Cream!

The company was constantly being measured in terms of postwar expansion by both James Ford Bell and Harry Bullis. The Vegetable Oil and Protein Division was established in 1943 with the purchase of a plant at Belmond, Iowa, designed to process vitally needed soybean oil and meal. That year also saw the acquisition of still another plant at Keokuk, Iowa, for the processing of starch and gluten, by-products of wheat flour.

In 1944 the company purchased a new plant at Oskaloosa, Iowa, for the production of packaged foods; and in 1945, General Mills leased the W. B. Anderson flour milling properties at Hopkinsville, Kentucky.

This continuing pattern of expansion and diversification required additional financing. In line with future growth potential, the preferred stockholders voted to authorize the issuance of twenty million dollars in low-interest debentures. The annual report for the fiscal year 1944-45 showed that General Mills was financially stronger than ever. A three-for-one stock split was proposed because GMI common stock had reached an unwieldy new high of one hundred and thirty-nine dollars a share. The result was an increase in total dividends, and enthusiastic buying soon sent each of the new shares up to fifty dollars apiece on the stock exchange.

On occasion after occasion, Harry Bullis was called upon to make speeches—sometimes as many as three in one day, when he visited various company divisions. He accepted the gruelling schedule as an appropriate part of "The Responsibility of the Chief Executive." In a speech by that title delivered at the annual convention of the Grocery Manufacturers of America in 1945 and later published in pamphlet form, Harry summed up his already far-reaching business philosophy. The engineer was speaking first, then the business humanitarian: "One of the most important tasks of the chief executive is to secure coordination and co-operation throughout the organization. He attempts to coordinate the operating executives, each of whom is a powerful dynamo, into a battery of dynamos in order to produce greater united power. . . . Perhaps the primary function of the chief executive today in his relation with his company's employees is to emphasize human relations. He must inspire enthusiasm throughout his organization and develop a high esprit de corps."

In his speeches, Bullis often found the quotations of Lincoln applicable to modern day problems. Millions of radio listeners sat in rapt silence on November 22, 1945, as he said: ". . . On this Thanksgiving Day we must all, as Abraham Lincoln said, dedicate ourselves to the unfinished task which lies ahead. Each of us must do his or her part to help heal the wounds of this war-ravaged world. We know that the peoples of the world want, above all else, peace. We know that they are looking to us for both spiritual and practical leadership. We know that if we can furnish this leadership, they will follow us eagerly and will not be led astray by selfish or brutal demagogues and dictators."

Dr. J. L. "Lew" Morrill was elected president of the University of Minnesota in 1945. Harry and Irma Bullis gave a very unique dinner for him and Mrs. Morrill at the Minikahda Club that fall. On the guest list were twelve leading citizens, each of whom spoke for five minutes regarding some phase of economic, religious and political life in Minnesota. The dinner was an outstanding success, because it gave the Morrills an intimate knowledge of the resources and various activities of the people of Minnesota.

Through all the industrial and political crises of World War II Harry Bullis kept his engaging sense of humor. When the research department threw a Gay Nineties party at Eaton's Ranch on August 26, 1944, Bullis was there in a high top hat and a Prince Albert coat, with a magnificent mustache bristling out on his upper lip. In a picture commemorating the event, he is gallantly tripping the "heavy fantastic" with a Ph.D. — one of the research department heads who was dressed as a damsel of the Gay Nineties.

Chapter Fourteen

Postwar Patterns

"You have always been a great source of inspiration to me and to everyone else. . . . I will never forget the kind solicitude of yourself and Irma for my mother during her lifetime. She always thought you were so natural, and as she said, 'just like a big boy of her own.' "

That is an excerpt from a Happy Birthday letter that Walter Barry wrote to Harry Bullis in 1945. Birthdays, weddings, holidays and anniversaries became special events around General Mills after Harry started the "personal appreciation" trend. He elevated personnel relations to the highest level of human relations.

There is a delightful note from Elsie Hawkinson, one of Mr. Bullis' long-time secretaries. When Elsie was married in New York City, Mr. and Mrs. Bullis added a special sparkle to the occasion by arranging for the bridal couple to stay in a suite at the Waldorf-Astoria as their guests. Elsie wrote glowingly of their finding "the lovely rooms and your wonderful flowers, together with your wire and letter—it was just too much!"

In 1945, plans were made to buy the twelve-story Hodgson Building in downtown Minneapolis and move the General Mills and Betty Crocker Kitchens to the spacious new quarters. For many years the General Mills offices were in the Chamber of Commerce Building.

The Hodgson Building was part of a twenty-two million dollar expansion program. The 1946 "Five Year Plan" also called for the erection of a new research building, and General Mills plants at Lodi, California, Los Angeles, and Buffalo, New York. President Harry Bullis' diary weaved along through a maze of planning conferences, addresses, inspection trips, radio and press interviews, and banquet speeches—all somehow humming straight ahead toward postwar acceleration for everyone on the "G.M.I. team."

Harry Bullis, in his year-end reports, usually had been optimistic, and he had an excellent "batting average" for being right about the state of the nation. A vast majority of Americans can look around them and realize that—despite the wails of the crepe-hangers—this is not exactly the worst country in the world.

Harry's year-end statement for Commercial West on January 11, 1947 injected a note of good cheer into the postwar economy. He pointed out that the vigor of the country had an almost miraculous quality. During a war in which we and our Allies had been victorious, we had produced all of our own military needs, plus fifty billion dollars' worth of munitions for our Allies. At the beginning of 1946, the output of automobiles was "not even a trickle," but by the end of the year, automobiles were rolling out of our factories at the rate of almost one hundred thousand a week. There were some unfavorable factors, including a rash of strikes, but in general the country was moving full speed ahead.

The postwar road was marked with a milestone of personal tragedy for the president of General Mills. His diary entry for January 15, 1947, says simply, "My wife, Irma Alexander Bullis, passed away this morning. She had been an invalid for almost six years. We had been married nearly twenty-eight years."

Even though he could look back with gratefulness upon the good and fine years of his life with Irma, the winter of 1947 was bleak without her. Early in February, Harry went to Nassau in the Bahamas. His good friend and veteran associate, Jim Selvage, president of the Southeastern Division at Atlanta, came to Nassau to be with Harry. Promptly the tables were turned. Selvage became violently ill with a kidney stone attack, and Harry spent his time hovering solicitously over him. Less than two weeks after he had gone to Nassau, Harry was rushing Jim back to Atlanta for an operation. It was a short vacation; Harry went back to his office.

In the life of a man like Harry Bullis, there are always some unusual revelations—he had often doubled as a handy volunteer nurse when his associates became ill. Once in awhile he even took care of "sick" friends who had imbibed too much. That was one reason why Harry was not a drinking man himself. He believed in the "live and let live" adage in the private lives of other individuals, but he thought that liquor was responsible for the deterioration and downfall of many a brilliant business executive.

In the early part of his career, Bullis was often asked why he was a nonsmoker and a teetotaler. When he was in his early teens, an older man whom he respected very much said to him, "Harry, if you do not smoke or drink until you are twenty-one, you never will smoke or drink." Harry followed that advice, and when he was twenty-one he was so busy that he had no desire to drink or smoke. When he went into the Army overseas, the vogue of smoking cigarettes was just becoming popular. Whenever he was pressured to try a cigarette, he turned it down.

After he started in the business world, Harry was criticized many times for not drinking. He credited his "stubborn nature" with coming to his rescue—the more often he was criticized, the stronger was his determination not to drink.

During the years following World War II, Harry Bullis took a deeply personal interest in the political situation. He sometimes conferred and traveled with another tall man named Harold E. Stassen who had become the youngest governor in the history of Minnesota in 1938. Stassen resigned as governor in 1943 to enter the navy where he served on the staff of Admiral William F. Halsey and saw action in the Pacific. In 1945, President Truman appointed him a member of the U. S. delegation to the founding conference of the United Nations in San Francisco.

When Harry Bullis spoke on "The Responsibility of the Chief Executive" at the convention of the Grocery Manufacturers of America in New York on November 7, 1945, he was pictured with Harold Stassen who was resplendent in his naval officer's uniform.

In February, 1946, Bullis appeared with Harold Stassen at the Milwaukee Association of Commerce. Afterward, at Neenah, Wisconsin, Stassen spoke to a group in a mansion belonging to an executive of the Kimberly-Clark Corporation.

Harold E. Stassen, of course, was campaigning at that time for the Republican nomination for president. During the trip to Milwaukee in 1946, Bullis noted in his diary that he had discussed "the wheat flour order" at length with Stassen.

The gray bread debacle probably tested Harry's "optimistic forbearance" more than anything that happened in his business career. Rare insight into Harry's character can be gained from the following sentence: "In February, 1946, my friend Clinton Anderson—the Secretary of Agriculture and now Senator from New Mexico—mistakenly got too excited about what he thought was a food crisis and a lack of wheat."

The grain of wheat was at the bottom of it all. After the war, England was trying to make the wheat kernel go farther by extracting eighty-five per cent of its component parts, with the presence of a noticeable percentage of husk fragments resulting in a darker flour. The U. S. Department of Agriculture decided to put out an eighty per cent extraction order in an effort to share more of our wheat harvest with a starving world.

Bullis co-operated with the government order by trying to improve the eighty per cent flour and urging other millers to do the same. The Home Service Department gamely went to work originating new dark flour recipes, and the manufacture of SoftAsilk and Bisquick was suspended. Bullis arranged for the emergency "equivalent" of Gold Medal to be called "All America," and the bakery flour became "King Wheat."

Co-operative as he was, Bullis did not suffer this outrage meekly. He let it be known that the new extraction order prevented the maintenance of uniformity controls, made the production of superior baked goods more difficult, coarsened the bread and affected the keeping quality of both bread and flour.

The administration believed that there was a "Flour Emergency" because of world-wide wheat crop failures. Despite three bumper crops in North America, there was a world wheat shortage. In large areas of Europe, war devastation and lack of manpower, together with poor crops, had left millions of people to face starvation unless we helped. The government thought wheat could be saved by milling it to produce more flour from the same amount of wheat. However, proper world-wide distribution channels were not laid out in advance, and the directive resulted in all sorts of hardships for the millers. With a record wheat crop harvested and a record corn crop in prospect, Agriculture Secretary Anderson removed all bans on the production of white flour on August 24, 1946, and eased government limitations on the use of grain, effective September 1, 1946.

Effective December 1, 1946, President Truman removed restrictions on the domestic use of flour and authorized millers to sell all the flour for domestic distribution that they could. They had been limited to eighty-five per cent of the average monthly distribution in 1945.

On September 17, 1947, when there was some suggestion that the nation go back to last year's "Gray Bread," Bullis said in a press interview: "Nobody gains and the public is fooled into believing that eighty per cent flour helps to relieve the European food shortage. Extracting eighty per cent of the wheat reduces the amount of mill feed and forces farmers to feed wheat to stock."

"Tampering with the freedom of the market place can only delay return of an ordered and balanced economy." In a number of articles and interviews during the postwar years, Harry Bullis declared himself in opposition to the continuance of price controls in peacetime.

After World War II, Bullis noted that the machinery of the Office of Price Administration had slowed up production at various times. "But this loss has certainly been offset many times over by the millions of dollars saved to the company by the control of prices of thousands of articles which it needed to purchase." During World War II, the cost of living advanced one-third, as contrasted with an advance of one hundred and ten per cent during World War I. Because national income increased beyond the controlled cost of living, Americans took pride in putting one hundred billion dollars into their World War II savings accounts. With the war over, they planned to spend part of those huge savings for civilian goods—clothing, radios, automobiles, houses. For that reason, Bullis pointed out, goods must be made available in sufficient quantities or prices would rise. "This means inflation, with the purchasing power of savings and wages greatly reduced. The only way to prevent inflation is to produce the goods needed, and labor will gain not only more jobs but more goods for its wage dollars."

Abundant production—not direct controls—should provide the necessary peace time balance. The economy can be regulated by the application of indirect controls, such as "stiffer taxation, tighter control over loan and mortgage credit, and prudent management of debt to avoid its conversion into cash for still more spending power," whenever such measures are necessary. "Incidentally," Harry Bullis added, "we do not need to be worried about inflation. We should be worried about deflation."

In August, 1946, even before it was ready for occupancy, Bullis set up a temporary office in the Hodgson Building, which had been re-christened the General Mills Building. By August, 1947, the tall structure housed almost six hundred administrative and service personnel. Its front had been remodeled and air and sound conditioning installed.

In addition to all the offices, new facilities included a service auditorium, health center, library, employee recreation space and reception area. The building was attractively and efficiently arranged. The "glamor center of enticing fragrances"—Betty Crocker's domain—was on the fifth floor.

And where was Harry Bullis, the president of General Mills? He was high above the city, in a handsome twelfth-floor office right next to the board of directors' room. Below him was the throbbing, bustling, prosperous city which had been propagated from "a grain of wheat" in the days of the first Washburn, the first Crosby, the first Pillsbury, and a dozen other founders of early milling companies.

In 1947, the incentive or profit sharing plan—an administrative equivalent to the employees' pension system—also became a reality with the distribution of the first bonus checks. Coming as a pleasant surprise to many of the executives of General Mills the bonus checks were given because the net earnings of the company for the twelve months ending May 31, 1947, were in excess of a certain set goal. The profit sharing system, which has been improved each year, has been in effect ever since 1946-47; however, there were two years when profits were not sufficient to provide profit-sharing checks.

Bullis was able to get James F. Bell, chairman of the board, to agree to the establishment of the executive profit sharing plan if Bullis would at the same time establish a suggestion system whereby employees would be rewarded for making worthwhile recommendations which could be put into effect in the company. From the top echelons to the bottom, all up and down the line, General Mills has fostered a program of appreciation for ability, intelligence and hard work. Its directors, who are specialists in many fields, receive generous salaries, rather than honorary stipends. An axiom of General Mills has been, "You get what you pay for," and the company has gone out of its way to get the best.

Even though Harry Bullis felt obliged to decline

two invitations to serve as a director of a great railroad, he became a member of the board of directors of Northwest Bancorporation on April 25, 1947. At a luncheon given in his honor that day, he reviewed the history of G.M.I. and its progress and achievements. He came to Banco loaded with enthusiasm, and his association with that estimable institution was a source of gratification in his life. Serving as chairman of the Finance and Budget Committee and more recently as vice chairman of the Finance Committee, Bullis promoted pension and deferred compensation profit sharing plans. He attended monthly meetings of the board regularly, at Banco's Minneapolis headquarters, and he faithfully — and enthusiastically — participated in Banco's annual field trips. There are seventy-seven Northwest Bancorporation banks in seven states.

The influence of the nuclear age crept stealthily into the General Mills premium department in 1947. It was a rare day in June when Bullis received a frantic emergency call from an old friend, General Julius Holmes, who had accompanied General Mark Clark on a cool-headed submarine scouting expedition to North Africa during the war. Sounding as distraught as any civilian father, General Holmes told Bullis that his young son had swallowed an "atomic ring" that had been offered as a Kix premium. "The doctor is here, and he wants to know whether the ring contains any uranium."

Bullis assured him it was doubtful that there was any uranium in a ring that could be obtained with a Kix box top and fifteen cents, but he said hold the phone and he would check. There was just one difficulty—Bullis was working "the second shift" again. Everyone in the premium department had gone home for the day. Finally Bullis contacted the general purchasing agent who told him that the ring glowed in the dark because it contained polonium which was absolutely harmless. Bullis hastened to forward the news to General Holmes at the Pentagon. The general interrupted almost immediately to confide that everything was all right—the boy had passed the ring.

With a snort and a chuckle, Bullis recalled the way he made a dash for the premium department the next morning to see just what they had in that place! It is one of the largest departments in the company, with hundreds of premiums listed, and many coupon-counters, packers and mailers.

A "Home-Town Echoes" cartoon, by E. Kessler, was widely reproduced in 1947. It shows a paper boy riding his bicycle along an old-time, small-town street. He is folding papers with an air of brash impudence, letting the handlebars take care of themselves. A pigtailed schoolgirl on the curb is exclaiming, "No hands!" A saucy little girl, riding past with her mother in a horse-drawn buggy, is saying with a disapproving sniff, "Harry Bullis thinks he's smart!" According to the caption, "Harry Bullis, president of General Mills, Inc., once delivered the Council Bluffs (Iowa) Nonpareil."

Harry's interest in keeping fit continued through the years. He still enjoyed taking long walks around the Lake of the Isles. Almost a thrice-weekly ritual, since 1935, were his turkish baths during the winter months at Ray Carciofini's Health Department at the Minneapolis Club.

Of historic significance was the "Olympic Games Trip" which Bullis took in June 1947. Its ostensible aim was to persuade the International Olympic Committee that Minneapolis would be an appropriate place to hold the 1952 Olympic games. The Minnesota delegation carried with it a replica—complete with enlargement revisions—of the stadium at the University of Minnesota where many of the events would be held if the invitation were accepted.

Harry Bullis and his good friend, Henry S. Kingman, president of the Farmers and Mechanics Savings Bank and a G.M.I. director, were on the fund-raising committee to publicize and finance the Olympic bid. Actually, it was noted in news stories that the major purpose of Bullis' trip to Europe was "to obtain firsthand and on-the-ground knowledge regarding food and economic conditions." Kingman planned to accompany him on the European tour.

The delegation from Minnesota was royally entertained in Stockholm, Sweden. In spite of much Minnesota eloquence, Helsinki was chosen as the site for the 1952 Olympic games. There was no resentment, because everyone admires Finland; and that country was unable to play host to the games during World War II. Minnesota was honored as the second choice and Harry Bullis' disappointment was tinged with relief—he was committed to raise one million dollars for the Olympic games if they were awarded to Minneapolis.

The king of Sweden and the Olympic committee gave a formal banquet for all the delegates in a magnificent hall at the Stadhuset. Harry confided impishly, "I sat next to a royal princess and gave her all my drinks which she consumed."

Chapter Fifteen

"Bread Cast Upon the Waters..."

Passport number 62503 was issued to a "business visitor" who was amply equipped with letters of introduction. On his itinerary, after the Olympic meeting in Stockholm, were cities in Denmark, The Netherlands, Belgium, France, Switzerland and England.

Bullis had always been a man who asked himself how the other fellow felt. About the time he and Henry Kingman started touring weary, war-torn Europe, a change came over the continent. Across the ocean in Bullis' homeland, Secretary of State George C. Marshall, in a speech at Harvard, had advocated plans for a European recovery program designed to revive and strengthen the economies of the war-devastated continent. The news fell like a benediction on shattered western Europe. "The result was electric," Bullis reported. "The plan was looked upon as 'the rise of a new sun for Europe.' " The faces of the people, forlorn and sick with apathy against the background of World War II rubble, suddenly became animated with hope as Bullis and Kingman watched. Renewed faith in the future stirred up an almost festive air of jubilation.

Even though he said in one of his speeches that he took a dim view of the so-called "expert" who traveled a few weeks in Europe and came back with a "solution" to all the problems of the continent, Harry Bullis' perceptive gaze took an accurate measurement of the economic and political climate of Europe. Many of these people, whose bootstraps were frayed to the breaking point, were ripe for any vainglorious promise of redemption—for socialism, communism, some form of totalitarianism.

The United States, Bullis began insisting, must come to the rescue. Such audacity required a tremendous amount of "bull-dogged courage" in 1947. Bullis could have shaken his head in sympathy and gone back to his office in the General Mills Building and kept quiet. Surely he would have been more popular with his fellow-Republicans and his fellow-businessmen. "We've pumped enough aid into Europe — it's like pouring money down the drain!" many conservative businessmen were saying.

But Bullis had a much-quoted answer to that statement. In speech after speech, he reminded the United States that "Between 1883 and 1913, Britain, France, Belgium, Holland, and Germany made investment advances of forty billion dollars to the rest of the world. The United States got half of it. That was a colossal amount of money compared to the national incomes of the countries which put up the money. Every American lives better today because our fathers and grandfathers had the use of this twenty billion dollars. With the aid of this capital they developed the production processes which we are now trying to help Europe establish."

In a press report early in August, 1947, Bullis asked, "How far should the power of the state go in planning the economic life of the country and how far should it be left to individual enterprise?" He reasoned that it was up to the United States to see that the issue was decided in favor of free enterprise. The United States "must support the Marshall Plan. . . . and insist that the governments requesting our assistance tell us what they will do to put their own house in order." Bullis emphasized that it would be vitally necessary to maintain a strong, vigorous, functioning economy here at home, and that a constructive information service should be established abroad.

In "Food and General Economic Conditions of Europe," delivered at a meeting of the Minneapolis branch of the Foreign Policy Association on August 7, 1947, Bullis told of his efforts to meet "plain John Citizen in Berlin, Stockholm, Paris and London. . . . Often the more important people try to gloss over the facts as they apply to John Citizen. On our trip, my traveling companion, Henry Kingman, and I attempted to learn something about John's thinking even while we talked with his political and business leaders."

In addition to interviewing many dignitaries—high public officials, industrialists, financiers, and American embassy officials—Bullis and Kingman sought out taxi drivers, hotel employees, and ordinary men on the street. Bullis believed they had gotten a "fairly representative cross-section of opinion," and he had some pertinent observations to make about the needs of each country.

Considering the punishment she had taken, England showed the greatest tendency to believe that "God helps those that help themselves." In England, bombed-out areas had been cleared of rubble; in Germany, by contrast, nothing had been done to remove the debris and wreckage of broken-down walls and entire buildings. Bullis did not agree that the British Empire was "doomed," in spite of the modifications in England's world power status. He believed that England was demonstrating a high degree of enlightenment "by the very democratic processes that have made for recent developments in India and the Far East."

The United States had been generous with aid to England in the past, and Bullis felt that it was a good investment because, "There is no need for anyone to worry about England going Communistic." Industrial methods needed to be modernized and production increased there, as in all the countries of Europe.

Sweden and Switzerland, both neutral during the war, were the most prosperous European countries. The people were working hard and would be all right, Bullis noted. He referred to Norway and Finland as mainly importing countries. Bullis marveled at the hardships that Finland was enduring in order to meet terrific Russian reparations; it was "a country with tremendous 'sisu,' which means they have what it takes. . . . They intend to pay the last cent of their debt."

Holland and Belgium deserved all the help possible. The people were "realists," and they were industrious. Especially notable was the Minneapolis oracle's comment, in 1947, about the Belgium-Netherlands-Luxembourg Customs Union which was being formed. "It may be the beginning of a customs union for all Western Europe in the years ahead, and it may be the spark that one day may ignite a new democracy over the whole of Europe."

From an economic point of view, he noted that "France had come back faster than any other country, but its financial situation is the worst." Frenchmen had no faith in the depreciated franc. People with money were living in semi-luxury while the remainder lived in poverty. Bullis must have looked horrified when he disclosed the scandalous news that "the bread being made in France at present is terrible! It consists of fifty per cent corn or rye and fifty per cent American flour."

One day, a tall man stalked along the bombed-out streets of Frankfurt, playing "hookey." Bullis had flown from Zurich, Switzerland to Frankfurt, Germany slightly ahead of the time he was supposed to arrive there. "I had one day when General Clay and his officers did not know I was in the American occupied zone. This gave me an opportunity to contact John Citizen and our American GIs. It was a great experience to be a common guy and a private in the rear ranks in Germany for twenty-four hours. I was given the old Army run-around, and I enjoyed it." When General Lucius Clay's officers discovered that Harry Bullis had arrived, his incognito interlude ended abruptly. They assigned him "the official works"—an officer, an Army chauffeur, and a Cadillac car in each city he visited.

Bullis reported that the American GIs were in good form. "The old saying is that as long as a GI can gripe, he is happy. Our boys are a very happy lot indeed!"

"In Berlin, at the Reichschancellory," Bullis said, "I stood on the balcony where Adolf Hitler used to exhort his followers. On all sides were ruins—the past glory of a dictator." He found Germany depressing, with people living in parts of bombed-out buildings. "Germany can be compared to a sick man—an individual who has been almost dismembered and is reeling from shock and pain." The industrial city of Stuttgart had been hardest hit. Germany's recovery would be necessary in order to have "a prosperous Western Europe."

The old-time barter system was returning to almost every country. European nations needed a stabilized currency—a common currency would accomplish wonders for Europe, Bullis declared. Almost everything was needed, from basic requirements of life to efficient machinery in industry.

Bullis was convinced that "the only way to defeat Communism is to make the lot of the common people more bearable—that is, improve their living conditions and permit them to purchase at least some of the necessities of life, especially food and clothing." After that, they would be in the mood to think in terms of the "dynamic economic progress" that is taken for granted in the United States.

"Food and General Economic Condition of Europe"

fairly bristled with world-wide implications for today and tomorrow. Although he had never favored Federal Government extravagance, Bullis noted that Speaker of the House Joseph Martin had said, in 1947, that our total food bill was costing us less than our government. "Perhaps this proves that bombers cost more than banquets. At any rate, I know that wherever government's costs are really low, relative to food, there you have a place that very few of us would want to live. None of us would want to live in Central Africa or in India."

Bullis saw the rehabilitation of Europe as a struggle for political power in the economic arena — between Communism and Socialism on one hand, and our free enterprise system on the other. This was the conclusion he drew when he realized that the Russians lacked enthusiasm for the "very special regional cooperation which is so necessary for Europe and which was envisaged within the United Nations charter."

Europe was "weak and ailing but by no means lost. . . . What will happen if we do not aid the patient, but turn ostrich-like and ignore his needs? In my opinion, the alternative is the horrible possibility of a United States of America armed to the hilt, with a Communistic Europe and a Communistic Asia pressing the continent of North America from two sides, and with a war of nerves pointing toward a cataclysm of terrible proportions. We must remember that failure to prepare and to participate in plans for an orderly world recently brought on an expenditure of 350 billion dollars, which was the price of World War II to us. Whatever the Marshall Plan costs . . . it will not pay us to be penny-wise and pound-foolish again," he warned.

Bullis reported that General Clay was doing an excellent job in Germany, but the challenge there was colossal. He learned that General Eisenhower was very popular, and Harold Stassen was viewed with considerable respect.

There were pictures that "burned themselves indelibly" in Bullis' mind during that observation tour of eight countries: the grim look of determination on the face of Britain's man-in-the-street as he moved doggedly ahead despite rationing and privation—the terrible devastation in cities of the former German Reich—the mighty mountains of unscathed Switzerland that cradled in their valleys peaceful villages that were a tribute to an industrious democracy.

Most of all, the president of General Mills, who had written so many letters to GIs, remembered the American Cemetery "Margraten," on the highway to Aachen, Germany, where he looked with brooding gaze on the "neat rows of some 18,000 crosses marking as many graves of American GIs, most of whom participated in the bitter assault upon Aachen." There he found himself pronouncing reverently and determinedly, "They shall not have died in vain." Every sympathetic comment, every practical and humanitarian observation that he made in "Food and General Economic Condition of Europe" was aimed at the ideal of ultimate world peace.

In spite of strong opposition and indifference, the president of General Mills kept "campaigning" for the Marshall Plan in speeches all over the country.

Undoubtedly Bullis' powers of persuasion drowned out some of the hue and cry against the Marshall Plan in influential quarters. People might have little respect for foreign aid, but they respected the judgment of the successful president of General Mills. It wasn't easy, but he had never chosen to drive straight ahead on an easy road. Even in his own company or in the policies of the United States of America or in international relations, he had not been satisfied with the "status quo.'"

In 1933, Bullis was one of the founders of the present National Association of Manufacturers. He was a director and officer of that conservative businessmen's association for the period from 1933 to 1947, fourteen years. During that period, in many speeches he made at annual meetings of the N.A.M., he recalls that he shocked the conservative members by what they thought were his too liberal ideas. Several years ago, one of the older members saw Harry Bullis and he said, "You know, Harry, back there in the early days of the N.A.M. we all thought that you were the most liberal business leader that we had ever had. However, the things that you advocated then which we thought were far too liberal have now become so conservative that all business leaders practically agree with them."

It was in that "shocked atmosphere" that Bullis was stumping for the Marshall Plan. On April 3, 1948, President Truman approved Congressional legislation authorizing the appropriation of about five and one-third billion dollars to finance the European recovery operations for the first year. Harry Bullis was pleased with the appointment of Paul Hoffman, another internationally alert businessman, to head the European Recovery Program.

In reviewing the history of the European Recovery Program from April, 1948, through August, 1953, it might be well to remember that World War II cost the United States about 350 billion dollars, aside from all the lives that were lost. Our Economic Co-operation Administration expended about twelve and one-half billion dollars on European rehabilitation. Of that amount, five and one-half billion were used to buy industrial commodities, mainly in the United States. Food and agricultural commodities accounted for slightly over five billion. Ocean freight costs totaled almost one billion. Approximately five hundred million went into the European Payments Union to facilitate the trade balances among the member states.

Did the Marshall Plan measure up to Bullis' expectations? Over-all industrial production, in the European countries affected, increased sixty-four per cent over the 1947 level and forty-one per cent over the prewar level. Amazing single industry gains since 1947 included steel, almost one hundred per cent; cement, ninety per cent; aluminum, sixty-nine per cent; coal, twenty-seven per cent; and foodstuffs, twenty-four per cent. A glance at today's newspapers will indicate how strong—how vigorous—how downright independent Europe has become!

The Marshall Plan and its successors might be likened to "bread cast upon the waters." In late 1952, Bullis was continuing to make important statements on behalf of foreign aid, at a time when many Americans, especially some businessmen, were not wholeheartedly in favor of the foreign aid program. Appearing before the Fifty-seventh Congress of American Industry in New York, he noted that, "It is a peculiar fact that the United States, which has poured out aid in such huge amounts, has not been weakened thereby. If anything, we have become stronger. . . . In undertaking the burdens of aid in other countries, we lifted our capacity to produce. As a result of continued high employment and high wages, we also lifted our capacity to consume. It is probable that the lack of production during the depression of the 1930's was more costly in a purely economic way than the production which we gave away in the 1940's. In any event, we have proved that we were able to give a great deal of aid to the rest of the world and at the same time enlarge our standard of living at home. In this area, we are moving along a new course for America. . . ."

Late in 1947, Bullis served on President Truman's Citizens' Food Committee. One of the committees' moments of high glory involved helping to promote the "Freedom Trains" that moved across the country collecting bulging carloads of "gift food" which was shipped to the hungry people of Europe.

All of this time, Bullis was also working early and late to keep the wheels of production moving at a fine clip in his own company. Wherever he went, he should have had six hands to take care of all the handshaking he did. "In fact," Bullis quipped last year, "I was shaking as many hands as Lyndon Johnson is shaking now!"

Naturally, Harry Bullis flew, or he would not have managed to be in so many places almost at the same time. He liked to fly, no matter how miserable the weather. When the plane was being buffeted and tossed by rough weather, he was often asked how he could look so unperturbed while other passengers trembled and quaked.

Perhaps his equanimity might be explained by the fact that he was a man with deep spiritual, mental and intellectual reserves. He had thrived on the adventure of "riding out a storm"—in business, in politics, in human and international relations, in blizzard-whipped hikes around the Lake of the Isles. His courage gave him a sense of equilibrium, on the ground and in the air; and perhaps he had the abiding consolation, whether he recognized it or not, of knowing that the country boy from Iowa had lived a good and rewarding life.

When James Ford Bell retired as chairman of the board of General Mills on January 1, 1948, the story in the Minneapolis Star was headlined, "Bell Gives in to 'Old Man Time' but He's Still on Job." The Star business reporter, Herb Paul, told of contacting the man whose milling life had started on his graduation from the University of Minnesota in 1901. Still brimful of interest and curiosity about the future, "the dean of American millers" was anxious to get to the office at the same time to take over his duties as chairman of the newly authorized General Mills Committee on Finance and Technological Progress. Referring to his new "retirement" position, Bell said, "A job is what a man makes of it, and I hope to keep on the job." He repeated a statement he had made at a recent board of directors meeting: "I have seen too many old men linger on to block the way of the new and younger generation. Old Man Time tells me I'm getting old and it's the spirit of our organization to keep the new and younger men alert by developing their responsibility and authority."

He offered a special tribute to one of his new and younger men, Harry A. Bullis: "His splendid record has been one of outstanding achievement and service, and no one could be better qualified or more deserving of this new position of exceptional trust," he said. Now the "mill hand" had reached the highest possible point, as chairman of the board of a company that was moving ahead with dynamic vigor.

Leslie Perrin, who had been instrumental in expanding Washburn Crosby's activities in the Central Division in Chicago before he was elected a vice president of General Mills, reached a gratifying height in his own career as president of General Mills in 1948.

On that memorable New Year's Day, four General Mills stalwarts named Leslie Perrin, "Spike" Kennedy, Walter Barry and Sam Gale came to the Bullis home bearing gifts of "two solid silver candelabra and a silver bowl, all from George Jensen of New York. It was Searle Mowat's idea," Bullis noted in his diary. Mowat was active in the Larrowe Division for many years.

Harry Bullis entertained his callers in the large home on West Lake of the Isles Boulevard which was now under the supervision of an extraordinary housekeeper. Irma's sister and brother-in-law and Harry's father had continued to come up and spend most of the summer with him; but two of Harry's very good friends, Mr. and Mrs. Kenneth Taylor, convinced him that he should employ a Polish lady named Countess Maria Smorczewska to supervise the household.

Countess Smorczewska, who had lived a series of nightmare lives during the Nazi bombardments and seizure of Poland and its joint-occupation by the Communists, was an expert at the gracious art of homemaking. Countess Smorczewska was a member of an old family—the Gruzinski family dated from 1129—which had contributed gallant knights, Kastelans and senators to the kingdom.

The Countess, whose second husband had died in 1932, was living on the Smorczewska estate when the Germans marched into Poland with two million troops. After her lands were seized by the German Kreisslandwirth and later by the Communists, she fled the lovely country estate where she had raised horses for the Polish cavalry, and went to Warsaw which was not a pleasant refuge, either. On occasions when she served as a member of the Polish underground, she had to dodge both the Gestapo and the Bolshevists. For a short period, she was able to return to her country home before another flight back to Warsaw. After an unsuccessful attempt at a great insurrection, vast multitudes of the Polish people were rounded up and taken prisoner by the Germans. Some were sent to prisoner of war camps; some were sent to do hard labor in Germany; some were sent to the gas chambers. Others were shot at once under the walls of bombarded houses.

The "lucky ones" were sent to Pruszkow Camp near Warsaw and the Germans selected from this group the individuals they wanted for certain services. A group of elderly women, sick-looking and exhausted, or just plain hungry and tired, were picked to work on Polish farms which were given to Germans whose farms had been bombarded by the Allies.

Maria Smorczewska would never forget the long, rugged miles of marching from place to place. With a couple of her friends, she had been sent after the Pruszkow Camp to Koniecpol Camp and there she was selected for farm labor. She worked on a farm until the end of the war.

After the Armistice, the foreign embassies returned to Warsaw. The American Ambassador, Arthur Bliss Lane, and his charming wife, Cornelia, returned to Warsaw. Mrs. Smorczewska left the farm she worked on which was taken over by the new Polish government and went to Warsaw to look for some of her family or friends, if they were alive, and to look for a job. She went to see Ambassador and Mrs. Lane. They were shocked to discover that Countess Maria Smorczewska had been deprived of her estates and was almost destitute. They had known each other during the "free and wonderful years" of Premier Paderewski when Mr. Arthur Bliss Lane was Third Secretary to Ambassador Hugh Gibson, back in 1919.

So after World War II, Mrs. Smorczewska became part companion, housekeeper and also interpreter to Mrs. Lane for a time. Mrs. Lane had considerable knowledge and mastered the Polish language quite well. Then Mrs. Stanley Hawks, Mrs. Lane's sister and also a friend of Mrs. Smorczewska from the "free and wonderful years of Premier Paderewski," advised her to leave Communist-dominated Poland and start life anew in her own home city of Minneapolis, Minnesota. The lady was afraid the Red government would not allow her to leave Poland. She said, "They will tell you 'yes'—then arrest you the next day." At last, with the assistance of friends who were devoted to her, she was able to reach free territory. In Minneapolis, she soon found employment as a housekeeper.

Later Mrs. Smorczewska was able to locate her daughter and son-in-law, her son and her brother, all in Great Britain—and during the war all of them were highly decorated and distinguished by Polish, British, French and Dutch governments. Hundreds of thousands of Polish soldiers escaped to Allied countries and continued to fight heroically.

So this was the background of the lady, Countess Smorczewska, who had come to preside over the Bullis home in 1947. Representative Walter Judd of Minnesota had introduced a special bill in Congress to permit her to remain in the United States, and it was signed by President Truman. There was some publicity in the papers, but Harry Bullis was mainly impressed by the fact that this aristocratic lady had the strength of character and the spirit of independence to insist on supporting herself. She was especially thoughtful and kind to Harry Bullis' father when he came from Council Bluffs for periodic visits.

Harry's first years as chairman of the board of General Mills were busy ones, as he and Perrin continued the expansion pattern. New Betty Crocker mixes were introduced, puffed goods capacity was increased, new products were being developed by research, and mill capacity was being enlarged. There was one gathering after another for Harry Bullis to address—Salesmen's Training Courses, Advertising Council, University of Wisconsin Foundation group, Traffic Executives, General Flour Branch Managers, General Mills Operating Board, Grocery Products contest winners—an almost incredible list. Early in the year he managed to get a few breaths of ocean air when he sailed from New Orleans to Guatemala on vacation.

In April, Mr. Bell and Mr. Bullis invited Dr. Deane Malott of Cornell to become "a knight of that round table" in the directors' room on the twelfth floor of General Mills. The president emeritus of Cornell is still serving as a director.

A signal honor, on May 5, 1948, was an invitation to deliver the Newcomen Society address at Buffalo, New York. Bullis' speech, "Buffalo—Its Flour Milling Heritage," was printed in a handsome brochure by the Princeton University Press, with a quotation about the ideals of the society. "Were American Newcomen to do naught else, our work is well done if we succeed in sharing with America a strengthened inspiration to continue the struggle toward a nobler civilization—through wider knowledge of the hopes, ambitions and deeds of leaders in the past who have upheld civilization's material progress. As we look backward, let us look forward."

No one could be more in agreement with those sentiments than Harry Bullis, who eloquently traced the history of the milling industry from the time when "the stripling nation that was to become America saw its first mill in Virginia in 1621, in New Amsterdam in 1626, in Boston and in the vicinity of what is now Albany in 1632." He noted that "The first grain to be ground was undoubtedly Indian corn, which was native to the country. Before long, wheat was grown and its flour produced as well." Bullis said it was fitting that the Niagara meeting should be a salute to the men who in the last fifty years had made Buffalo "the premier flour milling center of the world."

On June 1, Bullis and other executives welcomed a group of five Harvard professors who had come to Minneapolis to give General Mills an "examination." On June 12, Bullis spoke on "Management's Responsibilities to Stockholders" at the annual conference of the Alumni Association of the Harvard Business School. In that speech he declared, "Under our freely competitive economy — our 'people's capitalism,' as Harold Stassen calls it—management acts as a balance wheel for the interests of employees, stockholders, and the consuming public. Management has the duty of seeing that no one group gains unreasonable advantage of the others."

Back in Minneapolis, Bullis conferred often with the Harvard educators, who spent eleven weeks studying the operations of General Mills. In their one hundred and fifteen page survey, containing observations on everything from production and industrial relations to market research and finance, the professors reported, "We found an organization that gets things done smoothly, with high morale, a fine spirit of cooperation, and a willingness to assume responsibility."

Harry Bullis, seeing the project as a "two-way street," commented, "To the educator it provides a practical way to learn the problems of business and this knowledge in turn can be passed on to the students who will be the business leaders of the future. To the executive it furnishes an objective perspective . . . from qualified men who have the advantage of a fresh approach from the outside."

Bullis continued with enthusiasm to support Harold E. Stassen's candidacy for the Republican nomination for president. On June 25, 1948, he took fifteen guests to the Republican convention in Philadelphia. Thomas E. Dewey won the nomination. "Dewey was too complacent and thought he had the election won," Harry recalled, "and he didn't campaign hard. If Stassen had been nominated, he would have campaigned hard and would probably have been elected president." After Harry Truman won the presidency in that surprising election in the fall, Bullis noted with a gleam in his eye that Truman had toured the Middle West during the last two weeks of the campaign and had promised the farmers "the moon." However, Bullis generously conceded that Harry Truman undoubtedly will go down in history as one of the major presidents in this century, because so many spectacular events and transformations occurred during his years in office.

In July, Bullis joined forces with Mrs. Peavey Heffelfinger in a campaign to collect Minneapolis' share of sixty million dollars for the Crusade for Children Fund, to feed the children of the world who were dying of starvation and malnutrition. "Let us break bread with the world," seemed to be the slogan of this dedicated miller who again emphasized the need for international free trade and foreign relief measures in "The World's Food Prospects," published in Dun's Review for July, 1948. A. D. Whiteside, president of Dun and Bradstreet, wrote that they were fortunate to have that article because, "It is extremely important that businessmen understand from the sources in which they have confidence just what the situation is in this key phase of the world economy."

Harold Stassen became a president, after all, in July. Bullis congratulated him when he became the youngest college president in Pennsylvania's history, at the age of forty-one.

In 1948, Bullis saw the complex panorama of management and labor relations as a vast seeding bed, fertile with opportunities for harvesting a bumper crop of good will which would be of ultimate profit to both employer and employee. He believed that employees should be given a complete financial picture of the company—that they must be shown that their security is related to the security of the company. "Let's correct erroneous notions of high earnings by showing their true relation to the sales dollar and to investors' funds. But let us show how earnings are used. And let us repeat again and again how employees have profited along with the company."

The employee craves satisfaction in his work and wants to feel as though he is a member of the team, Bullis said. "Consider the desire for recognition, for participation—how important it is in the science of human engineering! Yet how often, instead of saying,

'Men, we are all on the team, and we will win together,' management seems to say, 'Men, I am the team!' Yes, it only seems to say it. It may think altogether otherwise. But good thoughts, unlike good deeds, do not speak for themselves, and the employee gets the wrong impression."

In our complex modern civilization, the desires of the employee are psychological as well as material. "They range," Bullis noted, "over the whole complex of human emotions, and they are changing constantly. . . . It is our job to create a favorable attitude toward business and the free enterprise system. We can, we shall—we must so conduct ourselves toward our employees that we will earn and deserve their enthusiastic support. . . . With every employee doing his public relations job, industry can so weave itself into the social fabric of America that the people will never let it down." This was the enlightened business philosophy of a "Champion American."

In his diary for December 29, 1948, Harry Bullis referred to a wedding that was scheduled for that day. Arthur Bliss Lane, former ambassador to Poland, and Mrs. Lane, had flown from Washington to Minneapolis to serve as best man and matron of honor.

Bishop and Mrs. Richard Raines had come all the way from Indianapolis for the occasion. Bishop Raines, whom Harry Bullis called "one of the great preachers of the Methodist Church," had been his minister at Hennepin Avenue Methodist Church. Two winters before, Richard Raines had written to congratulate Harry on one of his business statements: ". . . it is quite evident that we are making very real progress, and you are in the vanguard, taking the insights and convictions and attitudes of the church and Christ, and carrying them with you as determinative lights for making decisions in your office."

Back of the stories on the society pages was Harry's pensive recollection of an "enchanted evening" at the beautiful home of Mr. and Mrs. Stanley Hawks the summer before. When Harry arrived there, he found himself admiring the queenly poise and charm of the guest of honor who was exquisitely gowned in black lace. He asked someone, "Who is that beautiful lady?" and was surprised to learn that she was his housekeeper. This was the Countess Maria Smorczewska, who had competently directed the affairs of a large estate, who had sought refuge in a potato cellar and escaped the Nazis in a peasant's cart, who had performed hazardous services for her country, who had survived the ordeals of the prison and farm labor camps, and who had been so unobtrusively capable as Harry Bullis' housekeeper that he did not immediately recognize her when she was in an atmosphere befitting a lady of her patrician lineage.

Chapter Sixteen

"As Ye Sow . . ."

In one of Harry Bullis' scrapbooks is the wedding announcement, with the Grudzinski coat-of-arms engraved above the formal phrases: "Colonel and Mrs. Anthony Grudzinski have the honor of announcing the marriage of their sister Countess Maria Robert Smorczewska to Harry Amos Bullis on Wednesday, December twenty-ninth, One thousand nine hundred and forty-eight."

About twenty relatives and close friends were present at the lovely evening wedding of the Polish countess and the Minneapolis industrialist.

This wedding, which had an almost picture-book quality for the press, inspired many types of journalistic treatment. All of the stories reviewed Maria Bullis' life as a countess, and her harrowing ordeals during the occupation of Poland. They retraced Harry's life as a young paper boy, farm laborer, and bookkeeper in Iowa, to the heights of achievement as chairman of the board of General Mills and a leader of consequence in many other areas. The New York Daily News, featuring a picture of the bride and groom walking back up the aisle from the candle-lighted altar, captioned the story, "New Dividend."

Because Countess Smorczewska was a Roman Catholic, the marriage ceremony was later performed by Monsignor George Ryan. Mrs. Stanley Hawks and Mrs. Arthur Bliss Lane were witnesses.

Again, Harry's second wife became more than a wife. She was a partner who encouraged him in every possible way. Throughout his complicated business career, Harry said he adopted the practice of never discussing his business problems at home. However, both Irma and Mary have been the sort of highly intelligent ladies who inspired and encouraged him in his aspirations and endeavors.

"Mary," as Harry affectionately called her, opened up a new era for the General Mills executive who had restricted his social life mainly to company-oriented and service activities. As a titled continental lady, many doors were opened to Mary Bullis by the distinguished society people of Minneapolis.

Harry described Mary as a lady of "courtly bearing"—extremely efficient, most attractive and sensitively considerate. He was one husband who thought it was fine for his wife to make "a new man of him." He confided that Mary kept him from turning into the "stuffed shirt" he sometimes feared he was becoming. For instance, she taught him to dance. According to Harry, Mary chuckled as she told about it: "At first Harry was like a baby learning to walk. Now I think he almost enjoys it."

Mrs. Bullis is "an artist of the cuisine." With her

Old World background of gracious living and entertaining, an invitation to visit the Bullis home became a delight worthy of eager anticipation. Soon her traditional Polish Easter breakfast was being described as "fabulous" by the fortunate guests. The table was laden with succulent sausages, hams, roasts, a suckling pig, decorated eggs, sauces, breads, and a breath-taking variety of sweets and pastries. The centerpiece was always a lamb molded of butter or pastry, holding a Polish flag. Mrs. Bullis is noted for treating both her food and her guests with "tender, loving care."

After his second marriage, Harry was glad that he had continued to live in the spacious West Lake of the Isles home. He still enjoyed those long walks around the lake. Irma had always been afraid of dogs, so they never had one. In 1947, Harry purchased a boxer pup named "Trigger," who became his great walking companion. Mary Bullis, an avid horsewoman and a lover of all animals, was not content with just one dog. Harry declared, "We now have three dogs, and they are all favorites of mine!"

Mr. and Mrs. Bullis enjoyed a brief honeymoon at the Edgewater Beach Hotel in Chicago. Six days after the wedding Bullis was in Hartford, Connecticut on January 5, 1949, addressing two large meetings — a luncheon meeting of investment analysts and a dinner meeting of insurance company presidents. He also visited insurance companies which owned General Mills stock. The next day, when he was in Boston speaking at luncheon and dinner meetings of investment and insurance firms owning General Mills stock, he said he encountered some really "brutal questions." Later he opined, with positive Bullis lustiness, "Boston investment men are tough!"

After several other business conferences in Washington and Minneapolis, Harry and Mary Bullis were able to start for a vacation at Chandler, Arizona, on January 28. The February 3 entry in Harry's diary is typical: "Mrs. George Cormack telephoned me that George Cormack, our former head miller, was seriously ill at Tucson and she asked me to come there and see her. On February 4 I spent the day at Tucson with Mr. and Mrs. Cormack. I made arrangements for the General Mills plane to pick up Mr. Cormack's doctor in Helena, Montana, and bring him to Tucson to treat Mr. Cormack."

On April 2, 1949, Harry A. Bullis and Neil H. Borden were announced as recipients of the 1949 Parlin Memorial Award. The award, sponsored by the Philadelphia chapter of the American Marketing Association, is given each year for outstanding contributions to the science of marketing. The presentation was made in Philadelphia on May 18. At the dinner honoring Charles Coolidge Parlin, the distinguished founder of modern market research, Harry Bullis described the manner in which General Mills has handled its fluctuating market trends—through periods of heavy flour consumption and through "lean years" when Americans considered bread more fattening than other foods containing the same number of calories.

Neil H. Borden, professor of advertising of the Harvard Graduate School of Business Administration, who shared the Parlin Award rostrum with Harry Bullis that evening, was one of the Harvard educators who had conducted the General Mills survey in the summer of 1948. His Parlin Award speech traced the original idea for that study back to the day in the fall of 1947 when James Ford Bell had said at a Harvard Business School luncheon: "I think that it would be a fine thing if groups of professors from schools of business administration might be employed to come into corporations such as my own to study the operations and to make an appraisal of the management job being done. We think that we have a good organization and conduct our business well. The thing we need to fear is complacency. It would be good to know how well our management would measure up under the investigation of an outside group like this, which has a detached, objective viewpoint. I think that a study of this kind would be good for teachers of business, and, in turn, it should be good for the business studied."

The significant conclusions have already been noted, and anyone who has an opportunity to examine General Mills through the medium of Harry Bullis' scrapbooks will realize that this organization does "get things done smoothly, with high morale, a fine spirit of co-operation, and a willingness to assume responsibility." This does not mean that everyone at General Mills goes around dancing the "Pollyanna Polka" all the time, but there has been a spirit of enlightened vitality even in the resolving of occasional points of disagreement.

A 1949 letter to Harry Bullis from John A. McWethy of the Wall Street Journal confirms the Harvard evidence: "I'm glad you liked my story on General Mills. For a long time I've thought in a general way that you people at General Mills do an outstanding job. But I certainly didn't realize until I dug into the material for the story just how far ahead of the parade you are in flour making, public relations, merchandising and many other fields. . . ."

On a sweltering July 29, 1949, Harry Bullis removed his coat and invited his audience of Northwestern Mutual Life Insurance Company agents to do the same. At this 69th annual meeting, held in Milwaukee, Bullis advised agents to "sell themselves" on the merits of life insurance before they tried to convince the customer of its multiple benefits. He said, "You know, gentlemen, it isn't what we say that is so important, it is what we feel that counts most."

On August 2, 1949, Harry Bullis was guest columnist for M. S. Rukeyser in the New York Journal-American. His "Gold Rush" article was widely reprinted. "One hundred years ago," he began, "there was a 'gold rush' that sent thousands of people scurrying westward across prairie and mountain in search of hidden wealth. The vast majority failed to find a way to easy wealth. Instead, they faced the hard reality of earning a living. And by learning that they had to work to earn a living, they created our western empire. The 'gold rush' was not in vain!"

Harry Bullis, who had always placed "intelligent hard work" high on the list of ingredients for success, noted in the Rukeyser column that "In America today, our long-range problem is to make clear the fallacy of attempting to achieve wealth and security, as something we can get for nothing. Our emotional wealth is measured by our national production. . . .

"In interviewing the class of '49, American business can well emphasize that there is no mysterious alchemy, no formula of 'something for nothing' by which success may be achieved. Now, as in the days of our pioneer forefathers, the sweat and brawn of engineer and farmer, office man and salesman, laborer and manager, blended together in American teamwork, is the formula for an expanding and developing United States of America. . . ."

On March 3, 1949, during Minnesota's Territorial Centennial, Harry Bullis received "A Testimonial of a Grateful State." He was designated one of "The One Hundred Living Great of Minnesota, selected by popular balloting among the people in appreciation of unselfish contribution to the progress of the State."

When she was President Truman's ambassador to Luxembourg, Perle Mesta was a well-known personage to newspaper readers. All aglow with satin and a-flutter with lace, a dazzling Amazon of a "girl" came swishing into the spotlight at a Rotary Club meeting one day in Minneapolis. With a dainty wave of a white-gloved hand and a lipsticked-grin, charming Harry Bullis convulsed the Rotarians with Perle's good-humored boast, "I'm the hostess with the mostest on the ball!"

On the more sober side, Bullis was honored as national chairman of United Nations Week, from October 16-24, 1950. On September 17 he officiated as chairman of a large meeting of twenty-four hundred people which was held in the ballroom of the Waldorf-Astoria in New York City. He introduced Mrs. Franklin D. Roosevelt, American ambassador to the United Nations Warren R. Austin, and Assistant Secretary of State John D. Hickerson. Before the evening meeting, Mr. and Mrs. Bullis gave a dinner for the American United Nations delegation. After the evening meeting, at a reception given for Mrs. Roosevelt, Bullis stood at her left and introduced the guests in the receiving line to her.

On February 26, 1951, Bullis presided at a meeting of the board of directors of General Mills. Then he flew to Chicago to officiate as co-chairman of the American Association for the United Nations Emergency Conference on Our Responsibility for World Leadership which was held in the ballroom of the Hotel Stevens. He presided at a large dinner meeting on that same evening and introduced the principal speaker, Governor Adlai Stevenson of Illinois, who had helped form the United Nations in San Francisco. The next day, Harry Bullis presided at the conference and made an important address which was broadcast on a national network.

During his eleven years as chairman of the board of General Mills, Bullis arranged to have the members of the board of directors hold at least one meeting annually in some city in which the company operated a plant.

Visitations at General Mills plants gave the directors close contact with the various operations of the company. On several occasions, the directors donned the miller's traditional uniform—visored cap and overalls—to tour the flour and cereal mills. It took some of the men back to the days of their young manhood when they had worn those outfits "for real" to earn their daily bread.

In addition to drafting organization plans in which Bell, Bullis and Perrin all took an active interest, Harry Bullis assumed the leadership position for the regional stockholders' meetings after he became chairman of the board of General Mills. During the previous ten years, James F. Bell had acted as host during the expeditions to key centers in the country. When Bell had inaugurated the unique "friendly visits" in 1939, he was bringing the company to the "doorsteps" of the investors.

The personal greetings, the programs dealing with "the state of the company" in which their money was invested, and the question-and-answer periods were lauded as a great step forward in better business relations with millions of "small American capitalists." Financial commentators urged other large corporations to follow General Mills' example.

Bullis had accompanied Bell on a number of early stockholders' tours. In 1948, the new chairman of the board took to the road "on his own." His righthand man was Gordon Ballhorn, one of his Wisconsin proteges, who became comptroller in 1939 and later vice president.

Bullis' enthusiastic efforts led to special recognition for "Meritorious Achievement in the Field of Management-Shareholder Relationship" in 1957. Benjamin Javits, older brother of Senator Jacob K. Javits, presented the United Shareholders Annual Meeting Award to him in New York.

Bullis represented General Mills at stockholders'

meetings every two years during his eleven years as chairman of the board. He took youthful pleasure in getting his message across by showing animated films that gave an exciting, quick picture of the year's operations.

Of special note was the color movie, "Assignment—General Mills" which was shown at the 1950 stockholders' meetings. Featured stars were Gail Davis and Robert Arthur who played the parts of two young college students majoring in business administration. Assigned to write term reports on the year's operation of a national company, they drew the name of General Mills out of a hat.

The script took them first for a visit with chairman of the board, Harry Bullis, in his office on the twelfth floor of the General Mills Building. Then they met James F. Bell, the founder of the company, and Leslie Perrin, president.

On a guided tour, with the cameras following closely, the pair visited departments at Minneapolis headquarters, including the famous home service kitchens where they met the home economists who personify the spirit of Betty Crocker. In the General Mills research department they found scientists hard at work developing additional uses for products of the soil.

After seeing how it all originated, Helen and Ted visited a retail store to observe the merchandising and selling techniques that pass General Mills products along to the consumer. Back in Mr. Bullis' office, they were introduced to "Mr. Black" and "Mr. Red," animated cartoon characters who "acted out" the 1949-50 financial statement, pointing out the sources of income and types of costs, and arriving at the company's profits for the year and its current net worth. The movie closed with "Professor" James F. Bell reading the students' finished term reports on the company.

Bullis was a man who always had a host of "overlapping" activities. Believing that businessmen and stockholders of the future deserved to be given some active "skull practice," he instituted "mock stockholders' meetings" in leading universities throughout the country. Bullis found that he got more "skull practice" than he had bargained for, but he enjoyed the sharp, penetrating questions fired at him by economics and business administration students at Michigan, Cornell, M.I.T., Harvard, Pennsylvania, Minnesota, Yale and Stanford.

Bullis always invited the students to think of themselves as owners of fifty or one hundred shares of stock —for the duration of the program. The Wall Street Journal headed a story, "General Mills Officials Peppered with Questions for an Hour," when the GMI cavalcade held a session at Massachusetts Institute of Technology in 1952. Arms shot up freely as the "classroom financiers" wanted to know how General Mills was using "our investment." Bullis noted, at that time, that General Mills had just authorized the building of a modern flour plant at Louisville, Kentucky. "General Mills," he said, "is the largest flour miller in the world with eighteen plants in the United States and buys eighty-five to ninety million bushels of wheat a year."

In 1952 and 1953, the company was at the height of its post-war diversification program. During stockholders' meetings, many questions were asked about the manufacture of items outside the flour and food category, such as chemicals, vitamins, sponges, meteorological instruments—and even high altitude balloons.

What was a flour company doing in the stratosphere? Operation Skyhook, an assignment from the Office of Naval Research, was even more of a "glamour project" than the World War II precision instruments. The huge, elongated plastic balloons were designed to carry two hundred and fifty pounds of recording equipment. Soaring to a height of twenty miles, they gathered data on cosmic rays and sources of atomic energy. They also attracted almost as much alarmed conjecture as the explosion of Cadwallader Washburn's "A" mill back in 1878. Originally classified top-secret in 1947, it was impossible for General Mills to relieve the anxiety about the "ectoplasmic objects" drifting wraith-like in the sky. After startled earth people were told what it was, Operation Skyhook no longer appeared spooky. "Those balloons," Harry Bullis told a student at Cornell in 1952, "are the result of research in plastics. They're part of the $20-million government business we're doing."

The informal stockholders' sessions were the most popular presentation of all, with the report being given in person in an atmosphere of honesty, good fellowship and mutual interest. Bullis saluted his chief's splendid choice of words in noting that Mr. Bell regarded the chairman of the board "as a personal ambassador of the stockholders to management." Shareholders have come as far as two hundred miles to attend the meetings in New York, Buffalo, Washington, Boston, Chicago, Detroit, Minneapolis, San Francisco and Los Angeles.

Since all the meetings were held within a period of about a month, the pace was often gruelling for everyone concerned; but a bubbling spirit of camaraderie prevailed.

During the stockholders' tours, and at the end of every calendar year, Bullis made economic forecasts. In his widely publicized forecast at the end of 1953, he predicted "a year of satisfaction, high employment, and continued good business." He was correct, because 1954 did prove to be the year of the end of the relatively small recession of 1953-54. The 1954 Federal tax cut caused an offsetting increase in the tax base, and tax collections actually increased. In less than two years, federal revenues were even higher than before because the economy boomed.

"Fortunately," Harry said, "the majority of my forecasts of the business cycle have proved to be substantially correct." This Week Magazine, in an issue in the latter part of December, 1952, had noted that Harry was a seer with a sense of humor:

"Harry A. Bullis, board chairman of General Mills, found at recent stockholder meetings that the most frequent questions concerned his view of the business future. Perennially optimistic, Bullis made a hopeful forecast for 1953, but cautiously prefaced it with this story: A waiter brought his customer fifty-five cents change in the form of a nickel and a fifty-cent piece. The customer studied the coins, then pocketed the big one. 'Okay,' the waiter laughed, 'I gambled and I lost.' "

It is small wonder that Bullis attracted the attention of so many business reporters during his travels around the country. He seemed to carry in his mind a massive accumulation of graphs, charts and figures with which to appraise centuries of business trends and cycles. Yet, he always managed to be a great human being, instead of a walking economics textbook.

Bullis' missions were so varied that it would be difficult to classify them, but he always took a zestful interest in visiting with people who were promoting the welfare of the company and the country. Because they referred to the quickening of a comradeship that would refresh and gladden Harry's life, the last two sentences in the following diary entry should be punctuated with exclamation points:

January 9, 1950. "In New York. I had separate conferences with H. S. Sturgis and F. A. O. Schwarz at which we discussed employees' stock purchase plan, bonus or profit sharing for executives, and succession. In the afternoon, I visited our office and talked with our executives there. In the evening, I attended the dinner given by Bill Burnham and Arthur Lawrence for General D. D. Eisenhower. I sat next to the General."

As Countess Smorczewska, Mrs. Bullis had met General Eisenhower in Poland in 1946. Harry Bullis remembered having had "a good visit" with the general when he was given a small dinner at the Minneapolis Club on the evening of September 1, 1947. The State of Minnesota had invited him to speak as guest of honor at "General Eisenhower Day at Minnesota State Fair."

Through the courtesy of Bill Burnham who was a great friend of the general's, Harry Bullis later was included in small dinner groups in New York when Burnham entertained in honor of General Eisenhower.

Perhaps a segment of the Eisenhower-Bullis relationship might be traced back to those moments of tense awareness on D-Day, June 6, 1944, when Bullis requested prayers for the success of the Normandy invasion. General Dwight D. Eisenhower was Supreme Commander of the Allied Expeditionary Forces in that historic operation.

Chapter Seventeen

"So Shall Ye Reap"

On October 7, 1890, a spanking new American citizen was born in Hastings, Nebraska; while he was still a small child, his parents moved to Council Bluffs, Iowa. On October 14, 1890, exactly a week after Harry Bullis was born, another American infant was welcomed into the home of David and Ida Eisenhower in Denison, Texas. Small Dwight David was a year old when the Eisenhower family moved to Abilene, Kans.

The two average American "country boys," growing up at quite a distance from each other, probably were doing similar chores and engaging in some of the same rural interests. As the years passed, both of them became men with warm, flashing grins and talents for serving their country with devotion in peace and war.

In Dwight D. Eisenhower, Bullis would see another "country boy" who had not been afraid to tackle the rough and rugged glory road and who had come home to the cheers of the multitude. He was a winner, and Bullis frankly admired people who drive straight ahead—in peace or war—to achieve the victories that make big men of average American boys.

In Bullis' "Eisenhower Scrapbooks" are letters and copies of speeches that indicate a common national and international point of view. Bullis was thinking of Dwight D. Eisenhower as the man he would most like to see living in the White House when he wrote to the general early in 1950: "As I travel around the country these days I find increasing sentiment for you to become standard bearer of the Republican party in 1952." Bullis enclosed a copy of "The Road to Business Leadership" which he had delivered at New York University on April 11.

The hero of World War II is mentioned again in Bullis' diary on June 9, 1950, when he and Bill Burnham were invited to have breakfast with the man who then was president of Columbia University.

Bullis was happy to accept the invitation. He arrived at former President Butler's home with Burnham about ten minutes before eight on June 9. From newspaper accounts, which featured many pictures of General Eisenhower giving out diplomas, the visitors were aware that the commencement exercises had been held at Columbia on the preceding day.

Because he was so punctual himself, Bullis noted with approval that General Eisenhower came walking down the steps at exactly eight o'clock. As he greeted his guests, he explained that breakfast was the only meal of the day that he could control because he went to so many luncheons and dinners.

Harry appreciated the humor behind the general's

remark as he told the elderly lady who was waiting to serve them, "Ann, bring on the breakfast. Commencement is over so I can really eat."

At that breakfast session, Bullis learned that the Harriman brothers, of whom Averill Harriman was one, had recently offered to present Arden House to Columbia University. Arden House, a mansion of nearly one hundred rooms, had been the home of their father, Edward Harriman, the famous railway magnate. The spacious mansion, crowning a hilltop on an estate of about one hundred acres, was located approximately seventy miles north of New York City.

The general explained that, assuming Columbia University accepted the gift of Arden House, he wanted to pioneer in the field of adult education. The mansion could accommodate assemblies lasting a week or so, to which about eighty representatives of education, business, labor, government, and other activities would be invited. General Eisenhower suggested that the first assembly should concentrate on the subject of "Nutrition" because he had been shocked at the poor physical condition of the young men who were examined for entrance into the United States Army.

The subject of education, on nutrition or anything else, was of deep concern to Bullis. However, he reminded the president of Columbia University that he had on his faculty the international authority on nutrition, Dr. Charles G. King.

Bullis then discovered that the general had another reason for inviting him to breakfast. General Eisenhower wanted to sound out a group of representative citizens on his Arden House Assembly ideas. Bullis, of course, assured the general that he would be honored to give a dinner for him.

In several letters, General Eisenhower mentioned that he was keenly anticipating his visit to Minneapolis in July. Harry and Mary Bullis were rolling out everything from the red carpet to the "flying carpet" for the eminent visitor. Wrote Eisenhower in June, ". . . You are more than kind to think of sending your plane to pick us up." On July 6, he flew to Minneapolis.

In Harry's "Eisenhower Scrapbooks" are some fine big "glossies" showing the general arriving at the airport and laughingly acknowledging a certificate electing him a Life Member of The National Bald-Headed Club. On another picture, he was listening solemnly as a police representative warned him about a "crank letter" threatening his life.

On July 7, neighbors who lived near the house at 2116 West Lake of the Isles Boulevard saw an affably grinning visitor arrive in a shiny limousine and hurry eagerly up the steps. Mary Bullis said the general captivated everyone in the house when he insisted on meeting all the menbers of the home staff and shaking hands with them.

General Eisenhower had arrived on a lovely summer day, and Mr. and Mrs. Bullis entertained at a reception in his honor. All the guests congregated in the garden, and Harry confided that Mary Bullis and Mrs. James F. Bell cornered the general long enough to tell him that he owed it to his country to become the Republican candidate for president of the United States.

That evening Harry Bullis presided at the dinner

for General Eisenhower in the Minneapolis Club. The guest list included forty-three influential businessmen and civic leaders. In explaining the Arden House proposal, the general told the group, "We believe that universities—and we want Columbia to take the lead—can be of more use to the world today, instead of just training leaders for twenty or twenty-five years from now. We think the problems of today, if studied with businessmen as well as scholars sitting in to consider them, will be answered in a disinterested way that will be useful to the world."

The Korean War had started several days before, and Seoul had already fallen to the North Korean Communists. The Minneapolis Tribune described Ike as looking optimistic and predicting that the Korean War would not become a third world war.

The next day, when Bullis drove the general to the airport, he again discussed his possible candidacy for the presidency.

The forward-march of history is apparent in the mounting accumulation of Eisenhower-Bullis correspondence. Harry Bullis wrote to the general on July 10, 1950, "Like Julius Caesar, you came, you saw, you conquered." The general expressed his appreciation in a handwritten note for the hospitable welcome in Minneapolis, and added, "Your nice note encourages me to believe that I did not bore the assembly with my convictions and enthusiasms—I'm too devoted to this country, and want so much to do something about it, that I fear I grow garrulous."

Although he was president of Columbia University from June 7, 1948, to January 19, 1953, Eisenhower took leave of absence in December, 1950, to serve as Supreme Allied Commander in Europe to organize the forces of NATO. Eisenhower and Bullis continued to exchange letters dealing with their mutual interest in the Columbia Conference Plan at Arden House, which had been renamed "American Assembly." In December, 1950, at the request of General Eisenhower, Bullis agreed to become the American Assembly's representative in the upper Middle West.

Bullis attended the organization meeting of the National Policy Board at Arden House on Sunday, May 20, 1951, and the opening of the first assembly on Monday, May 21. He heard Senator Robert A. Taft and Paul Douglas make the kick-off speeches after dinner on May 21.

Bullis' interest in the "adult education" project continued through the years. On September 26, 1957, he was elected to a new group of trustees of the American Assembly which had just been granted a charter from the United States Board of Regents.

The Minneapolis man, who was a member of the governing body of the American Assembly from its formation, attended the semi-annual meetings regularly in New York. And it all began as a breakfast table topic in 1950. On February 15, 1951, Bullis' distinguished friend wrote, "Just before I take off to Europe this evening, I must send you a note of thanks for the very great help you have been to me during the past year or so. . . . I am not only grateful for the very constructive and helpful interest you have taken in the American Assembly, but for the fine work that you have done in bringing information concerning it to the attention of many others. I look forward with real pleasure to the opportunity of seeing you again, one of these days. . . ."

While General Eisenhower was serving as Supreme Commander in charge of organizing the defense of Western Europe, conjectures about his becoming a presidential candidate continued to be editorially prominent in his homeland; but General Eisenhower went energetically about his business in Europe. When he was pressed for an answer, he was reluctant to commit himself. His commander-in-chief, President Truman, had appointed him to a post involving grave responsibilities. He explained, "It is not always easy to determine where the path of duty lies. A man can do no more than his best."

When the NATO commander finally announced that he would accept the G.O.P. nod if he were drafted, Bullis was among the Republicans most anxious to get "General Ike" home. Back in Minnesota, Bullis had been in charge of raising funds for the Eisenhower campaign. He was also raising enthusiasm wherever he went.

The whole nation looked toward Minnesota in astonishment after the returns of the state primary were tabulated. The unprecedented had occurred. On March 23, 1952, the Minneapolis Sunday Tribune announced in large type, "If Ike Wins, State Republicans May Be Number One Reason." A masterpiece of journalism, by-lined Rolf Felstad, described that political miracle:

"The presidential puzzle of 1952 may have been solved on that wild and wonderful day when Minnesota voters, refusing to be slush-bound, overshoed to polling places, took pencils in hand and wrote things on the presidential primary ballots.

"They wrote things like Izenour, Eisenour, Isenhower, Izenhower, Eisinhower and President Ike. No matter how they spelled it, their scribblings added up to 110,000 votes for the man who wasn't there.

"The state, the nation, the world looked, listened and gasped."

Newspapers over the country and the world were asking how it could have happened. General Eisenhower was a famous war hero, of course; but James A. Farley, an old hand at assessing political trends, figured that "the Eisenhower group had a good organization working in Minnesota—things like that in politics don't just happen."

Favorite son Harold Stassen was running again, so Bullis was frankly supporting two good Republican candidates with encouragement and financial contributions.

Eisenhower received clearance to leave his European post on June 1, 1952, which allowed him slightly more than a month to campaign before the Republican convention. Meanwhile an exhilarating wave of "I Like Ike" sentiment was sweeping the country.

Equipped with tickets for one of the choice boxes, and additional tickets for their guests on the first floor, Mr. and Mrs. Harry Bullis attended the Republican convention in July. Behind the tumultuous demonstrations and fiery oratory depicted on television and reported in newspapers, top Republicans were "measuring the prospects" for a Republican victory in 1952. Bullis exulted in General Eisenhower's obvious popularity, as a war hero and as a leader with a personality that would attract the votes on the man on the street and the man at the board of directors' table. For the first time in two decades, it was apparent that the Republicans had an almost sure-fire winner.

More inspired than calculated were the tumultuous demonstrations of the Eisenhower standard-bearers as they surged through convention hall again and again. Meanwhile, Bullis and other influential Minnesotans were conferring with Harold Stassen and the Minnesota delegation. By the time Minnesota was ready to report, Stassen's nineteen votes belonged to "General Ike."

The Chicago Daily News, on July 11, 1952, called it an "Amateur's Triumph." The story of the "Eisenhower Landslide" was subtitled, "Nineteen Stassen Votes Do it." After that, "Everybody rushed for the nearest exit from the Taft camp."

Prominent on front pages were huge pictures of "Ike," his arms upraised in a characteristic victory salute. Before the day was over, the top of the Republican ticket was complete—Dwight D. Eisenhower and Richard M. Nixon.

Hoarse-voiced delegates went home to gargle and get their voices in shape for a major campaign. Astute Republicans realized that nothing must be left to chance this time. The battle would not be a complete "pushover" — there would be too many voters who would say, "Yes, Eisenhower was a great general—but is he qualified to be president of the United States?" They would say, "Stevenson is a man who knows politics; Eisenhower is a new man to this game." It would be folly to say that the general couldn't be beaten; that was what they had said about Dewey in 1948, and the "racket-busting hero" had been defeated.

Three days after the convention, Harry Bullis invited "General Ike" to highlight the start of his campaign with a Labor Day appearance in Minnesota, where he had received his first impressive write-in vote. There was no doubt that General Eisenhower could depend on Harry Bullis right down the line. We can visualize Bullis, sitting erect in his office, speaking earnestly as he dictated the last sentence of that letter: "I pledge you my continued support and co-operation in your campaign for the presidency of the United States."

Bullis was not Eisenhower's only dedicated booster, but his was a one-hundred per cent positive pledge, in terms of comprehensive strategy, enthusiasm, encouragement, and notable contributions to the campaign chest. Bullis used his influence to raise funds and arouse support for his candidate. He also set about "mending fences" immediately. Harry was able to report to "General Ike" that "Harold Stassen was going to work very hard for your election." Stassen was glad that Bullis had brought Eisenhower and him together, and the former governor thought it was "a wonderful thing" that General Eisenhower had walked across the street to Taft after he had won the nomination.

Bullis wore a large, blue ribbon with the word "Committee" on it when Minnesota Republicans welcomed General Eisenhower on Labor Day in 1952. The occasion was the annual plowing contest in southern Minnesota—an inspired location, with plenty of wide open spaces to accommodate the multitudes who came to see and hear the two major presidential candidates. Part of the day was devoted to an exhibition of skillful plowing in the rich Minnesota farm soil, but the prime attraction on September 6, 1952, was the arrival of the Plowville motorcade from Rochester, Minnesota, where General Eisenhower's plane had landed. Ike's speech before the huge rural audience was broadcast nationwide. The papers reported all the events of the day, including the chicken dinner for the Eisenhower party at the Snow farmhouse.

Harry Bullis was with General Eisenhower in northern Minnesota after the Plowville speech. The Minneapolis publisher, John Cowles, had invited them to spend the week end at the Star and Tribune's Glendalough Game Farm. In Bullis' scrapbooks are several splendid pictures of General Eisenhower, Bullis, Cowles, Governor C. Elmer Anderson, and other members of the small group.

Almost overnight, Minnesota blossomed like a garden with "I Like Ike" buttons of every size. Campaign headquarters were set up in almost every town and hamlet. All across the land there was a spontaneous, nonpartisan stirring of imaginations as November 4 neared. A major subject of discussion was General Eisenhower's promise to go to war-devastated Korea if he were elected.

Harry Bullis was with General and Mrs. Eisenhower in Boston on the eve of election day. The Eisenhower-Bullis paths had crossed on a number of occasions during the campaign, because Harry was continually traveling on business and stockholders' trips.

Thomas E. Stephens, the general's secretary, arranged for the two men to visit when they were together in various cities.

Huge headlines in the Boston Herald for November 5, 1952, proclaimed, "Ike Wins By Landslide." It was a magnificent victory, nationwide in pattern. Eisenhower had cracked the "Solid South." Drawing heavy support from labor, the farm belt and industry, he had won the largest popular vote in the history of the nation, tabulating four hundred and forty-two electoral votes to Stevenson's eighty-nine.

On a number of occasions after the election, President Eisenhower wrote to express his interest in Bullis' views on financial matters. Edward F. Greene, personal assistant to the president, wrote that Bullis' letters would go straight through to the president unopened, and telephone calls would be transmitted with equal dispatch. On November 20, 1952, President Eisenhower wrote to thank Harry for recommending the names of several economists and for forwarding a copy of his remarks before a recent meeting of the board of directors of the Chamber of Commerce of the United States.

That speech, delivered in Washington on November 14, was a warning to businessmen "not to sell themselves down the river by getting too self-interested." The brave Mr. Bullis waded into a sensitive area when he continued: "Let's face the facts of our new opportunity. Some businessmen think everything now is hunkydory, just because Ike is moving into the White House. They think we can shut the economic-window that looks out on the world. They forget that the millions of people who wanted a change and put their hopes in our great leader—the same millions who decide whether our annual statements will be red or black—indirectly elected us business leaders to help the new president carry out their hopes for that change for the better."

The conservative National Chamber had usually opposed the administrations of Franklin D. Roosevelt and Harry S. Truman. In 1952, Bullis believed that businessmen could look forward to a more favorable climate for the risk system of profit and loss. But millions of working men and their families and white collar workers and their families would be waiting to see if there would be an improvement in the economic and international situation. Some of the businessmen in Bullis' audience undoubtedly shuddered when the stouthearted chairman of the board of General Mills dared to suggest that this vote of confidence might not be permanent—that the average voter in the nation might be saying, "Fail, and we will drag you out of this saddle and you can go back to walking for the rest of your lives."

Co-operation — with business, labor and government driving straight ahead for the benefit and welfare of everyone—was the theme of Bullis' message. Now, he said immediately after President Eisenhower's election, is the time to prove false the former public suspicion of big business—to demonstrate that the aims of business and the welfare of the American people are the same thing. He urged his fellow Chamber of Commerce directors not to be a group of "Agin-ers," but to help Ike in his effort to attain international harmony and to secure a more stable economic security for all, not for just a few Americans. Bullis pointed out that the millions of people who voted for President Eisenhower liked him personally. "They respect him. But he has to face the downbeat music of their mass economic doubt. They want to know about their jobs, their homes, their savings accounts and their sons of draft age."

Probably the most penetrating paragraph in that speech was the one in which Bullis reminded his audience of the election of 1932, which swept the Republicans out of the White House for a long, lean period of twenty years. "The masses suspected businessmen of being reactionary, against social progress, tarred with standpat philosophies, being isolationists in a time of need for worldwide thinking, and subscribers to their own selfish version of the profit system."

Bullis suggested that "tight credit" policies be enforced to check inflation and that taxes be reduced—slowly, carefully, prudently, to stimulate business activity and assure high productive employment. Bullis told the Chamber that trying to keep the budget balanced in the face of a slight recession will only make the recession worse. He referred to 1937 "when we almost had a balanced budget, yet we had over eight million Americans unemployed and our productive plant was operating at only sixty-seven per cent of its capacity." Thus spoke Bullis—"the measuring man"—fitting figures out of the past into the economic picture of yesterday, today and tomorrow.

Looking in every direction, 1952 was a terrific "bonanza year" for Harry Amos Bullis. His favorite candidate was elected president of this mighty land by an overwhelming flood of votes.

That was also the year when the former Countess Maria Smorczewska became a naturalized citizen of the United States of America. As soon as the five-year waiting period was over, Mrs. Bullis was ready to pledge allegiance to her adopted country. Harry noted in his diary on July 1, 1952, that he had attended the ceremony in Judge Joyce's courtroom in the Federal Building. On September 16, Harry reported proudly that he was not the only orator in the family: "Mrs. Bullis received her Certificate of Naturalization. She was a featured speaker at the large New Citizens Meeting at the Court House. I heard her speech."

In 1952, Harry Bullis became "a grandfather by marriage." When the Bullises heard that Mrs. Bullis' daughter-in-law was expecting a baby, they arranged for her to come to Minneapolis from South America so the child would be born an American citizen. Earlier in the year, Mrs. Bullis' daughter had come from London with her husband.

On May 28 Harry Bullis enjoyed the thrill of being a "Grandpa" at last. In a wonderfully heartwarming article, "God is My Senior Partner," which Harry wrote for The American Magazine in November, 1952, he counted the baby as one of the great blessings that God had sent him. "To be born under the American flag," he declared, "is today the world's greatest birthright. The little girl was born a few months ago, and my once rather stiff and silent house is lively now with the rich confusion and excitement a baby brings."

Inside General Mills in 1952 Leslie Perrin retired,

and Charles H. Bell was elected president. In the words of the chairman of the board, Harry Bullis, James Ford Bell's son was "the outstanding candidate among the young executives. Charles H. Bell has carried on with great efficiency the Bell tradition in General Mills." While he was the company's executive vice president, the younger Mr. Bell had toured all of the General Mills installations from coast to coast, spending months becoming personally acquainted with the people and plants. In July, 1952, Charles Bell started his "top echelon activities" by negotiating the acquisition of O-Cel-O, Inc., manufacturers of cellulose household sponges.

The mere act of reading about all of Harry Bullis' activities would tax the endurance of the average forty-hour-a-week person. General Mills business continued to be his chief occupation and avocation, involving speaking tours in which he addressed audiences of from two hundred to seven or eight hundred people—sometimes twice in one day. When the new "Betty Crocker's Picture Cook Book" came off the press, Harry took pride in sending a copy to Mrs. Dwight D. Eisenhower. General Mills was continuing its dynamic march ahead, with the Korean war situation bringing a wave of consumer buying.

A scholar as well as a businessman, Harry Bullis received the degrees of Doctor of Commercial Science from New York University in 1950 and Doctor of Laws from Macalester College in St. Paul in 1952—the third and fourth in a list that would add up to a round dozen during the next ten years.

On December 5, Mr. and Mrs. America opened

their newspapers and noted with personal gratification that President-elect Eisenhower had wasted no time fulfilling a major campaign promise. Somehow he had slipped out of the country and was suddenly pictured in the midst of a group of "tickled-looking" GIs in Korea.

On December 30, 1952, Harry Bullis received a letter from John J. McCloy who wrote, "Yesterday, Paul Hoffman and I were lunching with General Eisenhower and your name came up in the course of it. You would have been very pleased to have heard the nice things that were said about you. . . ."

By 1952, Harry Bullis had made hundreds of speeches that were unique in their point of view. Because there is nothing routine and ordinary about them, they deserve to be quoted liberally in many books instead of being compressed into the limited text of one biography. Many of the Bullis speeches have been published in small brochures which have been in great demand.

In 1952, Bullis became the author of his first hardcover book, "A Businessman Views a Changing World." In that small volume he proved his stature as a magnificent citizen of the nation and the world. In every way—mentally, physically and spiritually—he was in favor of flinging our windows open wide for the peace and good health of humanity.

"A Businessman Views a Changing World" originated from a series of five interviews early in 1952 on Dwight Cooke's radio program, "You and the World." Mr. Cooke believed that his Columbia Broadcasting System audience would be interested in hearing the views of a businessman on the complexities of our modern civilization. The choice of Harry Bullis showed visionary judgment on the part of Mr. Cooke, because Bullis was a man with a knack for analyzing departures from the "status quo."

On the dedication page Bullis champions the cause of "the many thousands of young men and young women who are struggling to achieve their hopes, ambitions and goals in every walk of life. If it helps a few of them to a better understanding of fundamental principles, it will have accomplished its purpose."

In the chapter on "Business and World Peace," Bullis emphasized the gigantic role that the American capitalist system must play in a tension filled world. Noting that war is outrageously costly, he said, "It is essential that we build up the economic and military strength of our own country and our allies. . . . Our free enterprise system depends on world peace for its continued existence."

In the chapter on "Business and Europe," Bullis said that the Marshall Plan idea should be extended to the Far East to help backward nations achieve independence in the world economy.

In "Business and Government," Bullis noted that "Freedom from government interference is a sacred American tradition," but he believes that we sometimes become "a bit muddleheaded about it." He invites the reader to open our history books and discover that "Right from the first Fourth of July, the United States government has been regulating our domestic and personal lives in some way."

On the other hand, he says, "American industry

today fears the galloping increase in controls that government is placing on our economic life. . . . Everyone knows that in our complex economic system someone has to make and enforce the rules of the game. . . . Once these rules are established, then the government's main function in the business field is ended. . . ."

Because he was mixed up in quite a bit of it himself, Bullis speaks as a man on familiar terms with labor: "It seems as though for the greater part of my career I have been working under a boss, so I consider myself a worker. I feel that I know the problems and aspirations of workers," he said in the section dealing with "Business and Labor."

Harmony between management and labor must be achieved or government will take over in order to keep things going. This did not mean that capital or labor should grovel to each other. "We must not be afraid of controversy between capital and labor. The only way to avoid controversy is to shackle our freedom. Without freedom there would be no controversy—and there would be no free labor unions or free business as we know them today."

In the stimulating chapter entitled "My Faith," Harry Bullis revealed once more that his steadfast communion with God is a "listening relationship." His faith gave him the power to expand his mind above and beyond the stifling confines of pettiness and despair. He starts right out with an apt evaluation: "It is fashionable today to be pessimistic — pessimistic about business, about public and private morals, about war—and even about God.

"I am unfashionable. I am an optimist about the future despite the hodge-podge of present conditions. My optimism is not the result of wishful thinking. . . . It has the toughest core any philosophy can possibly have. I believe in God. My mother, who was both a very religious and a very practical woman, taught me early in life that a man cannot go it alone in this world. He needs help. I have never found any reason to doubt what she told me."

Instead of merely hoping that everything would come out all right, he had a seven-point formula for solving major problems:

1. I consider with great care and patience all the evidence that I have in connection with the problem.

2. I then get the opinions of one or more interested persons. But I always hold this group to a very small number.

3. I pray daily for guidance to solve this problem.

4. Having done these things, I wrap up the problem, put it on the shelf and try to forget about it.

5. I watch for some sign of the voice of God during the next week or ten days. It usually comes out of a clear sky while I am talking with someone or taking a walk, or often when I am reading a book.

6. I follow what I believe to be God's prompting.

7. I then forget about every other possible solution to the problem.

When Bullis had followed this course, his efforts were crowned with success. Hesitation and doubt have inevitably brought complications. "In other words," he said, "I had to be tough-minded if my reliance on a hunch from God was to help me lick my problem."

Tough-mindedness and faith in God are completely compatible, Bullis believed. He affirmed Tolstoy's positive declaration, "Faith is the force of life." Being tough-minded about his faith had made Bullis self-confident and optimistic. "Tough-mindedness is an evidence of spiritual optimism, of self-respect and a belief in order and progress. It is comprised in part of a steadfast conviction that God is an orderly God, not a capricious force, and that God wants men and women to live full and successful and satisfying lives."

Pessimism, Bullis thought, is a departure from the bold, aggressive self-confidence of the pioneers. Pessimism makes men timid, too easily satisfied with the safety of a little security. "If everyone tried to play it safe in life and business, there would be no safety for anyone. The optimist always seems to have room in his plans for the other fellow—his optimism makes him more generous and more willing to do something for others."

Bullis' pessimist is easy to recognize, because everyone knows his counterpart. "Your worried pessimist, whether in industry or government or science, narrows his interest down to his own personal lot. He wants success merely for his own security. He cannot bring himself to include his fellow workers or neighbors or fellow citizens in his plans. He plays his cards so close to his chest that he gets nearsighted in regard to human values."

Bullis saw Communism as a pessimistic philosophy. By poisoning our American philosophy of life with pessimism and self-distrust, he said, the Communists are "hell-bent on banishing from men's minds any reliance on the supernatural and destroying any strength from prayer and any guidance from faith." Against this threat Bullis had the defense of the faith his mother taught him: "Very simply it is this—I believe that by prayer and by periods of listening silence we can learn the will of God. In these periods we can say with Samuel, 'Speak, Lord, for Thy servant heareth.'" He insisted, "It is just as possible for a businessman in his office to listen to God as it is for a man in a cloister."

Faith in God gives a man the spunk to speak in favor of "the ultimate decency of things" when everyone else is forecasting doom. Bullis' faith was not a blind one. He had grown up with it, achieving a spiritual maturity that gave him the courage and fortitude to see sunrise beyond the tempest.

The chairman of the board of General Mills had often said that he did not climb that step ladder to success by his own efforts. God had been his "Senior Partner."

Bullis drew no lines of "religious partisanship." His was the ecumenical spirit of the Good Samaritan. During a discussion about religion, the name of Pope John came into the conversation. Harry Bullis' voice was spontaneously exuberant as he exclaimed, "Isn't he wonderful — isn't he great!" He seemed to be thanking God for sending the benevolent pontiff who made "goodness" popular, when the world sorely needed legions of men who believed in "the ultimate decency of things." Pope John was an optimist too.

Chapter Eighteen

"Dear President Ike"

When President Dwight D. Eisenhower took the oath of office and delivered his inaugural address, Mr. and Mrs. Harry Bullis were seated near enough to feel personally involved in that major hour in history.

Early in 1953, after President Eisenhower had appointed Harold E. Stassen to the post of Mutual Security Director, Bullis was asked to head a five-man evaluation team to study the security situation on Formosa. The Formosa team was one of eleven groups of businessmen assigned to visit eleven countries.

In spite of the discomfort of multiple inoculations and a miserable attack of influenza en route, Harry Bullis was pictured smiling his way through Formosa. Because he wanted advice from top authorities, he had personally selected the men who accompanied him. They were: Dr. Raymond T. Moyer, former chief of the Mutual Security Mission to China and Formosa, and at that time with the Ford Foundation at Pasadena, California; Major General William A. Worton, Los Angeles, a retired Marine Corps general with years of experience in the Far East, and former chief of police at Los Angeles; Norman F. Allman, past consul at Shanghai and head of a former law firm in Shanghai, China, living in New York City; and Clinton Morrison, Minneapolis, major in Quartermaster Corps, U. S. Army, World War II, and an investment banker. The secretary of the team was John J. Capece, a government employee in Washington.

In the report to Harold Stassen, which Bullis spent many hours compiling in Honolulu and on the plane trip home, his evaluation team recommended that the United States pursue an "aggressive positive policy" with respect to Formosa. Bullis noted that a majority of businessmen were in favor of reducing foreign aid at that time, but he was very much opposed to abandoning Formosa to the Reds. He said it would be "economic and political nonsense of the most dangerous order."

Bullis and his team members met with numerous Taiwan businessmen and government officials. They toured the two hundred mile length of the country, visiting manufacturing plants, talking to farmers, and inspecting the troops and equipment on the Oriental island fortress.

There were two audiences with Generalissimo Chiang Kai-shek, the president of Nationalist China. When Bullis asked Chiang what he thought about the election of President Eisenhower, the Generalissimo's face lighted up. "Yes, I think it was a wonderful choice. It may even have hastened the passing of Joseph Stalin —certainly he had less to live for after your election."

The continuing broad range of Harry Bullis' interests included everything from 4-H Clubs and Junior Achievement to church and Sunday school activities. He was an organizer of the first Junior Achievement group in Minneapolis; and in 1953, he served as chairman of National Sunday School Week and National Bible Week.

As a founder of the present National Association of Manufacturers in 1933, he left an indelible mark as a liberal business leader on that conservative group. He must have made them like it, because he was saluted as N.A.M.'s man of the year in 1953.

In a speech entitled "Industry Must Speak" in 1936, Bullis told his fellow businessmen that there would be more co-operation between management and labor if employees were educated to an over-all picture of company activities. "Business is a little like the woman who had neglected to tell her husband that she had at an earlier time been a snake charmer. When he upbraided her for not telling him, she replied, 'But you never asked me.' "

In 1945, Harry took affectionate pleasure in presenting the N.A.M. charter membership certificate to "my good friend, John S. Pillsbury," who accepted it on behalf of the Pillsbury Company.

Bullis served for fifteen years as a director of the National Association of Manufacturers, from 1932 to 1947. During the last half of that time he also served as a National officer of the N.A.M. and made many speeches urging his colleagues to be vigilantly conscious of the needs of "this changing world."

As chairman of the board after 1948, Bullis kept

taking an active interest in the "miracles of General Mills."

New plants, new products, new methods—all kept adding up to new horizons of prosperity for General Mills. Marching toward the middle 1950's, Bullis was still presiding over the stockholders' meetings with a beaming smile; and he was also answering questions in "General Mills Horizons," the attractive magazine published for GMI stockholders. The employees were reading about the progress of the company in the excellent General Mills publication, "The Modern Millwheel."

In packages so colorful that they seemed ready to zoom off the shelf, new "wake-up" products were being introduced to breakfasting America. Said President C. H. Bell, "Our ready-to-eat cereals occupy a high rank in the total breakfast cereal business." With the company efficiently organized in seven divisions, he felt that General Mills was "geared for Tomorrow."

Perennially optimistic, Bullis radiated faith in the future in his frequent letters to President Eisenhower. In February, 1953, when he heartily endorsed President Ike's recommendations that direct wage and price controls be dropped immediately, Bullis reminded the president that this was not a new subject to them. In 1950, Bullis was one of fifty industrialists and bankers who attended an all-day session of the College Presidents' Conference in New York. "Barney Baruch and Dwight Eisenhower talked," Bullis said. "I debated with Baruch and opposed his 'Controls Clear Across the Board' idea." Bullis enjoyed recalling that Dr. Milton Eisenhower said he took on the "Champ" when he tackled Barney Baruch.

The "country boy from Council Bluffs" received an impressive number of invitations to dine at the White House. One of the famous "stag dinners" on June 22, 1953, was a tuxedo affair. The guests were greeted by both the President and Mrs. Eisenhower before the gentlemen withdrew to the State dining room.

During each of President Eisenhower's administrations, Bullis expressed himself at length on agriculture, business, and national and international trade and aid. He also remembered to wish "President Ike" a happy birthday, and he was probably one of the most anxious private citizens in the country during President Eisenhower's periods of illness. Both sides of the Bullis-Eisenhower correspondence have been preserved in Harry's "Eisenhower Scrapbooks."

When Bullis received a birthday message from the president, he noted that "President Ike" had a similar anniversary coming up one week later. "I know because I am just one week older than you to the day. That is the only thing in which I am ahead of the President of the United States!" He congratulated Eisenhower on a recent speech in which he "again brought to the American people the actual facts concerning our international relations."

In January Mr. and Mrs. Bullis were again invited to some special events in Washington. "D. E." enclosed a special message to Harry and Mary: "With the official invitation to the inaugural ceremonies which accompanies this letter comes also the hope that you will be the personal guests of Mamie and myself for the various functions to be held on January twenty-first." In the "Eisenhower Scrapbooks" are invitations to the pre-inaugural service, the inaugural ceremony, the inaugural festival, the gala inaugural concert, the inaugural parade and the inaugural ball—all bearing the words "Honored Guest."

It was a time for heartfelt rejoicing for two historic reasons. On September 25, 1955, the world had held its breath as it read the headlines. President Eisenhower, after playing twenty-seven holes of golf, had suffered "a mild coronary thrombosis," and political theorists wondered if he would be able to seek re-election in 1956.

Harry Bullis, who shared the discomforts of those who were dear to him, was stricken with deep personal anxiety. When he sent President Eisenhower the traditional birthday message on October 14, he referred to "the tremendous wave of appreciation and joy throughout the nation and the world that you are making such a rapid recovery from your recent illness. . . .

"Now we want you to relax and get well, and for the next few months enjoy with Mamie, that great partner of yours, the peaceful life of a gentleman farmer on that rolling country estate of yours at Gettysburg. A soldier, a five-star general, a university president, the President of the United States, and now just for a few weeks a farmer before you and Mamie return to the battlefield of Washington. You have earned this leave, Ike. Enjoy it to the fullest."

Mrs. Mamie Eisenhower replied on October 17, "I read your birthday letter to Ike on Friday morning. Both of us commented that rarely had he received such a fine and understanding note. We are grateful for your friendship and your thought of him."

After the Eisenhowers had appeared in the Twin Cities on October 16, 1956, Bullis wrote the President, ". . . Your visit has put new life into the Republican organization here, and everyone is now working with renewed enthusiasm for a Republican victory on November 6." In spite of that critical interlude, Eisenhower was heading up the campaign trail toward another colossal victory.

President Eisenhower often expressed his gratitude to Harry Bullis for his "unswerving support of administration policies." When the President wanted to launch his People-to-People Program in 1956, Bullis was one of the thirty-four American leaders invited to the first conference. Bullis became chairman of the business organization committee of the program and later served on the board of trustees of which Dwight Eisenhower was chairman, He also continued to be active on the national Crusade for Freedom committee. A number of General Mills executives, including Samuel Gale and Nate Crabtree, were instrumental in creating the Freedom Bell and arranging for General Mills balloons to drop free world information behind the Iron Curtain.

In 1953, at the request of an executive of the Eisenhower administration, Bullis inaugurated a committee for a national trade policy to promote world exchange and commerce. He served as vice chairman of that committee for several years.

In 1958 President Eisenhower appointed Harry Bullis to the important post of chairman of the International Development Advisory Board. As soon as the appointment had been confirmed by the United States Senate in 1959, the President named twelve members —distinguished leaders of American business, labor, agriculture and education—and the board became operative. Bullis noted that numerous meetings were held during 1959, but the crucial one occurred on September 17, 1959, when the board resigned en masse because Congress refused to provide any of the one hundred thousand dollars requested for the board's expenses. The board felt that its effectiveness would be hampered by this lack of congressional confidence in the program.

In 1958 Bullis was appointed a member of the Advisory Council on Public Assistance which published an exhaustive report in 1959.

In October, 1959, President Eisenhower chose Harry Bullis to head a three-man commission to choose a site for a government-sponsored World's Fair in 1964.

The three-man commission noted that 1964 was especially meaningful in the history of New York City. It would mark the 300th anniversary of the establishment and naming of the city and the fifteenth anniversary of its becoming the home of the United Nations. The chairman of the commission reported, with something like glee, that it had acted with streamlined dispatch. "The commission was appointed less than three weeks before making its report to the President, which he immediately accepted and which recommended that a 1964 World's Fair be held in New York City."

He and Mary attended a white tie state dinner at the White House on December 1, 1960. The ninety-four guests had "a wonderfully good time, filled with friendliness and nostalgia."

Harry recalled that "At 10:00 p.m. the Marine Corps orchestra started playing for dancing in the East Room. . . . While I had been in the White House many times, I achieved a first that evening by dancing in the East Room under the well-known large chandeliers. . . . It was a truly sentimental evening, with just a trace of sadness."

On August 22, 1958, Bullis wrote to "President Ike" about a thrilling visit to Abilene, Kansas. As Minnesota director for the Presidential Library, Bullis wanted to tour the Eisenhower Center in Abilene with some members of his committee and view the site for the library. In his group were Dr. Donald J. Cowling, president-emeritus of Carleton College; Senator Gerald T. Mullin, president of the Minneapolis Gas Company; Patrick Butler of St. Paul, mining and steel executive; and Nate L. Crabtree, director of public relations of General Mills.

Bullis rhapsodized about "the typical Kansas hospitality." Of the Eisenhower family home, he said, "It brought to mind many recollections of my youth when I lived in Council Bluffs, Iowa, which my brother and I fondly referred to as 'The Capital of the World.' " The Eisenhower brothers had insisted on keeping the family home just as it was, with the same kettles on the stove and the same old magazines and books in the living room.

By November, Bullis had announced the appointment of several additional committee members: H. H. Corey, Rudolph T. Elstad, Daniel C. Gainey, F. Peavey

Heffelfinger, Archibald Jackson and Harry Zinsmaster. Bullis also said that both Senator Hubert Humphrey and Senator Ed Thye would assist him as chairman of the state drive, indicating the non-partisan spirit of the campaign. The committee distinguished itself by making Minnesota the first state, except for Kansas, to go "over the top" in raising its Eisenhower library quota.

Bullis was among several citizens invited to tour the Eisenhower Museum with the President and Mrs. Eisenhower. The museum contains everything from Ike's high school diploma to the chair and table he used while planning the invasion of France.

October 13, 1959, was the day of the groundbreaking ceremony for the building which would become the magnificent new library, with its handsome wall mural depicting many of the dramatic moments in the life of President Eisenhower. On the cover of the Winter, 1959, issue of "General Mills Horizons" is a picture of President and Mrs. Eisenhower standing with Harry Bullis in front of the colorful wall. The Eisenhower Presidential Library has asked for the three Eisenhower-Bullis scrapbooks.

In his "groundbreaking" speech, the President expressed hope that scholars of the future would be concerned primarily with ideals, principles and trends that provide guides to a free, rich, peaceful future in which all peoples can achieve ever-rising levels of human well-being.

Harry and Mary Bullis had ridden the Union Pacific "Eisenhower Library Special Train" from Kansas City. Harry stayed to help Ike celebrate his birthday and then flew on to Washington with the President and Dr. Milton Eisenhower in the President's jet plane which took them half way across the country in slightly more than two hours.

Harry noted anxiously that Mary had caught a severe cold in the raw wind. Ill with pneumonia by the time she arrived back in Minneapolis, Mary was glad to reach a warm haven, the lovely Bullis country home at Charleston Acres, near Wayzata.

Chapter Nineteen

Championship Performance

After 1956, the Bullis address was no longer 2116 West Lake of the Isles Boulevard. Mary Bullis—like the great American cowboy of her adopted land—did not want to be "fenced in." It had started with a small summer place on seventeen acres near Wayzata, where Mary had loved to seek solitude, planting flowers and shrubs in the good earth and enjoying the company of birds, pheasants, chipmunks, and even an occasional deer. She had been accustomed to a large country estate in Poland, and Charleston Acres seemed to be "a little bit of old Poland" to her.

Harry Bullis had said, with a pleased grin, that Mary knew all along that they would make their permanent home in the country, but it took him three years to find it out. Now there is a spacious home on twenty-two acres of gently rolling land; and there is a small house over the stable that is an exact replica of a modest Polish cottage.

A skillful equestrienne from her childhood days, Mrs. Bullis wanted to live in a place where she could keep some horses. When her little granddaughter came for a visit, Mary Bullis made certain that she would have a pony and learn to ride while she was there. When the "animal population" at the Bullis country estate was at its highest count, there were four Arabian horses, two Shetland ponies, three dogs—and an enchanting Persian cat with a supercilious expression on its face.

Harry Bullis took pride in the attractive home at Charleston Acres and enjoyed being the expansive, congenial host when he and Mary entertained. However, his days and evenings were crowded with business, politics, and "human relations" interests.

Harry merited respect and admiration in every area in which he served. He believed in teamwork, enthusiastic co-operation, and esprit de corps—but not to the extent of bootlicking or compromising his convictions. In a mood of righteous indignation, he sometimes fumed, "I won't let them get by with this—it isn't right!" or, "This is an abuse of democratic freedom!" Bullis was a born dragon-slayer who could often convince the dragon that this was for his own good.

Many of Harry Bullis' greatest progressive speeches were addressed to chamber of commerce groups because he felt that their influence could rejuvenate musty reactionary traditions. From 1946 to 1958, Bullis was a director of the National Chamber of Commerce. During three of those years he was national vice president.

To be asked, just once, to become president of the National Chamber is an honor of rare distinction. In 1954, 1955, and 1956, the nominating committee urged the General Mills chairman to accept the office. After consultations with his fellow executives each time, he declined because of heavy company responsibilities. The major executives wanted Harry to continue as chairman of the board for several more years, he said.

Harry sounded almost wistful when he confided to Dr. Deane Malott, president of Cornell, in 1956: ". . . It is probably too much to expect that the nominating committee will offer me the same opportunity next year. However, if such a miracle should occur, I will say to you that I will accept. . . . Because, along with any other red-blooded American who is thankful for the many blessings which he has received as a citizen of the United States of America, I do want to make my contribution to my country and to our free enterprise system before taps are finally sounded."

Dr. Malott took "violent issue" with Harry's statement about wanting to make a contribution "before taps finally sounded." "Every day," he scolded affectionately, "you contribute to the country and the free enterprise system—by what you do, what you say, the leadership you exert, the traveling you do, the stimulation you give to others in your conversations. . . ."

While he served on the board of directors of the National Chamber, Bullis was a member of the executive committee, a chairman of the important committee on economic policy which published many bulletins, and a member of other chamber activities. He addressed many of the important annual meetings in Washington, D.C., and he served as chairman of the Canada-United States Chambers of Commerce groups. During his term as a director of the National Chamber, Harry Bullis also was a director and a vice president of the Minneapolis Chamber of Commerce.

One of Harry's finest speeches was the one called "The Showcase of Democracy" which he delivered as an introduction to an address by Dr. Lawrence M. Gould, the distinguished president of Carleton College, before delegates to the Junior Chamber of Commerce International World Congress convening in Minneapolis in 1958.

He asked the delegates who were seeing the United States for the first time to look into our showcase and see the fruits of production in this consumer's paradise—the television sets, the automatic washing and drying machines, the new cars thronging the streets. "Look at our 'spiritual showcase,'" he said. "We have more churches per capita than any other nation in the world. . . . More important, they are well attended." There were the schools we were building and the modern houses, to say nothing of the "glittering gems" that our supermarkets are. "Nowhere in the world is a nation better nourished and better fed."

Back of a recent honor that gave Harry Bullis "the thrill of a lifetime" were decades of loyalty and dedication. "For many years I've been on the committee to choose the Wisconsin Alumnus of the Year. As soon as I retired, they chose me!" he sputtered, trying to conceal the emotion he felt.

The salute from his beloved alma mater proclaims: "This Citation for Distinguished Service is awarded to Harry A. Bullis, Wisconsin Alumnus of the Year, for his inspirational leadership in the fields of industry and public service; for his dedication to furthering the

American ideal and the free enterprise system; for his strength of purpose which has served as a shining example for countless Wisconsin alumni; for his unbounded energy in contributing to the enrichment of the University of Wisconsin."

In June, 1935, Bullis had been elected to the board of directors of the Wisconsin Alumni Association. As president of the Alumni Association in 1936 he fought Governor Philip LaFollette's attempts to control the University of Wisconsin by "packing" the Board of Regents and trying to oust Dr. Glenn Frank as president of the university. There is a plaque on Bascom Hall on the campus of the University of Wisconsin, and Harry knew its inscription by heart:

"Whatever may be the limitations which trammel inquiry elsewhere, we believe that the great State University of Wisconsin should ever encourage that continual and fearless sifting and winnowing by which alone the truth can be found."

Harry often emphasized that "we should think in positive terms of freedom to embrace knowledge and truth, for knowledge and truth are elements which banish fear."

"Politics must not control the university," Alumni President Bullis insisted in the October 1936 issue of "The Wisconsin Alumnus." He pointed out that it would be tragic if political expediency were to dictate the interpretation of history, the freedom to discuss contemporary affairs, and the pursuit of truth in research. He believed that no political party—whether Republican, Democratic or Progressive — should attempt to control the appointments and policies of the university.

While the packed LaFollette Board of Regents ousted Dr. Glenn Frank as president of the university, Bullis believed that the unfavorable publicity, aroused during the trial of Dr. Frank, helped to defeat Governor LaFollette at the next election.

Bullis helped to double the membership of the Wisconsin Alumni Association during his first fourteen months as president by organizing a good promotion program. He reached out with a long arm toward the graduates of his alma mater, mailing letters far and wide. He chuckled about one resulting episode. A doctor and his new wife, living next door to the Bullis home on Lake of the Isles Boulevard, had just returned from a honeymoon trip around the world. They said to Bullis one night over the fence, "Harry, do you know you are known in Moscow?"

"Moscow, Iowa?" Bullis inquired.

"No. Moscow, Russia." They explained that a chance encounter in Moscow, Russia, had led to a dinner invitation from Ambassador Joseph Davies, a Wisconsin alumnus, and his wife.

During the course of the meal, Ambassador Davies asked Dr. Strauchaeur, "Do you know Harry Bullis in Minneapolis?"

They said they lived right next door to the Bullises.

"Well," said the ambassador, "I have just received a letter from Harry asking for one hundred dollars for the Wisconsin Alumni Association."

"Well, you'd better send him the one hundred dollars," the Minneapolis doctor advised.

The ambassador replied, "Knowing Harry Bullis as well as I do, I have already sent him my check for one hundred dollars."

"You see," Bullis' neighbor said, "you are well known in Moscow, Russia."

As a founding member of the University of Wisconsin Foundation in 1945, Bullis immediately began serving as a director and as first vice president. The foundation has built the Wisconsin Center on the campus and has established many scholarships and several distinguished professorships. Since 1949 it has made grants to the school totaling over thirty-five million dollars, including annual grants for research and new buildings.

Bullis was active as one of the ten eminent Wisconsin alumni who composed the board of trustees of the Wisconsin Alumni Research Foundation. "WARF grants-in-aid have played a significant role in development of the university's widely recognized research efforts; they have stimulated or 'primed' many valuable grants from other sources, and attracted outstanding scholars to Wisconsin."

In countless forums where the progress and enrichment of education have been promoted, Harry Bullis has been among those present. On August 26, 1953, he became a director of a new non-profit corporation called the Council for Financial Aid to Education, Inc. Organized by Alfred Sloan, Irving Olds, and Frank Abrams, it is supported by four principal foundations. Its objective is to encourage business corporations and individuals to provide financial support for institutions of higher learning.

Bullis also believed that industry should become conscious of elementary education. In the early 1950's he spoke enthusiastically about General Mills' program of basic economics teaching integrated into the social studies courses. "The results have been astonishing. We have proved that youngsters in the fourth, fifth and sixth grades can understand and appreciate such basic economic concepts as freedom of choice, the importance of investments, the function of capital, and the production miracle of industry and labor working together. . . . It is the story of America, of achievement under freedom, and under the economic climate which our founding fathers said was our endowment from our Creator."

In many addresses, Bullis urged industry to "invest" in higher education. When he spoke on "Increased Corporate Aid for Higher Education as a Sound Business Investment" at the University of Akron in 1962, he congratulated Akron industry on its support of educational programs. However, he believed that industry in general, elsewhere, was not contributing as much as it should and could.

Bullis made thousands of statements that might be classified under the title of "An Educated Electorate: The Hope for Human Survival." In a 1962 article of that title he made the point that news media and parents and teachers should work together to banish the demand for mediocre entertainment and strive to produce "an electorate which wants to read about, listen to, and see TV material on the stakes of life or death for civilization."

Interest in education had made Bullis an active

trustee on the boards of two Methodist institutions, Hamline University in St. Paul, Minnesota, and Simpson College in Indianola, Iowa.

When this new businessman—this herald of the future—delivered the opening address at the Fourth National UNESCO Conference in Minneapolis in 1953, he referred to UNESCO's program "as one of world-wide slum clearance—to wipe out physical and spiritual slums in order to free the bodies and minds of men from squalor, hopelessness and raging intolerance."

In 1961, at the invitation of University of Michigan President Harlan Thatcher, Harry Bullis joined a small group, which included Sir Arnold Toynbee and George Romney, at Fair Lane, the former home of Henry Ford, Senior. The group recommended that the University of Michigan should use Fair Lane as Arden House is being used—for adult education assemblies.

In a stirring speech at the annual meeting of the Wisconsin Alumni Association on June 2, 1962, Harry Bullis had advocated the formation of a "University of the Later Years." Soon after, he became the chairman of the newly organized Oliver Wendell Holmes Association which is described as "A New Adventure in Higher Learning: Emeriti Professors and Emeriti Laymen." It recognizes "the need to provide opportunity for those whose business and professional careers are largely behind them, to continue learning for learning's sake and to make education a lifelong experience."

Among Harry Bullis' papers are many vitally significant commencement addresses. He had been awarded the honorary degree of Doctor of Laws by the University of Wisconsin, Macalester College, Creighton University, Jamestown College, Hamline University, Simpson College, the University of Chattanooga, Occidental College and the University of Akron. From Simpson College he also received a doctorate in Business Administration, from New York University the degree of Doctor of Commercial Science, and from Rockford College the degree of Doctor of Humane Letters.

The list of city, state, national and international organizations in Harry Bullis' life has been phenomenal. Because he took his responsibilities seriously each could fill a fascinating chapter in a book. He had been both an active and an honorary Rotarian. He was elected as a general trustee of the National Trust for Historic Preservation when it was formed in Washington in 1946.

Bullis served as a member of the Salvation Army advisory board since 1952. For years he was a member of the national advisory committee for CARE. He was a director of the Fund for Adult Education, sponsored by the Ford Foundation, from 1953 to 1961. In 1961, he served as chairman of the Minneapolis area Sumner H. Slichter Fund Committee, honoring the noted Harvard economist.

The Minneapolis industrialist was elected treasurer and a member of the board of trustees of the National Planning Association in 1951. That same year he was also elected a member of the National Industrial Conference Board. He served as a member of the board of trustees of The Farm Foundation from 1948 until 1958. In 1954 and 1955 he was a member of the Task Force on Overseas Economic Operations for the Hoover Commission.

It was a great day for 4-H Clubs all over the nation when Minnesota's T. H. "Dad" Erickson was brought into General Mills, Inc. and told to write and develop programs for the benefit of the 4-H Clubs that he loved so well. On June 18, 1958, Harry Bullis was invited to the National 4-H Conference in Washington to receive a special citation:

"For his sincere interest in and strong support of 4-H through the national dairy and food preparation awards programs and for his service to club members and local leaders through arranging for his firm's employment of T. A. Erickson. Erickson's 4-H booklets have far-reaching influence in helping young people become good citizens and lead happy, useful lives."

In July, 1961, Bullis became a charter member of the advisory council of the International Movement for Atlantic Union, Inc. In October, 1961, he was elected a member of the board of trustees of the Center for International Economic Growth. Early in 1962, he served as president of the Freedom from Hunger Foundation which listed Adlai Stevenson, Eleanor Roosevelt and other leading Americans on its board of trustees.

Harry Bullis was selected to be the first honorary marshal of the Minneapolis Aquatennial in its twenty-two year history. When he and Mary Bullis rode at the head of the Aquatennial parade on July 15, 1961, it was the first time Harry had been in a parade since he had led that company of Washburn Crosby ex-soldiers from World War I up Nicollet Avenue in 1920.

One development is apparent. After Harry Bullis' retirement from General Mills was announced late in December, 1958, the latent tide of chairmanships and offices of distinction came flooding in, as though at a signal. As his old friend, S. Marshall Kempner, observed in a 1961 letter, "he does three men's work each day."

When he was asked why he continued to be so active with various organizations after his "retirement," he said, "I am so thankful for the opportunities which have come to me that I want to spend the rest of my life in public service endeavoring to make a contribution to the United States of America and to the free enterprise system for all the blessings I have received."

On the night of December 22, 1958, when Bullis' associates honored him at a testimonial dinner on the occasion of his retirement, Charles H. Bell was host for the evening and Orson Bean, famous humorist, appeared on the program. The hilarious feature of the evening was a skit depicting the struggles and triumphs in the career of one of the last "true Horatio Alger heroes," Harry Bullis.

Bullis smiled broadly and enjoyed "kidding" back and forth with his chief, James F. Bell, with Charles Bell, Gerald Kennedy, and all the colleagues who had been a familiar part of his life for many years. Referring to Gerald "Spike" Kennedy, who was acting as emcee, Bullis said, "Even though he has ribbed me and exposed parts of my past to your wholesome sense of humor, and let me add to my own amusement as well as yours, and even though in these latter years he always beats me at golf, nevertheless he has been one of my best friends for a third of a century, and I congratulate the board of directors on their wisdom in electing him. I said to the directors this morning that I do not know of anyone I would rather have take my place than Spike."

Thus Gerald Kennedy, an Irish lad from St. Thomas College in St. Paul and a World War I veteran who had served his apprenticeship in the Buffalo plant, succeeded Harry Bullis as chairman of the board.

During that "swan song" speech, Harry remarked, "I noticed running through a large part of the program this evening, as a sort of theme, was my personal motto, 'Drive Straight Ahead with a Positive Mental Attitude.' My good wife Mary has often kidded me about that motto," he said. "The other day she asked me to hang a plaque in our amusement room. She handed me a hammer and nail and said, 'Now drive that nail Straight Ahead with a Positive Mental Attitude.' Incidentally, the plaque read, 'The opinions expressed by the husband in this house are not necessarily those of the management.' "

Bullis expressed his esteem for many of his close associates. Recalling the day in 1919 when he first met James F. Bell, he said that he sensed then, and later learned from experience, that he is "a big man in every way." "It can well be said that General Mills is the lengthened shadow of a great man—James F. Bell."

At the conclusion of his speech, Bullis had the last word about that motto. "Gentlemen, good night, a Merry Christmas, Happy New Year, and, oh yes, just one last thought—Drive Straight Ahead with a Positive Mental Attitude!"

Bullis was presented that night with a fine antique silver tazza made in England in 1710, and a handsome bronze plaque inscribed with an inspiring tribute to Harry Bullis which said in part: ". . . . The organization will miss the eternal optimism and unfailing urge to progress which he radiates, the loyalty and devotion and generous outpouring of his rare personality in many accomplishments. He has paid the price. He has earned the overflowing respect, honor and affection of his associates. . . ."

Press, radio and television representatives gathered the next day to interview Harry Bullis about his retirement as chairman of the board of General Mills.

Chapter Twenty

"This Guy Bullis"

It was typical of Harry Bullis to get in touch with me as soon as my publisher notified him that I would be writing his biography for the Men of Achievement series. Reading his first letter I was amazed at the outpouring of his friendly personality.

Here was a distinguished businessman who had opened a copy of my Charles F. Kettering biography the evening before and had read it all before he went to sleep. "Mr. Kettering," Harry Bullis wrote, "has always been one of my heroes. I had the pleasure of hearing him speak several times. One of the attributes that I always enjoyed about Mr. Kettering was that in addition to being one of America's inventive geniuses he had a delightful sense of humor."

In that letter Harry broke the news to me about the gigantic collection of a hundred scrapbooks dealing with his multiple activities, which his secretaries had been compiling over the years. "In my opinion," Mr. Bullis wrote in that first letter, "you should plan to spend a week or ten days in Minneapolis going over these scrapbooks."

It may be assumed that I have had opportunities to write Men of Achievement biographies about international figures who have been in the headlines more often than Harry Bullis had, but I leaped at the opportunity to write the story of his life. I knew that he had performed with distinction as president and chairman of the board of General Mills. But it was the other side of "this fellow Bullis"—he often referred to himself in the third person—that intrigued me. This gentleman—whose honors included the "American Success Story" plaque which was awarded to him in 1957 by the Free Enterprise Awards Association—sounded as though he must indeed be an extraordinary businessman.

In the January 23, 1954 issue of "The Saturday Review," Leo Cherne had written a profile called "Harry A. Bullis: Portrait of the 'New Businessman,'" in which he had quoted that devastating speech Harry delivered to the board of directors of the United States Chamber of Commerce immediately after President Eisenhower's election: "Let's not sell ourselves down the river by getting too self-interested. . ." he had said.

Here was an amazingly successful leader of a great enterprise telling Mr. Cherne for publication that "Complaints about government frequently depend upon whose ox is being gored. You have to be larger than the personal interest of your own company or your own pocketbook. . . . The worker is not only a member of the productive team, but also the great American customer. Some of the old war horses in industry haven't learned this, but the intelligent businessman has known it for some time."

Here was an opportunity for me to tackle some

provocative questions that Mr. Cherne had posed back in 1954: "What made him this way? Why is he Bullis, not Babbitt, even though, as he moves forward, the shadows of Babbitt, Dodsworth, and Jefferson Selleck dance around him? Unfortunately, the mainspring of a man's drive must remain a mystery. What makes a successful businessman is the subject for a social scientist's speculation. What gives him international perspective is anybody's guess."

It might be concluded that "the new businessman," as typified by Harry Bullis, is stimulated by the complete panorama of history, as much as by the daily items of business on his desk. For some indefinable reason he was born with an overpowering sense of creative curiosity. He wanted to analyze everything, including himself, and the analysis led to the conclusion that there was always room for improvement—and that improvement was both practical and possible. Trying to explain "what made him that way" merely leads back to another question. What is the origin of any unusual talent? Harry Bullis approached life from a creative point of view; he poured the powers of his genius into General Mills with all the intellectual dexterity of an artist at his easel, concentrating on the present masterpiece but entirely alive to everything outside the boundaries of that canvas. To the true artist, the world and all infinity are part of the landscape he paints. References to the hungry world beyond our boundaries, and our prospects for space exploration, were a part of this miller's everyday language.

"Of course man will get to the moon!" he told me. Even his faith had progressive overtones. It was not lessened by his belief that God had become Universal, as man's knowledge of the universe had expanded.

"The Saturday Review" for March 24, 1962, featured a review of Harry's "free enterprise classic," "Manifesto for Americans," published by McGraw-Hill. Reviewer Kytle's description of Harry Bullis was perfect: "It may be hard to picture Harry A. Bullis on a Wheaties carton. There is, nevertheless, much about him that bears an inescapable resemblance to the goodness of his company's favorite product. He neither smokes nor drinks; at seventy he is still trim, robust, glowing . . . he has the champion's philosophy—'Drive straight ahead with a positive mental attitude.' "

Mr. Kytle deserves cheers for pointing out that ". . . the fact that there are businessmen like Harry Bullis needs to be better understood, not only by critics of business in the U. S. but most particularly by leaders of rising young countries overseas," and " 'Manifesto for Americans' can do much to correct the unpopular image of U. S. business abroad. Let's hope the U.S.I.S. makes the most of it."

The New York Times reviewer, Louis M. Hacker, said, "His book is as sound as a nut. 'Manifesto for Americans' demonstrates that he is a man of intelligence, truly devoted to freedom, and desirous of expanding the reach and effectiveness of the free world."

Mr. Hacker suggested, however, that Mr. Bullis had not been active enough "in those arenas of debate and contest where the policies that fundamentally affect our nation are determined."

The brave Mr. Bullis had not hesitated to denounce Senator Joseph McCarthy's "unwarranted attacks" and "abuses." And then there were all those Marshall Plan speeches and hundreds of others in which he appealed for harmony between business and labor and a better understanding and appreciation of the free enterprise system. Wanting to share his ideas for a better world, Bullis published many of those speeches in small brochures and sent them out to people he hoped would read them.

In the final analysis, it will be ascertained that Harry Bullis did "associate himself with that fight for freedom about which he speaks so knowledgeably and eloquently." Perhaps he put his finger on the difficulty when he said in one of his speeches, ". . . We businessmen do tell our story, but usually we tell it to other businessmen. This probably accounts for the recent article in 'Fortune' which says in effect, 'You dopes—you're talking to yourselves!' " That was the arena in which Harry Bullis operated, and it will be left to history to judge whether or not he had the biggest dragon of all by the tail.

There are many splendid reactions to "Manifesto for Americans" in Harry Bullis' scrapbooks—most of them from editors, educators, and people in politics. Francis C. Pray of the Council for Financial Aid to Education wrote: ". . . Your advice to educators who seek business support certainly is sound. . . . But I think I enjoyed most your chapter 'One World.' . . ." William Benton of "Encyclopedia Britannica" told Harry, "You are a great leader. Very few in the business community can rival you. I congratulate you on your statesmanship—and your courage. . . ." Norman Cousins, the editor of "The Saturday Review," assured

Harry that "It is one of the most stimulating forthright and affirmative surveys and prospects that I have seen. I might add that it is an extremely clear and readable work, free of obfuscation and of the compulsion to parade knowledge."

In his letter, Dr. Milton Eisenhower was especially interested in the chapter on education. Lester Pearson wrote from Ottawa where he was Leader of the Opposition at that time, "You will know how much I have valued our work and association together in the cause which we both support, some of which you deal with so effectively in your book."

There are pages and pages of highly quotable observations. All of the reviewers agreed that it should be widely read.

"Manifesto for Americans" should be on the required reading lists of all the young people who will decide our country's future and our position in the world leadership arena.

Executives and management people should read "Manifesto for Americans" so they will be able to explain themselves. "Manifesto for Americans" analyzes capitalism in a manner that makes an American proud to be a citizen of a free enterprise nation, with its dynamic potential for the propagation of an abundant economy in an enlightened World of Tomorrow.

Anyone who attempts to quote "the best portions" of "Manifesto for Americans" would need to copy the entire book! Here can be found Bullis' definition of a successful man: "I think it is fair to say that a human being is a success when he uses his life well and contributes something good to his fellows; when he leaves behind him no residue of unhappiness, no dissipated energy or underdeveloped talent, and when he thus achieves for himself inner peace and deep satisfaction."

When Harry Bullis spoke about "Manifesto for Americans" on KUOM, the University of Minnesota station, in March, 1962, he continued to "plug" for the free-choice economic system: In wondering what sort of manifesto Marx would write today, he noted, "We are not a socialist state, and yet we are advancing welfare legislation even while we safeguard a mainly privately owned economy. I believe we should try to persuade Russia and mainland China to accept the virtues of this revolutionary creation."

Erect and undaunted, Bullis waded into the Cuban question during that same radio address. "Let us look at the example of Cuba. For too long the desperate hunger and need of ninety per cent of the Cubans was ignored. Americans passed by on the other side of the street—except when we made money on deals with Batista. . . ."

One of his major themes in "Manifesto" is freedom, which he emphasized is "indivisible." "It is impossible to preserve our political freedom if economic freedom is suppressed—whether for capital's benefit by irresponsible profit-taking or for labor's benefit by irresponsible and wasteful work rules, or for the state's convenience by confiscatory taxes and unreasonable government controls. . . ."

Bullis told me that education became one of his hobbies, "because I had such a long, drawn-out, difficult time in completing my formal education." In the chapter called "Education: The Race for Inner Space,"

Bullis said, "Our future will be decided not in outer space but in inner space, the space between the ears. . . . We are faced with a national emergency now in education; we are lagging behind that part of the world we cannot describe as free. . . ."

In the chapter entitled "One World," Bullis declared emphatically that "No single existing international or supranational institution is so important to peace and understanding as the United Nations. Its miraculous power for good lies in the fact that delegates from even the smallest nations can stand up and speak. . . ."

Retirement did not lessen Harry Bullis' interest in the business of General Mills. He continued to attend the board of directors' and stockholders' meetings regularly and kept in touch with his colleagues.

On May 7, 1961, not many weeks before the founder of General Mills died, Harry took some color pictures of James Ford Bell in his garden. Harry also recalled, "I had talked over the telephone with Mr. Bell at his home about three days before his death. . . . I did my best to 'pep' him up, but it was evident that he had almost run his course."

Bullis, who worked closely with James F. Bell for so many decades, paid tribute to the man who had employed him in 1919: "His fairness, his intuitive insight into the emotions of people and his practice of spreading to others the fruits of his constructive ability enabled him to establish a good morale and to win a high degree of personal loyalty among his executives and employees. He was the greatest businessman I have ever known." Bullis considered it appropriate that the impressive new General Mills Research Center is named in honor of the illustrious James F. Bell, a leader with "a strong scientific and research outlook."

Charles H. Bell was elected chairman of the board of General Mills in December, 1961, after the retirement of Gerald Kennedy. General Edwin W. Rawlings, U. S. Air Force, retired, became the sixth president of General Mills.

Harry kept up communications with the new executives, often extending compliments on the continued high rate of progress within the company. In a letter to Charles Bell on August 22, 1962, Bullis marveled at "another demonstration of our modern age" when the stockholders' meetings at New York, Boston, Detroit, Chicago and San Francisco were conducted through a private network broadcast originating in Minneapolis on August 21. ". . . In other words, for the first time, you completed the formal stockholder meeting and six informal stockholders' meetings all in one afternoon. . . . You, President Ed Rawlings, and Vice President Nate Crabtree deserve the highest praise for the success of this pioneering achievement."

This paragraph in on his early letters endeared Harry Bullis to me: "If you should come to Florida before February 21 when we leave for Minneapolis, I shall be glad to meet you and have you 'size up' this guy Bullis! Since I voluntarily lost thirty pounds during the last two years, when I am taking long walks in my bathing suit on the sand by the ocean, I see myself in every old retired man with tall thin legs who is walking on the beach. . . ."

After that delightful introduction, I was happy to

have an opportunity to meet Mr. and Mrs. Harry Bullis in Palm Beach one day in February. There was that moment of instant recognition in the hotel lobby and the warmth of instant friendship. I was immediately drawn into the charmed circle of those two vividly interesting people, Mary and Harry Bullis.

After lunch, Harry and I strolled up and down the street of entrancing shops while Mary went shopping. Harry began to talk about many of the episodes in his life—about his service in the army, his experiences overseas, and his marriage to Irma Alexander. He talked a great deal about Mary and spoke of how much she and her family meant to him.

When Mary came out of Bonwit Teller, she had shopped for a lovely gift for me. I discovered that this was typical of Mary and Harry.

While he was driving us around Palm Beach, Harry mentioned the motto that had been his lifelong guide to success: "Drive Straight Ahead with a Positive Mental Attitude." I couldn't resist telling him he'd better not drive straight ahead at that point or we'd end up in the ocean.

As life would have it, I had never seen the Atlantic Ocean before. Harry immediately decided that I should see seventeen miles of it, so he took the ocean road down to Delray Beach. The conversation was spirited all the way. The liveliness of his anecdotes did not interfere with Harry's skill as a driver.

While we were having tea at their apartment at The Talbot, Harry began to talk about their country place at Wayzata. He often described it as "Mary's Animal

Farm," and teased Mrs. Bullis by adding, "and Bullis is one of the animals!"

"Harry, you must not say such things!" Mary would reprove him, worried perhaps that it might get into a book some day.

Harry spoke with great pride of Mary's skill as a horsewoman. Picking up the Fall issue of "Harp and Hound," published by The Irish Wolfhound Club of America, he told of a dramatic moment at the 1962 Arabian Horse Show in Minneapolis. "All of a sudden," he exclaimed with a wave of his long arm, "these beautiful characters came dashing into the arena!" On the cover of "Harp and Hound" was a picture entitled "In Days of Yore." It was a reproduction of a hunting scene described in "The Richest Hours of the Duc de Barry." The book is in the Musee Conde and Mrs. Bullis has a copy. Authentically impersonating Blance de Montferrat, gowned in a velvet costume from "the days of yore," Mrs. Bullis was riding her beautiful Arab, Bonnie. Miss Helen Dalton, who wore the costume of the Duc de Barry, was riding Bonnie's daughter, Naja. Their page, in jerkin and hose with a plume in his hat, was played by Macalester College student, Jim McComb. McComb was holding two handsome Irish Wolfhounds, one of which was Mrs. Bullis' champion, Hillaway's Finnbar. As in "olden times," the wolfhounds wore antique collars and were held by real chains, according to the story in "Harp and Hound."

After a completely congenial afternoon during which I came to realize how much I would enjoy writing about "this guy Bullis," Mary and Harry returned me to my motel. We parted with mutual feelings of good cheer about our anticipated reunion in Minneapolis.

Shortly after they had started back, I was mortified to realize that I had left my glasses in the Bullis' apartment when I was reading about Mary in "Harp and Hound." Although I called Harry and told him most emphatically to send my glasses to my home address—I would be leaving on a flight later that night and had a substitute pair at home—he insisted on getting into the car and driving all the way up to Palm Beach, after dark, for the third round-trip that day.

Mary had even sent some fruit along for me to eat on the way home. "Harry," I blurted out, "you needn't have done this. I thought you were wonderful already!"

Instead of a reprimand, he said quite solemnly, "Everybody makes mistakes. I'm glad to know you're human like the rest of us."

I was flabbergasted!

On that first day Harry Bullis had talked at length about the Council on World Tensions in which he was deeply engrossed. Here was his international forum for the propagation of the ideas he had often expressed in his speeches, brochures and books.

In 1959, Bullis was elected chairman of World Brotherhood. He said he took a critical look at that name and got it changed at the first meeting because "Business corporations are reluctant to support 'do-gooder' organizations." In this rapidly fluctuating world, "Council on World Tensions" was a more appropriate name. Harry invested much time and personal money in this "labor of love," as did many other distinguished members of the organization. The Council on World Tensions is supported by contributions from foundations, corporations and individuals.

According to the descriptive folder Bullis prepared in 1962: "The Council on World Tensions is a private organization conducting high-level, university-centered studies and conferences on practical steps toward peace, based on better economic and social conditions for all people. . . ."

Among the "responsible men and women of the highest caliber" who participate as directors of the council are: Lester B. Pearson, Konrad Adenauer, Paul Hoffman, Vijaya Lakshmi Pandit, Carlos P. Romulo, Paul-Henri Spaak, Adlai Stevenson, Everett Clinchy, Margaret Grant, and other international figures.

In 1960, Chairman Harry Bullis attended the three-day conference at the University of Chicago and then traveled with Dr. Everett Clinchy, president of the council, to Geneva, Switzerland, where they attended the two-day session.

A 1961 conference was held at the University of Minnesota, and then Mr. and Mrs. Bullis went to the conference at Oxford University. Harry's imagination was stirred by the black delegates from the newly-formed African nations who came dressed in their red and blue robes and speaking perfect English. Most of them were graduates of either Oxford or Cambridge.

After the week-long conference, Harry flew back to the United States. Mary presently joined her friend, Mrs. Rena Goldsbury, for a tour of France and Switzerland.

Harry Bullis traveled with Dr. Clinchy to the 1962 Conference on World Tensions which was held at the University of Bahia in Salvador, Brazil. The next World Conference will be held in Kuala Lumpur, Malaya.

"What do we hope to accomplish with these World Conferences? Well," said Harry Bullis, "the delegates, many of them at war with each other, find out by living with each other for a week that they make just as much noise eating soup as the other fellow! By helping them understand a little better the other fellow's problems, we hope to have the old world move just a little farther along the road to world peace!"

When he was in South America he prowled around behind the handsome facades on the luxury streets and surveyed with horror the squalor and distress of the impoverished, who seem to be punished for being born.

"Tensions," Bullis often declared, "are not all undesirable. They can lead to constructive advances in human society. Out of tension and competition can come the stimulation for growth, the prodding for progress, and the prompting for invention. Out of the dangerous pressures that are today forced upon us we will be driven to build a better world or to destroy ourselves. The building of a better world can come as we learn to use our powers of creation and direction to manage the tensions we must face. It is not reasonable to expect or to wish to eliminate tensions; the realistic objective must be the control and guidance of the energies created by these tensions into constructive channels."

On March 14, Harry wrote that he had attended a

rather strenuous session of the 19th Annual White House Conference for The Advertising Council. He had been invited to the conferences all through the Eisenhower and into the Kennedy administrations. The president and vice president, and most of the cabinet members, were on the program. Some of Bullis' comments included: "As usual, McNamara made the best impression of any of the participants. . . . While I am a Republican and outside of Dillon and McNamara they were all Democrats, I could not help but have the feeling that the men in high places in our present administration are all dedicated Americans doing their very best to cope with the problems of the times. . . ."

A "Resolution of Appreciation" was presented to Harry Bullis when he attended his last Northwest Bancorporation board of directors meeting on March 28, 1963, after sixteen years of lively participation. One of the gratifying highlights of his career as a "Banco enthusiast" was his selection as a "Banco Man of the Year." His beaming smile lighted up the cover of the "Banco Yearly Times" for 1961. Grace Dwight, Banco Times editor, collected vivid impressions about Harry from a wide circle of acquaintances.

Harry said that he hadn't played much golf lately because his score was too high. One uproarious paragraph in "Banco Times" described Harry's extraordinary approach to the game: "As a golfer, Bullis leaves nothing to be desired, if you are interested in a relaxed, informal, sociable game. His opponents usually have to watch his score, for he is absent-minded about counting and will needlessly add a stroke or two to his score if there is any question in his mind. He has been known to do rather unorthodox things on a golf course, such as playing with a red ball in the snow, or joining up with a foursome. With his penchant for doing bold things he once agreed to a proposition where five men teed off at the same time, and the one who got to the hole first, regardless of the number of strokes, was the winner. Reports are that Bullis drove straight down the fairway, through balls flying in all directions, and got to the hole first. Though he took about 22 strokes, he won and his attitude was positive all the way."

In the letters section of Banco Times, General Eisenhower wrote: "Harry Bullis is one of the truly dedicated men of our country. . . . I am fortunate to consider myself his warm personal friend." His esteemed associate on the Council of World Tensions, Paul G. Hoffman, wrote that Harry "richly merits this tribute. No American I know has devoted himself more unselfishly to promoting international understanding and also understanding of the American economic system."

I was looking forward to seeing the Bullises again. When Harry met me at the Twin Cities airport, he was a bit more pale than he had been when I had seen him in Florida, but I knew that he had suffered a short period of illness after he arrived home.

At the Woman's Club, Mary Bullis was waiting to welcome me to my suite of rooms. Beautifully furnished as they were, she had added many delightful items to contribute to my comfort and convenience. Mary had been ill too. Coming back on the train—as usual—from Florida, she had gotten off for a few minutes in Chicago, taken a deep, deep breath of the piercing winter air, and in a flash—pneumonia again.

In the large sitting room with its spacious work table I had my first glimpse of the mammoth collection of Bullis scrapbooks. Harry had been apprehensive about my possible reaction, but I was fascinated to the point of wishing I could do proper justice to all that material. I soon realized that trying to squeeze merely the "high points" into one book would be like trying to capture Niagara Falls in an eye-dropper.

In a 1941 letter to Ray McLaughlin, president of the central division, Bullis made one of his earliest references to the growing collection of memorabilia: "I have in those scrapbooks many interesting and inspirational letters from you on all sorts of subjects, such as philosophy, literature, as well as business. Occasionally at home at night, just before retiring, I pull down one or more of these scrapbooks and drink in some of the inspiration, courage and friendliness which I find in the communications and documents assembled there."

The deeper into the scrapbooks I delved, the more I appreciated the achievements and philosophy of "this guy Bullis." His secretary, Miss Gladys Leight, came over in rain and shine to be of assistance.

Mr. and Mrs. Bullis had already made plans for pleasant interludes. As Harry put it, "You'll go nuts if you coop yourself up with those scrapbooks all the time!" Actually, I loved those scrapbooks. Almost every morning Harry Bullis would call to ask about my progress, his hearty voice booming over the telephone, "Good morning, Gladys! Well, now . . ." And usually there would be another diversion to keep me from "going nuts."

At the Minikahda Club Harry showed me his picture in the Presidents' book after we ate. Although he couldn't have found two more reluctant models anywhere, Harry insisted on taking some pictures of Mary and me on the lawn near the Minikahda Clubhouse. Mary is also fond of the Wayzata Country Club "because they have horses there," and the Sunday "brunch" is a substantial version of nectar and ambrosia.

The Minneapolis Club, with its dark paneling and atmosphere of well-bred security, was of special interest because Harry had "given dinners" for so many notable personages there.

Harry told about the time he had startled some of the members of the Minneapolis Club by proposing the name of Senator Hubert Humphrey—whose party is not very well represented there—for honorary membership. "He's our senior senator, and I got him in, too!" Bullis declared triumphantly. When someone once suggested that Harry run against Humphrey for office, Harry refused on the grounds that "No businessman could ever beat Humphrey!" Besides, they were good friends.

After dinner at the Minneapolis Club, we attended a performance of "Everybody Loves Opal" at the Old Log Theatre, with Harry driving skillfully through the rain of a Minnesota spring night, and reminiscing at the same time.

Harry shook with laughter at some of the "earthy" jokes in the play. A comment about the spectacularly fine performances of the cast brought forth the proud boast that "This is the only professional theater in this part of the country!"

Harry Bullis, of course, was showing me all the places that were dear to his and Mary's hearts. All during the writing of his biography I would have a mental picture of the Minneapolis Club, the Minikahda and Wayzata Country Clubs, and the Minnetonka area. When I would write about his taking long rambling walks of five or six miles around the country roads at Charleston Acres, with his three dogs and all the others in the neighborhood that joined up with them, I would see those small hills and the trees and the places where the road curved around. And I would remember Harry's saying, "I like to walk. But I know that some people can't do a lot of walking—their feet hurt."

There was a memorable afternoon when Harry drove me to the General Mills executive offices which are no longer housed in that twelve-story building in downtown Minneapolis. In 1958, a magnificent new glass-and-aluminum structure, out in the wide open spaces on Wayzata Boulevard, was dedicated. On June 4, open house day, Board Chairman Harry Bullis stayed in his office all day and shook hands with thousands of visitors.

Now it was five years later. Bullis, sitting erect in the driver's seat, slowed the Cadillac as we neared the flag pole. I could almost sense an urge to salute as he raised his eyes toward the flag of his country, with the blue and gold General Mills banner unfurled in the breeze beside it.

Wondering what Cadwallader Washburn would have thought of this bright, handsome building, we made our way through the wide halls to the Home Service Department where we were greeted by gracious Mrs. Mildred Kranz, who had been employed by Harry Bullis a number of years ago. The reception area adjoining the Betty Crocker Kitchens is attractively decorated with a huge, curved sofa upholstered in hand-blocked linen. Above an antique Chinese chest hangs a portrait of the new "modern Betty Crocker," created in 1955 by artist Hilda Taylor.

The Betty Crocker Kitchens, as thousands of visitors know, are a homemaker's dream of efficiency in a charming setting. Completely fabulous are the test kitchens with their handy ovens, cabinets, surface burners, freezers, refrigerators, mixers, dish washers, and every conceivable kitchen convenience. The attractive Home Service girls looked as though they had come straight from a beauty pageant, and it was obvious that they could cook too.

Harry "initiated" the first kitchen in December, 1958, when he prepared his favorite dish, beef chateaubriand under the attentive eye of Mrs. Helen Hallbert, director of the department. The first three Betty Crocker kitchens are devoted to the business of cooking, baking, developing and testing new recipes. In the fourth, the Kamera Kitchen, picture-book foods become models for the photographer. Nearby is a large, complete photography department.

An important unit of the Betty Crocker kitchens is the office, a long, cheerful room of many desks where "Betty Crocker" answers thousands of letters every month, compiles cook book material and conducts other departmental business.

The charm of the transplanted Old New England dining room has been preserved in the new building.

Among other antique furnishings it boasts a grandfather's clock and an artist's conception of the great explosion of Cadwallader Washburn's "A" mill in 1878.

As we set out on a tour of some of the other offices we paused several times to admire the open-air court in the center of the building. Suddenly we entered a reception hall that might be called "the presidents' gallery." On the walls were portraits of the great leaders of General Mills—presidents and chairmen of the board for many decades past. Prominent among them was Harry Bullis—a life-sized portrait painted by Fritz Werner at the Minneapolis Institute of Art in 1947.

It was past closing time as we rounded up our tour and headed for the garage. We passed countless empty offices, deserted until morning. At last, in one cubicle, we glimpsed a lone worker, his head still bent in deep concentration over the work on his desk. Harry grinned roguishly. "That fellow might be president of General Mills some day." He had seen the shadow of young Harry Bullis there.

On the way to the Bullis home at Charleston Acres that afternoon, Harry talked about "The Betty Crocker Search." The American Table Dinner would be held in Minneapolis for the first time on April 26, rather than in Washington or New York.

"The Betty Crocker All-American Homemaker of Tomorrow" is the subject of the search program. The project was started in 1955 when 190,000 senior girls in eight thousand high schools across the nation enrolled in the first Betty Crocker Search sponsored by General Mills. Examinations were held in the Fall to select the state winners. During the following Spring

General Mills invited each of the state winners, accompanied by a teacher or chaperone, to enjoy a tour in the east. A group of judges also made the trip, studying the girls and searching for the one best qualified to be "The Betty Crocker All-American Homemaker of Tomorrow."

By this time we had reached Charleston Acres. As we turned into the Bullis estate I was thrilled to see a genuine old millstone propped up like a monument on the lawn! It was Harry's pride and joy, transported from the garden at the West Lake of the Isles home.

Below us, in white-fenced corrals, were Bonnie and Naja and two other beautiful horses. They stood attentively watching the car arrive. Mary Bullis feels that they are very intelligent animals. "When I am depressed, I go down to the stable and sit and talk to them," she said. "Then I feel better."

Mary, the perfect hostess, greeted us, and she and Harry took me from room to room in the home that is low and rambling and has a pleasant air of warmth and welcome. Mary treasures some small miniatures from "the good and wonderful old years in Poland." On the wall in the central hallway hangs a picture from some good and wonderful years in Minneapolis. Harry arranged to have Mary sit for a Fritz Werner portrait soon after their marriage. She is wearing the lovely black lace gown that she wore on the night of the dinner at the Stanley Hawks home in 1948. Artist Werner has captured more than the delicate, patrician curve of the high cheekbones, the indefinable air of good breeding. There is also that wistful, haunting aura of sadness that adds a soft glow of radiance.

Harry took me down to the basement to see his book-lined den with its fine big desk and many of the mementoes of a long and honorable career.

There were just five of us—my publisher, Mr. Lawrence Brings and his wife, Nettie, the Bullises, and I—who were there for the superb dinner which had been prepared under Mary's careful supervision. I remember the unusual beet broth and the sirloin tip roast with mushrooms. Mostly I remember that Harry talked volubly, as though he had much to say and time was passing too swiftly.

Nettie Brings and I were especially intrigued with the Bullis' Irish Wolfhound who is about one size smaller than a horse and kept coming into the living room for chocolates in spite of Mary's efforts to discourage him. Mr. Brings got chummy with the boxer; they made faces at each other. It was an evening of good fun and pleasant companionship, with no "stuffy" moments.

One afternoon I was invited to call on Harry Bullis in his own handsomely sedate office in the building where he had spent much of his active executive life. On his wall was the framed motto that guided his life: "Drive Straight Ahead with a Positive Mental Attitude." This is the same office in which he had officiated as president of General Mills.

On the cover of "General Mills Horizons" for July, 1947, is a picture of "A Room with a View." It shows James F. Bell and Harry Bullis standing at the high twelfth-floor window of the former General Mills board of directors' room, next door to Bullis' office.

The General Mills directors no longer meet there, but it is furnished in the same way.

When Harry and I went out on the railed roof top, he pointed out some of the recent "face-lifting projects" in downtown Minneapolis. There was a fine view of the Mississippi river milling area, scene of flour-making history for almost a century.

After we said good afternoon to Mr. Bullis' secretary, we went down to the street to be jostled by the homeward-bound workers of the city, none of whom seemed anxious to burn the midnight oil in their offices. "Well," Harry observed, "everybody doesn't want to be a general, and they need a lot of privates in every army."

Almost too soon, before I had done justice to all those scrapbooks, it was the night of the American Table Dinner. The next day I would fly out to Oregon to visit my mother and other members of my family, while I started writing the story of "this guy Bullis" who had given me his blessing. "Mothers are great institutions, and sons and daughters should contact them as often as possible," he had written in a delightful "Welcome to Minneapolis" letter. Harry would never forget that he had lost his own mother when he was a young man.

On the way to the Radisson Hotel where the 1963 "Betty Crocker Search" would reach its grand climax, Mary recalled those early years "when the winners would kiss Harry." It was an evening of stimulating, contagious suspense. As we started up into the banquet room, Harry looked at the bevy of "Betty Crocker candidates" flitting through the hall in their lovely ballet-length formals and observed, "Some of them are a little heftier this year."

During the earlier years, the girls had sat at a long, elevated table facing the banquet room. In 1963, each of many guest tables was allotted a state winner. We were charmed to have lovely little Susan Graper, Miss Indiana, with us.

Harry escorted Mr. Charles Bell, chairman of the board, and General E. W. Rawlings, president of General Mills, over from a nearby table to meet me—so I would have a "mental picture" of them too.

Jovial Lanny Ross was the emcee for the evening. The superb program also featured Alice Lon, the Air Force Academy Chorale, and the Radisson Hotel Golden Strings.

Mr. and Mrs. Harry Bullis were among the notables invited to stand and take a bow for their years of dedicated interest in the creation and promotion of the American Table Dinner.

All of the food was supremely worthy of identification with Betty Crocker. Looking back, the dinner seemed to have been building up to the awesome moment when the huge banquet room was darkened. The music quickened, and from entrances at either end, two gentlemen dressed as bakers and carrying flaming torches marched into the room. Behind them came a parade of young ladies, each carrying a Lemon Velvet Chantilly Cake. That cake deserved to be served with a flourish.

Then the "high moment of destiny" arrived. As her name was called, each girl approached the stage, circled around gracefully, bowed to the assembled guests, and took her place on the upper level of the stage.

Before he began to open the envelopes prepared by the judges, Mr. Charles Bell announced the amounts of the awards. Each state winner receives a $1,500 scholarship and her runner-up a $500 award. The All-America Homemaker of Tomorrow has her scholarship raised to $5,000; and the second, third and fourth place winners in the nation receive a grand total of $4,000, $3,000, and $2,000 in scholarship awards.

The air in the room seemed to vibrate with tension as Mr. Bell called out the name of the fourth place winner—Caroline Treat Davidson from the state of Washington. Third place winner was Cecilia Ziemba of New York. Catherine Dunham, from Vermont, stepped forward to receive the $4,000 second place award.

Mr. Bell procrastinated for a teasing moment with the final envelope. On the cover of the May issue of "The Modern Millwheel" is a picture of an ecstatically rapturous young lady with an armful of roses, with her advisor sharing her moment of incredulous bliss. The caption reads, "Excitement reigned supreme as Rae Jean Dell was named Betty Crocker All-American Homemaker of Tomorrow for 1963. Rae is a senior at Lincoln Northeast High School in Lincoln, Nebraska."

"Well," said Harry Bullis, "that's fine with me. She's a girl from the state where I was born—Nebraska!"

Flash-bulbs were popping, and the gentlemen of the press were gathering around the winners as we left the banquet room. "Now that young lady will go home a celebrity!" Harry declared.

The next afternoon, it was time for me to leave the Woman's Club where I had been treated with such friendly consideration for more than two weeks. Mrs. Bullis, who had spent the morning in town, joined me at the club. When Harry saw her he saluted her with a kiss and an affectionate greeting, as though they had been separated for days, "How's my beautiful lady? I haven't seen you since early this morning!"

The hallways and stairs are fairly interminable in the fine new Twin Cities airport. Mary chose to sit down and rest, but Harry insisted in escorting me to the proper gate. When I said goodbye, I tried to thank him for all the grand memories of him and Mary that I would cherish always. I knew that my life had been "enriched" by the hours I had spent in their stimulating company.

Before I went out to the plane, I looked back and saw Harry Bullis, tall and erect, marching up the long hall. Driving straight ahead with a positive mental attitude.

Chapter Twenty-one

"Best Regards"

In all his conversations, Harry had made many affectionate references to Mary. She had grown up with culture, while he had been cultivating corn and keeping books—but he had always made a valiant effort to catch up. With his expansive, receptive mind, Bullis was eager to familiarize himself with all the great creative art forms, and he took a true Minneapolitan's pride in the Guthrie Theater when he pointed it out to me.

There was some delightful "cultural spoofing" in a letter of May 13. Harry wrote that he and Mary would be attending a black tie dinner and reception at the Minikahda Club before the Metropolitan Opera performance of "Othello." He commented, "I understand that as is usual in such plays, Mr. Othello in the last act, believing that his wife was unfaithful to him, strangles her. Then, when he finds out that he was mistaken, he kills himself. I do not recall ever having seen a play, given by the Metropolitan Opera which has been coming here for years, that did not have at least one death in the last act."

That letter was bursting with Bullis exuberance. ". . . This morning started out as what my secretary, Miss Gladys Leight, calls an 'egg beater morning'—as though a giant egg beater were stirring up incessant telephone calls, callers, mail and what-have-you! . . ." On Friday he would fly to Madison, Wisconsin, to attend meetings of the Wisconsin Alumni Research Foundation. On Sunday, a military car would take Mary and him to Fort Snelling for the closing ceremony of Armed Forces Week. As civilian aide to the Secretary of the Army for the State of Minnesota, Harry would assist in reviewing the troops. Later he wrote, "During the proceedings when the troops of all services marched past the reviewing stand, I thought I was back in the days of World War I."

A comment in my next letter brought forth bits of Bullis whimsey: "Yes, we have Shakespeare all over the place here in Minneapolis. The other noon at a meeting of the finance committee of the Hennepin Avenue Methodist Church I made a motion to take a certain action which a minority of the committee opposed. I started my comments by saying, 'Since we have gone Shakesperean around here in Minneapolis, I am going to quote from Macbeth, Act I: "If it were done, when 'tis done, then it were well it were done quickly." ' Then I made a motion which was carried."

He told about having lunch with his distinguished fellow members of the board of trustees of the Wisconsin Research Foundation on the previous Saturday. They had toasted him as the "Wisconsin Alumnus of the Year for 1963." After they had drunk their champagne, they sang "For He's a Jolly Good Fellow" and ended up by singing "On Wisconsin!" Harry commented with mellow good cheer, "It really seemed like the old Wisconsin Days."

Shortly afterward there were several days of disturbing silence. Then Miss Leight wrote to say that Mr. Bullis was in the hospital. It was good to remember that Harry had been saluted with "For He's a Jolly Good Fellow" at that luncheon in May, because he was unable to attend the scheduled festivities at the University of Wisconsin in June.

In spite of his illness, he dictated many letters from "dry dock"—letters filled with information, humor and encouragement for me. In the midst of his illness, he bothered to keep my morale high. "Congratulations for having your sixth book off the press! I take off my hat to anyone who can write six books and who is now working on her seventh book." And I couldn't think of anyone I would rather have take off his hat to me than Mr. Harry Bullis!

In his letters Harry spoke of Mary's thoughtfulness. "She has been and is a wonderful wife. She visited me every afternoon when I was in the hospital, and, of course, she is a great tower of strength to me during this period of my convalescence."

The man with many friends received many letters from people who were anxious about him. "Artistically sublime" was a message from John Rood, Minnesota's eminent contribution to the world of modern art, who wrote: "A young friend of mine, Jim Hancock, is program director of the Minneapolis branch of Junior Achievement. Some weeks ago, I gave him your 'Manifesto for Americans' to read. He was so impressed by it that he took it to a meeting in New York—of the top Junior Achievement program directors—and made the others read it. They shared in his enthusiasm. As a result, they have contacted your publisher with the hope that they can arrange to buy enough of the books to place them in the hands of every boy working in the Junior Achievement program—90,000 of them!"

In his letter, Mr. Rood continued, "I thought this would please you—to know that your words have fallen on receptive ears, and undoubtedly will bear fruit in the future. It isn't everyone who is privileged thus to have an effect on young people. Too, it isn't everyone who could write such a book! . . ." Mr. Rood's letter inspires profound rejoicing on the part of anyone who is familiar with "Manifesto for Americans."

With his "warm personal regard," General Eisenhower wrote Harry, "I sincerely hope you are following the doctor's orders—they do wonders these days. Of course, I feel as though I am an expert on this subject as I have had a couple of battles with the doctors in the past. And now I am working as hard or even harder than before my so-called retirement!"

In his conversations and correspondence with me, Harry Bullis seemed driven by an urgent compulsion to convey a clear picture of his philosophy. A conservative-appearing businessman, generally somber except when a humorous observation came sputtering out, Harry took pride in referring to himself as a Liberal. To him, being a Liberal meant that he had rejected the straitjacket of the "standpatter." Liberalism, to him, meant progress in every direction—today, tomorrow, and far into a better, more humane world of the future.

He classified himself as a "Conservative Liberal or a Liberal Capitalist"—not as a "pie-in-the-sky" radical Liberal. He never lived in the groove of past tradition. He looked farther ahead than today—and far out beyond the unknown tomorrow—because he was always aware that all institutions and the whole world are constantly changing.

Bullis chose to be an optimist, recognizing that there is a choice, but his optimism was realistic. He was a fighting optimist—a happy warrior; and he witnessed the wide acceptance of many of the things for which he struggled.

Bullis continually asked searching questions: "Is industry planning well ahead to absorb future job hunters? Is it giving equal opportunity to everyone, regardless of race, color or creed? Is it providing opportunities for the handicapped? How much of its profits is industry turning back into research? Is industry contributing money in the form of grants-in-aid, endowments and scholarships to underwrite American education? Is industry carrying its share in guaranteeing a large supply of intellectually mature young citizens to take over and guide America's economic and social future?"

Bullis was especially impatient with immensely wealthy people who were niggardly about supporting education. "Do they think they are going to live forever!" he rumbled. He spoke admiringly of a Twin Cities industrialist who is famed for his liberal gifts to Catholic schools and colleges. "A million here—two million there—that fellow has more darned fun with his money!"

Like a good accountant, he kept his "books" in balance. Even while he was asking labor to beware of wage-price inflation and to produce abundantly through "intelligent hard work," he was speaking over his shoulder to management, declaring, "This does not mean the 'speed-up' or 'sweating' of labor. As a matter-of-fact," he said, "it is management that must do most of the sweating."

In one sentence in "Maintaining a Strong Domestic Economy," Bullis said, "We must not permit excessive taxation to destroy the incentives that have made our country great." Two sentences later, he dealt with the other side of the story, "The proponents of free enterprise should not always register head-on opposition to all social welfare measures."

It is obvious that Harry Bullis took pride in being a "Liberal," but what kind of a businessman was he? Is it possible for a member of this breed of "new, liberal businessmen" to be highly successful in the marketplace?

When Bullis had received offers from some larger companies, he had chosen to remain with Washburn Crosby and General Mills. The atmosphere was good; there was room for his mental breathing and range for his restless curiosity. It suited the friendly, expansive personality of the big fellow who saw that "the sky was the limit" there—for men who were not afraid of "intelligent hard work." There is something special about General Mills; Harry had to use all the tact and gentle persuasion at his command to convince some of the elderly executives that it was time to retire. It has been noted that Harry was not an easy man to retire when his turn came. General Mills was his life, and he put his heart and soul into it and into the human beings around him.

Harry has noted that he would be the last to claim any credit, but he took justifiable pride in being "at least a substantial factor" in the progress made during his terms of stewardship as president and chairman of the board of General Mills. During the time he served as president, from 1943 to 1948, the total capitalization, including reserves, increased from $62,000,000 to approximately $90,000,000. At the end of his eleven-year administration as chairman of the board in 1959, the capitalization figures had risen to $159,000,000.

During his term as president, the total annual sales rose from $217,000,000 to $458,000,000. When he retired as chairman of the board in 1959, the annual sales figure had leaped beyond the half-billion mark—$546,000,000. The net earnings of the company in 1943 were $5,366,000. In 1948, after Bullis had served as president for five years, they were $13,068,000. By the end of fiscal 1959, they were $16,817,000. The number of stockholders increased from 9,690 to 14,560 during his two terms of service. These figures undoubtedly indicate that Bullis was no "pie-in-the-sky" Liberal. He was a solid, substantial "pie-on-the-table" Liberal.

Harry kept emphasizing that no progressive company can be a "one-man-show." He always took pride in the co-operation he received from dozens of talented executives and thousands of fine, enthusiastic employees.

Harry Bullis mentioned a number of times that General Mills has the distinction of being one of the companies listed on the New York Stock Exchange which have paid regular, substantial dividends all through the depression years and the precarious World War II years, right up to the present.

By the end of June, Harry was feeling chipper enough to dictate some significant appraisals of the present economic situation. I had asked him about the drain on our gold supply, a subject of vital interest. He noted that our international accounts show complete adequacy in our balance of trade. "A surplus or favorable balance of $4.8 billion was achieved last year. It is our balance of payments that causes the trouble. It is running adverse by a rate of $3.3 in the first quarter this year compared to $2.2 billion for all of 1962.

"The loss of gold has immensely sobered the people of the United States. So we have held wages down admirably for the past three and one-half years. We are holding our price levels down better than other nations. In that way we gain a favorable ratio in our prices to foreign prices.

"What is needed most is to induce our now prosperous Allies of Western Europe to take over a greater share of all military expenditures made for our collective defense and to take over at least one billion dollars a year in aid to underdeveloped countries."

Harry was more than a businessman with a twinkle in his eye when he told one audience, "We all know that man cannot live by bread alone—though we in General Mills sometimes wish he did."

Harry often quoted the Bible. One of the bulwarks

of his faith was his "Personal Prayer" which he used daily:

"Oh God, I ask not for easier tasks. I ask for stronger aptitudes and greater talents to meet any tasks which may come my way. Help me to help others so that their lives may be made easier and happier. Strengthen my confidence in my fellowmen in spite of what they may do or say. Give me strength to live according to the Golden Rule, enthusiasm to inspire those around me, sympathy to help lighten the burdens of those who suffer, and a spirit of joy and gladness to share with others. Help me to make a worthwhile contribution to the world. Give me courage and confidence to meet adversity with a smile and wisdom to see good in all things. Renew in me the resolve to do Thy will honestly and fearlessly and grant me a peaceful mind."

Among the many wonderful "get-well" letters Harry received was one dated July 8. It was not from a "competitor"—it was from a lifelong friend, John S. Pillsbury, Sr., past chairman of the board of Pillsbury Mills, Inc., whom Harry considered "the senior outstanding flour miller" and "one of the great citizens of this midwest area."

In addition to wishing Harry well, Mr. Pillsbury recalled, "As I have told many people, when you assumed control of General Mills, there was never a more popular election among the trade and among competitors. Everyone had complete confidence in your integrity and when you were on a committee there was always the assurance the best interests of the industry would be served."

Harry Bullis was due to retire as a director of General Mills in August, 1963. It was reassuring to hear that he was able to attend the board meeting on July 22, and even make a speech. He noted that it was just about thirty-three and one-half years ago since he had been elected a director of General Mills in 1930. "I am sure that being a member of this board has benefited me more than I have benefited General Mills. During this period of a third of a century, the company has left some mighty big footprints in the business life of the nation. . . ."

Harry looked at "the new young men" with approval. "We have great leaders in Charles H. Bell, chairman of the board, who is getting more like his father every day, and our wonderful president, General Edwin W. Rawlings, who is one of the great presidents of our company."

The citation, which Harry's fellow board members presented in absentia at the annual stockholders' meeting on August 22, 1963 has the rhythm of poetry and the sincerity of a great moment of truth:

"To Our Friend and Associate
HARRY A. BULLIS

"Character, ability, integrity, dedication. These are the words that best describe the Harry A. Bullis we have known during his forty-four years of outstanding service to General Mills, Inc., and its predecessor, the Washburn Crosby Company.

"His life is an American saga. From newsboy to Phi Beta Kappa . . . from mill hand to president and chairman of the board . . . from private citizen to world leader, all this while retaining those human characteristics that make a man loved as well as respected: intelligence, dependability, unswerving dedication to the positive approach in all things . . . the sympathy, understanding and interest in others that have made him the friend of porters and presidents.

"It has been a joy and a privilege to be associated with Harry A. Bullis. His absence from our meetings, after an unequaled record of faithful attendance over thirty-three years, will be sorely felt. His spirit and his example will remain with us as a priceless legacy."

George E. Swarbreck, editor of "The Northwestern Miller," quoted the citation in full on September 2 in a splendid salute entitled: "Let Us Now Praise Famous Men."

The last paragraph is a fine short, short story about a tall, tall man: "Harry Bullis, someone once said, is an incurable optimist who doesn't want to be cured. One of his greatest gifts is the ability to transmit his optimism to all those who have the good fortune to come into contact with him. . . ."

On September 10, Harry Bullis signed a letter to me for the last time, and I could see that it had been an effort. His mental attitude was positive enough, but his handwriting was unsteady. He always ended his letters with "Best regards." Then, "Sincerely," and the large, clear signature, "Harry Bullis" in green ink.

Early in the last week of September Harry's secretary wrote to say that he had seen the galleys of the first few chapters of this book and had thought they were "wonderful."

On the following Saturday night Harry Bullis died,

slightly over a week before his seventy-third birthday. Like a good soldier, Harry obeyed when taps were sounded. There is a feeling of unreality about it, because he was so youthfully interested in life and living, a few short months ago. A fact is a fact, but it is a great consolation to remember Harry Bullis marching ahead up that long, long hallway at the airport, shoulders square, head up, erect—a Champion American.

It must have been necessary to re-arrange the front page of Mr. John Cowles' Minneapolis Sunday Tribune during the night of September 28. Few people rate such huge headlines and a story of such length. Harry, who had one hundred scrapbooks filled with choice letters, souvenirs and clippings on many subjects, would have prized that story. He would have been pleased to see himself described as the "former president and chairman of the board of General Mills, Inc., and a dedicated champion of human rights" in the very first paragraph.

The funeral was on Tuesday, October 1, at Hennepin Avenue Methodist Church where he had served as a faithful steward from 1947 to 1961. True to his faith in God and the pursuit of knowledge, almost half of his estate will go eventually to Hennepin Avenue Methodist Church, the University of Wisconsin, Simpson College and Hamline University. Perhaps Harry Bullis' greatest legacy now, and for many years to come, is a book called "Manifesto for Americans."

Let this be my requiem. Harry Bullis is the only businessman I have heard speaking with the tongues of angels and Carl Sandburg. In his reference to the "masses," Bullis also saw the faces of individuals marching to work and to war. Put this Bullis quotation into free verse, and most people would guess incorrectly that Sandburg had written it: "Often the more important people try to gloss over the facts as they apply to John Citizen." A man who knew just about everything there was to know about business, Bullis never tired of repeating, "The humanities of business are more important than the techniques of business."

Some men, through the articulate intensity of their convictions, achieve a share of earthly immortality. "This fellow Bullis" won't have finished talking for a long while yet—not when there are so many people who need to hear what he had to say. Wait until those young Junior Achievement people start shoving "Manifesto for Americans" at their parents and friends.

Several people have suggested that Harry Bullis fancied himself as something of a "king-maker." Is that bad? He and Mary treated me as though I were a queen, and it was a "noble" sensation! Of all the generous and extravagant things Harry Bullis did for me, there is a certain memory that will always bring a lump to my throat. He made that third round-trip to bring my glasses to me. He was always making the extra gesture, I've learned—giving of himself with his gifts of thoughtfulness. He was not a man to make a good impression once—and expect it to last forever.

Considering that he was only one man, Harry made a great many people feel as though they were kings or queens or at least a bit more valuable than they had ever thought they were. You see, Harry Bullis had this wonderful faculty for putting himself in the other fellow's shoes. He knew how those shoes felt, walking the paper route, trudging behind the plow, clamped around the legs of a bookkeeper's stool, bearing the weight of flour sacks at the mills. They were his feet and his brother's feet. "Spike" Kennedy had taken the measure of "the measuring man" whom he knew so well, when he said in a letter dated December 23, 1958:

". . . I want to repeat that old quotation which says better than any words of mine what all of us really think of Harry Bullis:

> 'He has walked among us these many years,
> A giant among men and yet—a brother
> to us all.' "